VOLUME 2

WISH YOU WERE HERE

FEDERAL BUREAU OF PHYSICS

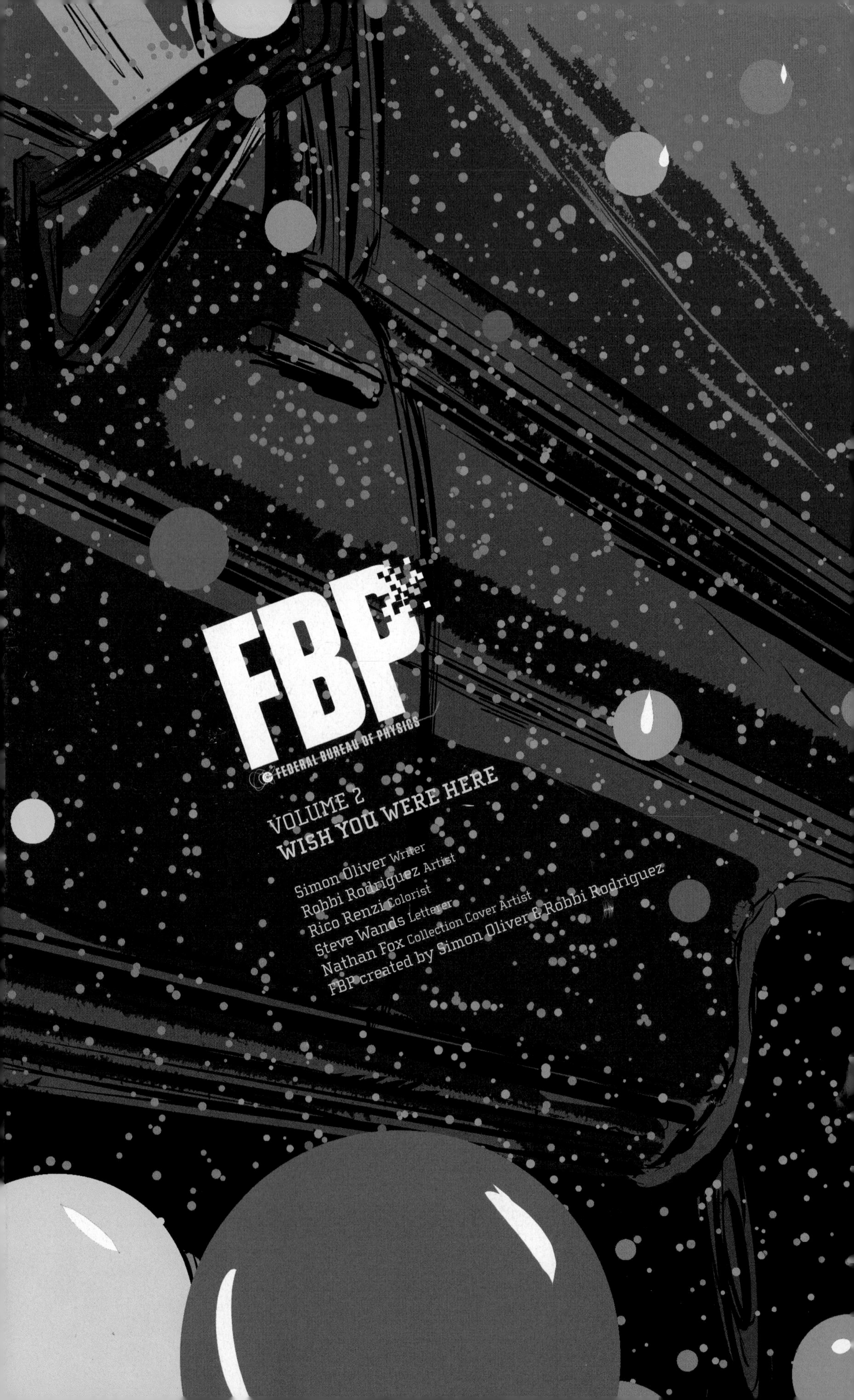

FBP

FEDERAL BUREAU OF PHYSICS

VOLUME 2
WISH YOU WERE HERE

Simon Oliver Writer
Robbi Rodriguez Artist
Rico Renzi Colorist
Steve Wands Letterer
Nathan Fox Collection Cover Artist
FBP created by Simon Oliver & Robbi Rodriguez

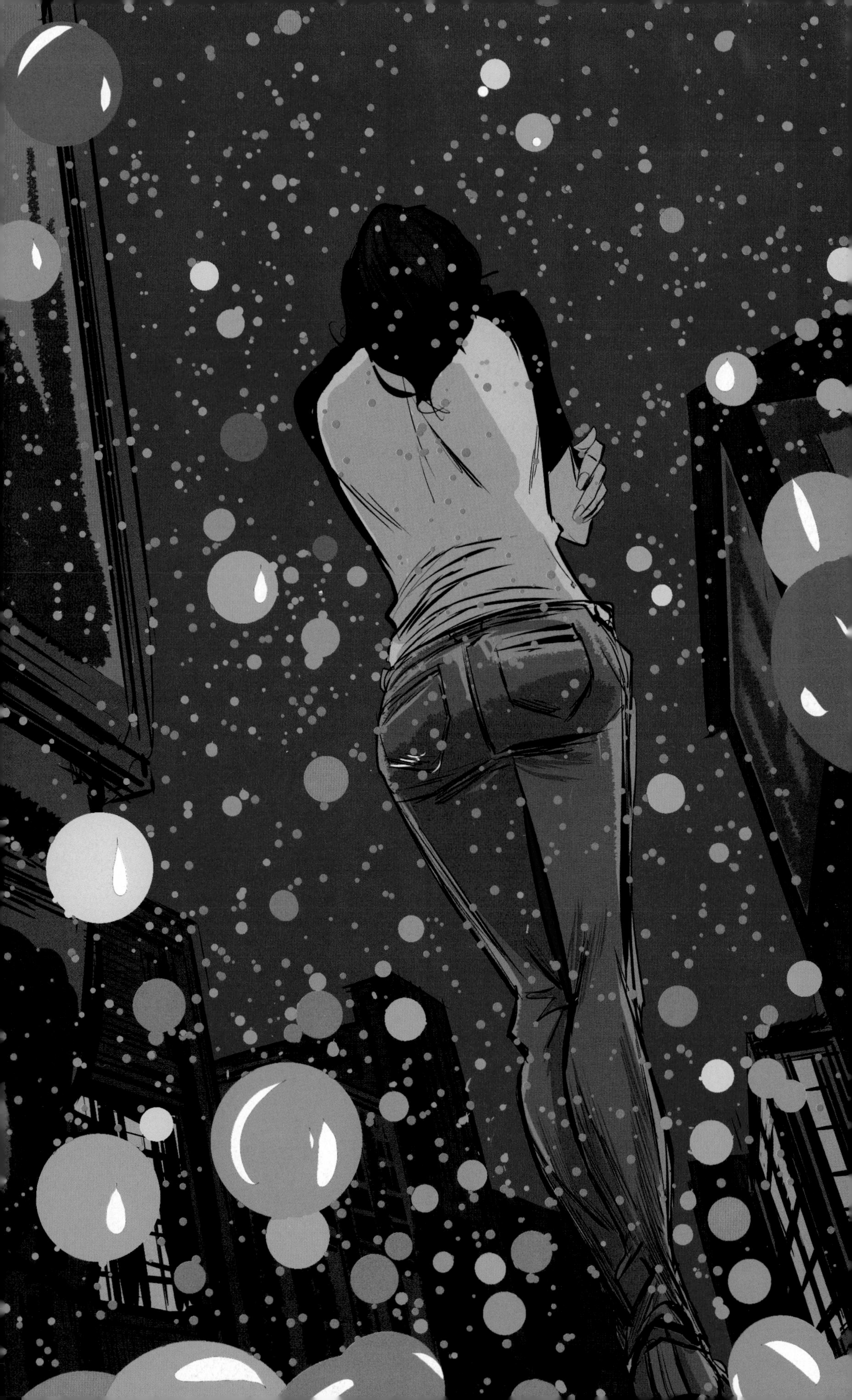

Mark Doyle and Greg Lockard Editors – Original Series
Sara Miller Assistant Editor – Original Series
Jeremy Bent Editor
Robbin Brosterman Design Director – Books
Chris Griggs Publication Design

Shelly Bond Executive Editor - Vertigo
Hank Kanalz Senior VP – Vertigo & Integrated Publishing

Diane Nelson President
Dan DiDio and Jim Lee Co-Publishers
Geoff Johns Chief Creative Officer
Amit Desai Senior VP – Marketing & Franchise Management
Amy Genkins Senior VP – Business & Legal Affairs
Nairi Gardiner Senior VP – Finance
Jeff Boison VP – Publishing Planning
Mark Chiarello VP – Art Direction & Design
John Cunningham VP – Marketing
Terri Cunningham VP – Editorial Administration
Larry Ganem VP – Talent Relations & Services
Alison Gill Senior VP – Manufacturing & Operations
Jay Kogan VP – Business & Legal Affairs, Publishing
Jack Mahan VP – Business Affairs, Talent
Nick Napolitano VP – Manufacturing Administration
Sue Pohja VP – Book Sales
Fred Ruiz VP – Manufacturing Operations
Courtney Simmons Senior VP – Publicity
Bob Wayne Senior VP – Sales

FBP VOLUME 2: WISH YOU WERE HERE

DC Comics, 1700 Broadway, New York, NY 10019
A Warner Bros. Entertainment Company.
Printed in the USA. First Printing.
ISBN: 978-1-4012-5067-6

SUSTAINABLE FORESTRY INITIATIVE
Certified Chain of Custody
20% Certified Forest Content, 80% Certified Sourcing
www.sfiprogram.org
SFI-01042
APPLIES TO TEXT STOCK ONLY

Library of Congress Cataloging-in-Publication Data

Oliver, Simon, author.
FBP : Federal Bureau of Physics. Volume 2, Wish You Were Here / Simon Oliver, Robbi Rodriguez.
pages cm
ISBN 978-1-4012-5067-6 (paperback)
1. Graphic novels. I. Rodriguez, Robbi, illustrator. II. Title. III. Title: Wish You Were Here.
PN6727.O5F38 2014
741.5'973—dc23

2014011938

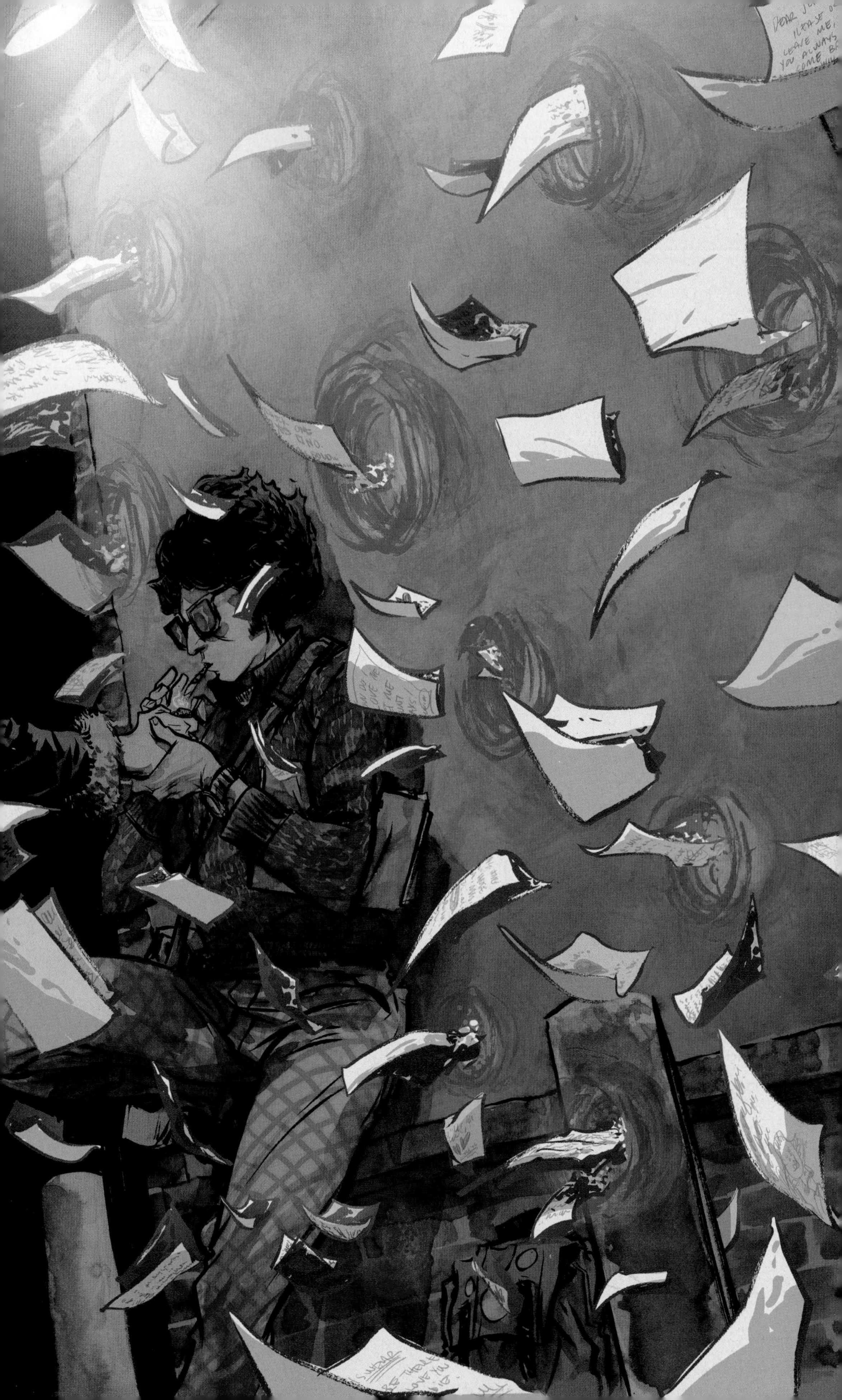
LEAVE ME,
YOU ALWAYS
BE THERE
LOVE YOU

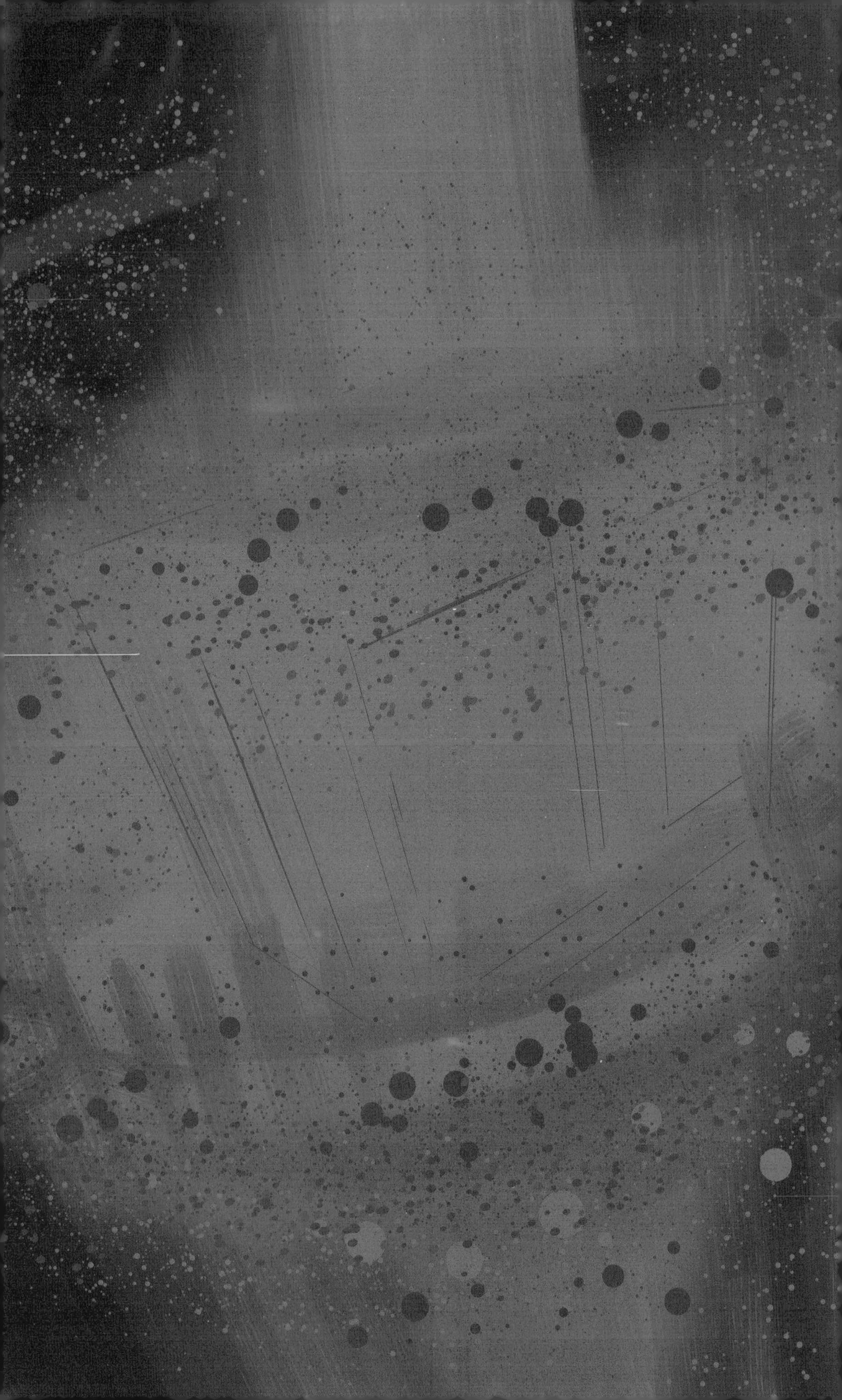

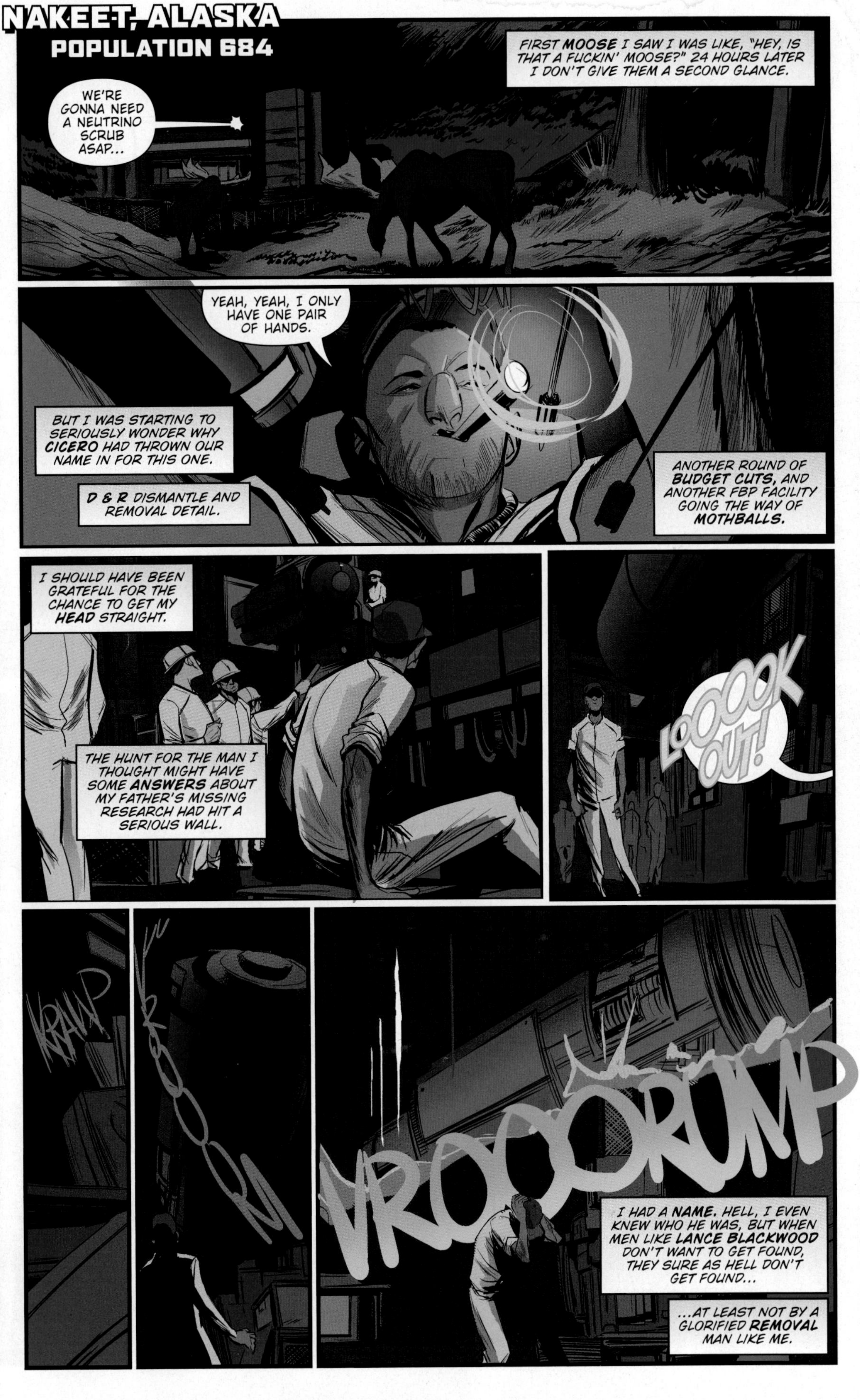
NAKEET, ALASKA
POPULATION 684
FIRST MOOSE I SAW I WAS LIKE, "HEY, IS THAT A FUCKIN' MOOSE?" 24 HOURS LATER I DON'T GIVE THEM A SECOND GLANCE.
WE'RE GONNA NEED A NEUTRINO SCRUB ASAP...
YEAH, YEAH, I ONLY HAVE ONE PAIR OF HANDS.
BUT I WAS STARTING TO SERIOUSLY WONDER WHY CICERO HAD THROWN OUR NAME IN FOR THIS ONE.
D & R DISMANTLE AND REMOVAL DETAIL.
ANOTHER ROUND OF BUDGET CUTS, AND ANOTHER FBP FACILITY GOING THE WAY OF MOTHBALLS.
I SHOULD HAVE BEEN GRATEFUL FOR THE CHANCE TO GET MY HEAD STRAIGHT.
THE HUNT FOR THE MAN I THOUGHT MIGHT HAVE SOME ANSWERS ABOUT MY FATHER'S MISSING RESEARCH HAD HIT A SERIOUS WALL.
LOOOOK OUT!
VROOORUMP
I HAD A NAME. HELL, I EVEN KNEW WHO HE WAS, BUT WHEN MEN LIKE LANCE BLACKWOOD DON'T WANT TO GET FOUND, THEY SURE AS HELL DON'T GET FOUND...
...AT LEAST NOT BY A GLORIFIED REMOVAL MAN LIKE ME.

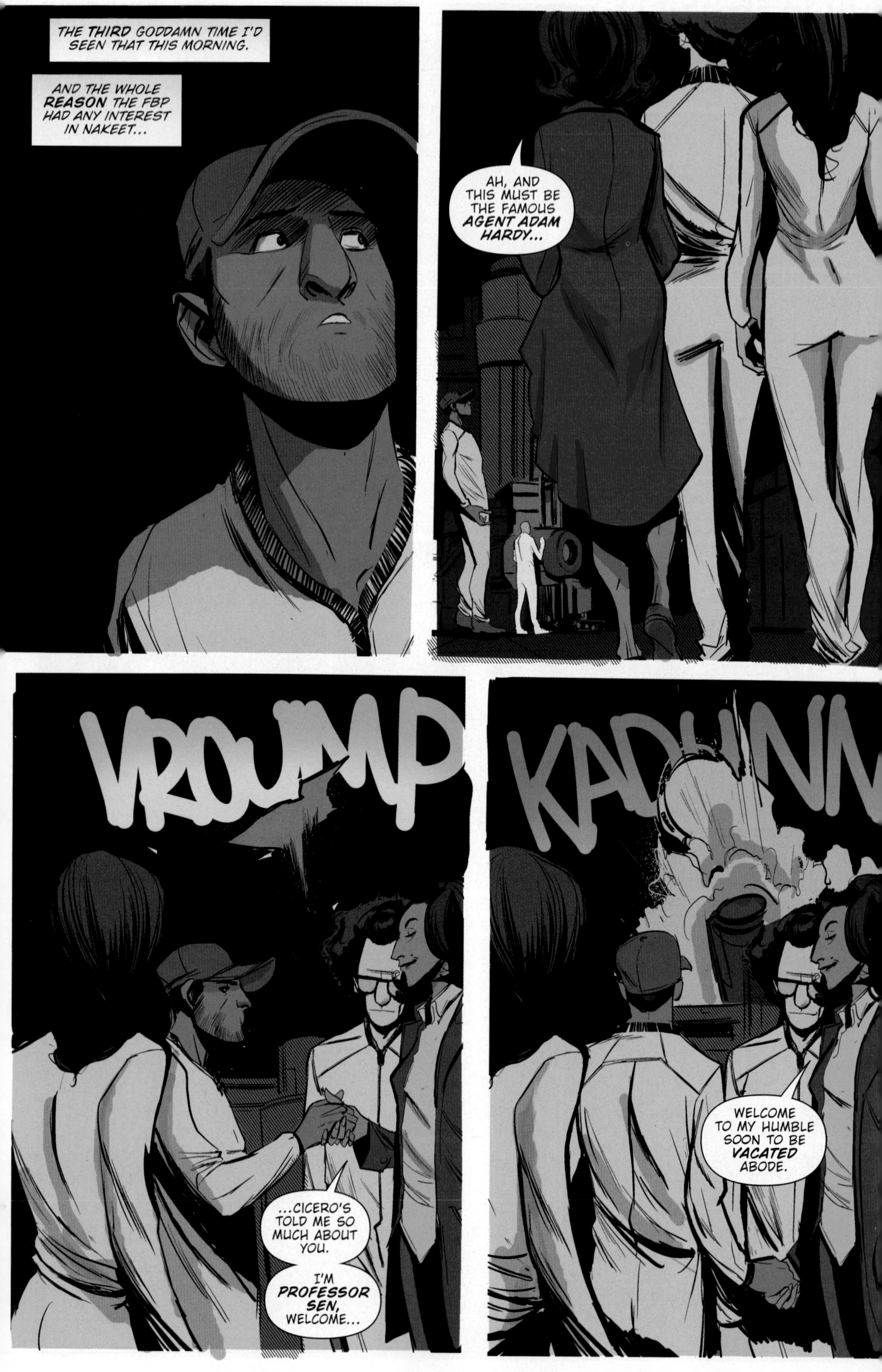
THE THIRD GODDAMN TIME I'D SEEN THAT THIS MORNING.
AND THE WHOLE REASON THE FBP HAD ANY INTEREST IN NAKEET...
AH, AND THIS MUST BE THE FAMOUS AGENT ADAM HARDY...
VROUMP
...CICERO'S TOLD ME SO MUCH ABOUT YOU.
I'M PROFESSOR SEN, WELCOME...
KADUNN
WELCOME TO MY HUMBLE SOON TO BE VACATED ABODE.

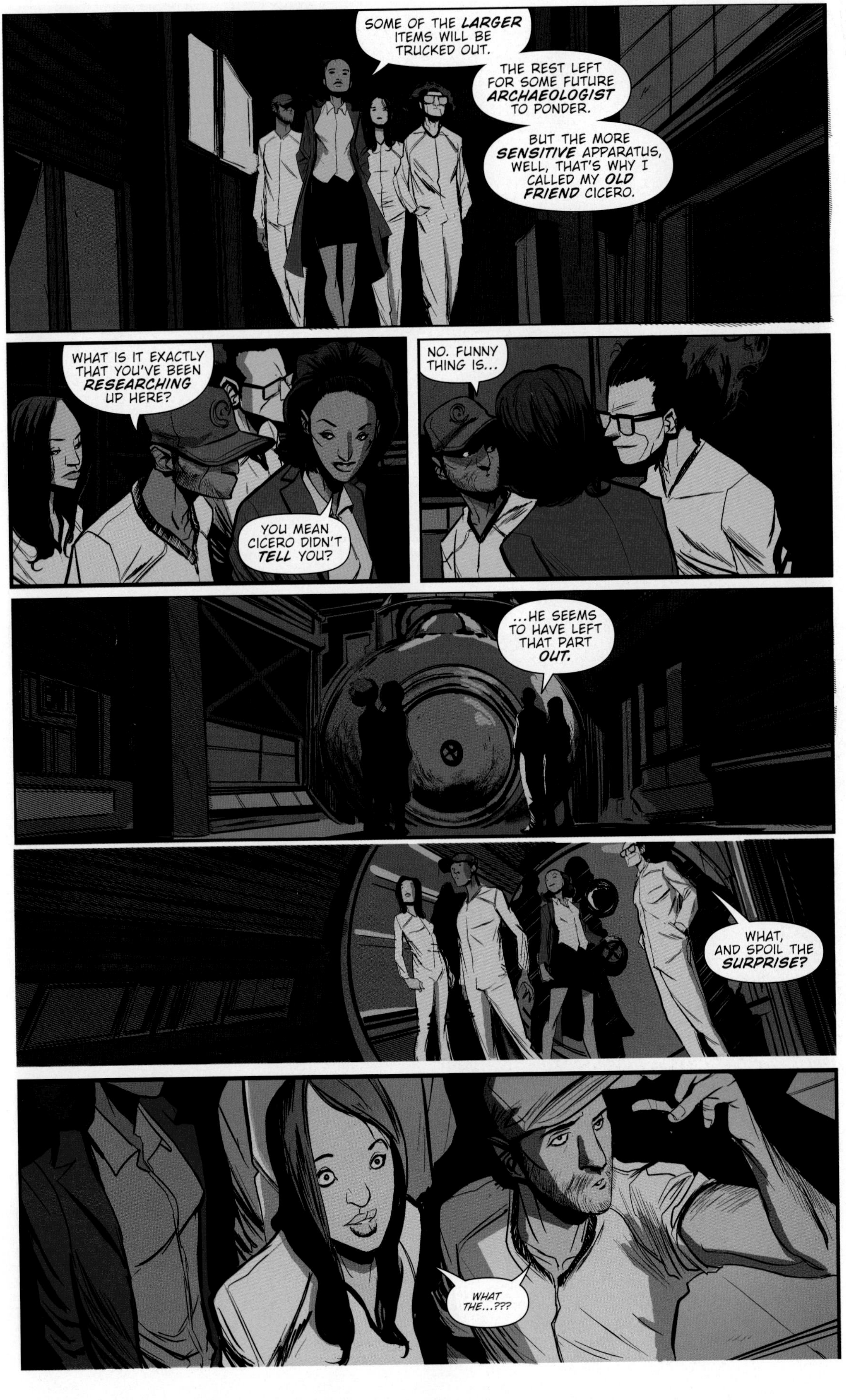
SOME OF THE LARGER ITEMS WILL BE TRUCKED OUT.
THE REST LEFT FOR SOME FUTURE ARCHAEOLOGIST TO PONDER.
BUT THE MORE SENSITIVE APPARATUS, WELL, THAT'S WHY I CALLED MY OLD FRIEND CICERO.
WHAT IS IT EXACTLY THAT YOU'VE BEEN RESEARCHING UP HERE?
YOU MEAN CICERO DIDN'T TELL YOU?
NO. FUNNY THING IS...
...HE SEEMS TO HAVE LEFT THAT PART OUT.
WHAT, AND SPOIL THE SURPRISE?
WHAT THE...???

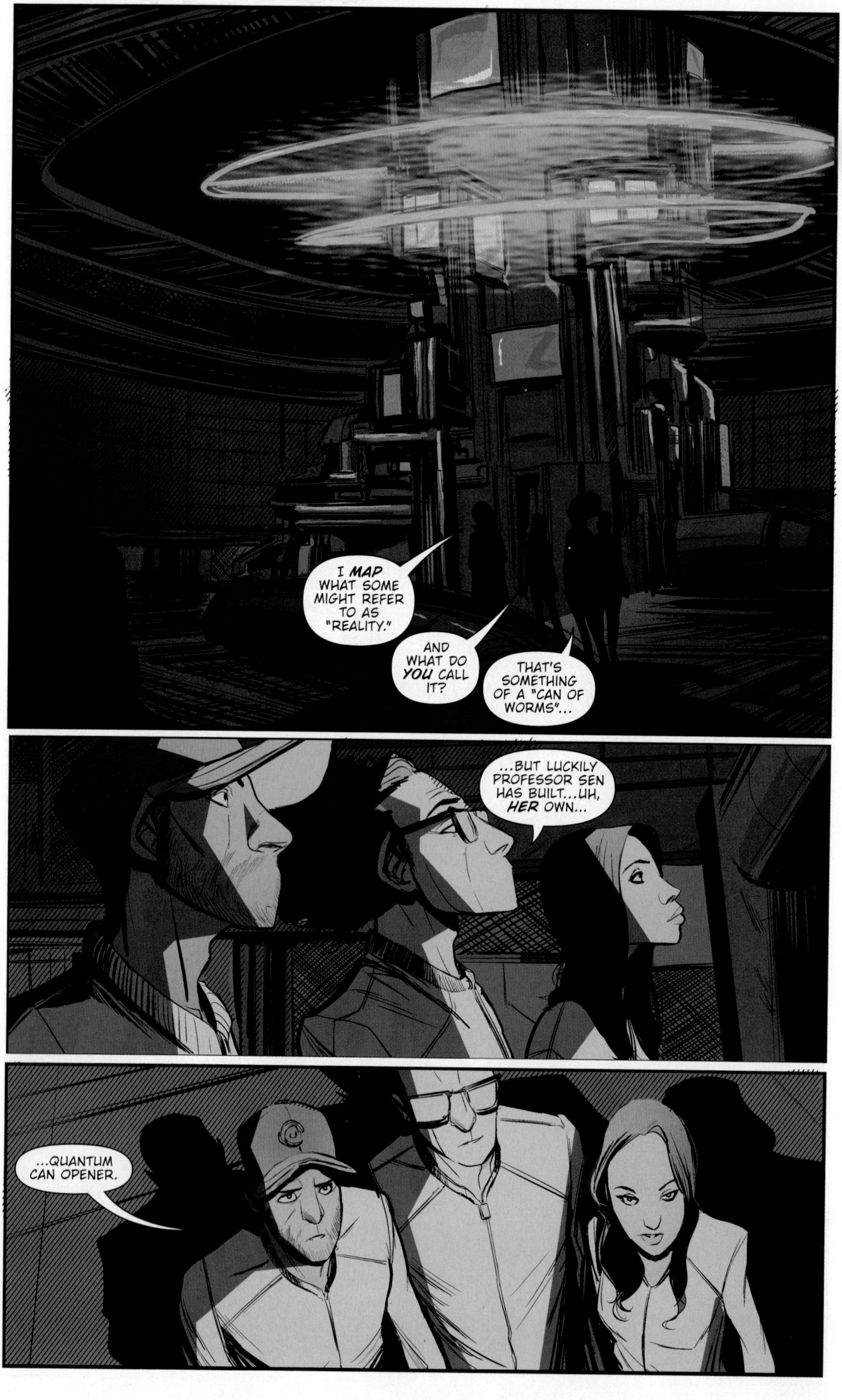
I MAP WHAT SOME MIGHT REFER TO AS "REALITY."
AND WHAT DO YOU CALL IT?
THAT'S SOMETHING OF A "CAN OF WORMS"...
...BUT LUCKILY PROFESSOR SEN HAS BUILT...UH, HER OWN...
...QUANTUM CAN OPENER.

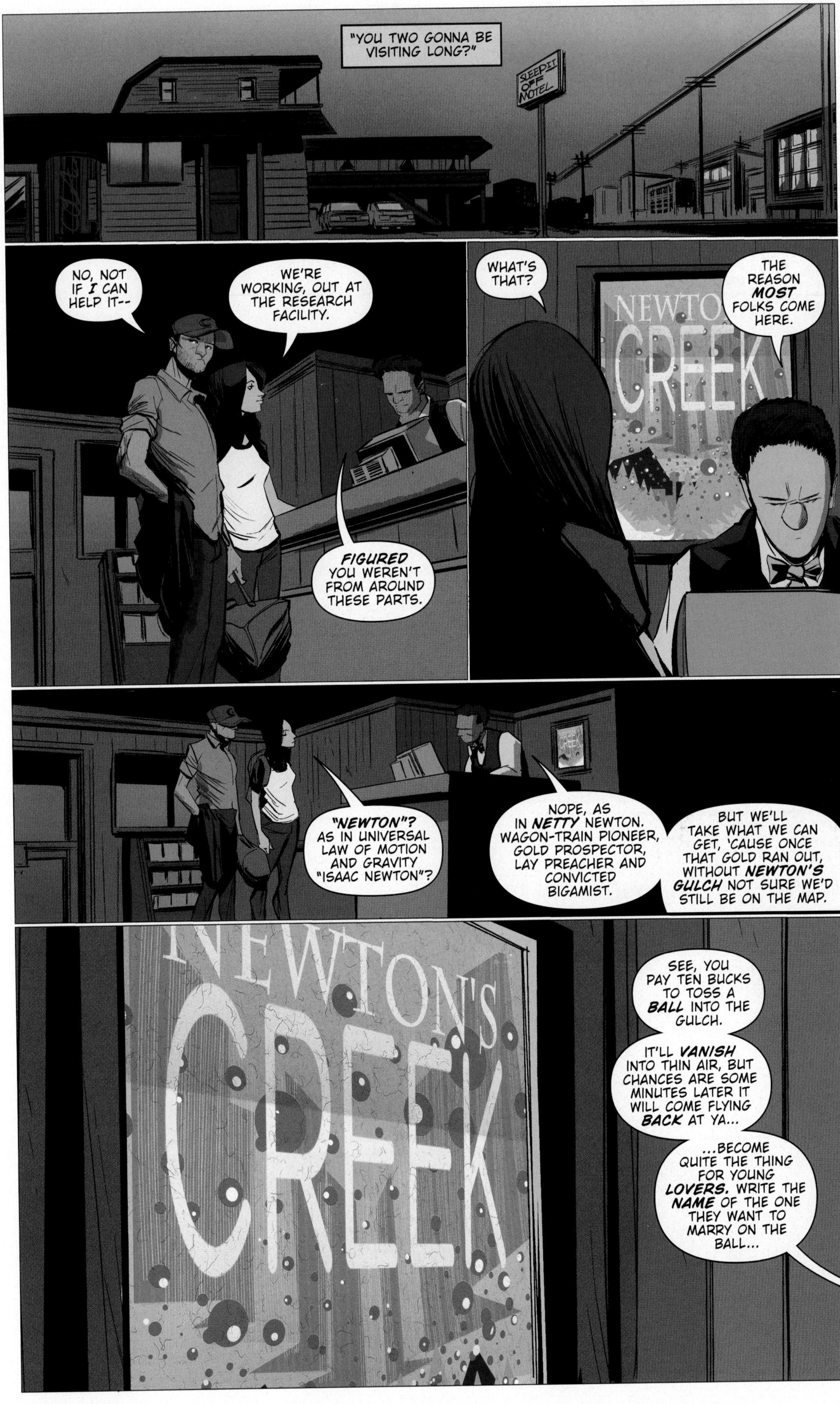
"YOU TWO GONNA BE VISITING LONG?"
SLEEP IT OFF MOTEL
NO, NOT IF *I* CAN HELP IT--
WE'RE WORKING, OUT AT THE RESEARCH FACILITY.
FIGURED YOU WEREN'T FROM AROUND THESE PARTS.
WHAT'S THAT?
THE REASON *MOST* FOLKS COME HERE.
NEWTON'S CREEK
"NEWTON"? AS IN UNIVERSAL LAW OF MOTION AND GRAVITY "ISAAC NEWTON"?
NOPE, AS IN *NETTY* NEWTON. WAGON-TRAIN PIONEER, GOLD PROSPECTOR, LAY PREACHER AND CONVICTED BIGAMIST.
BUT WE'LL TAKE WHAT WE CAN GET, 'CAUSE ONCE THAT GOLD RAN OUT, WITHOUT *NEWTON'S GULCH* NOT SURE WE'D STILL BE ON THE MAP.
NEWTON'S CREEK
SEE, YOU PAY TEN BUCKS TO TOSS A *BALL* INTO THE GULCH.
IT'LL *VANISH* INTO THIN AIR, BUT CHANCES ARE SOME MINUTES LATER IT WILL COME FLYING *BACK* AT YA...
...BECOME QUITE THE THING FOR YOUNG *LOVERS.* WRITE THE *NAME* OF THE ONE THEY WANT TO MARRY ON THE BALL...

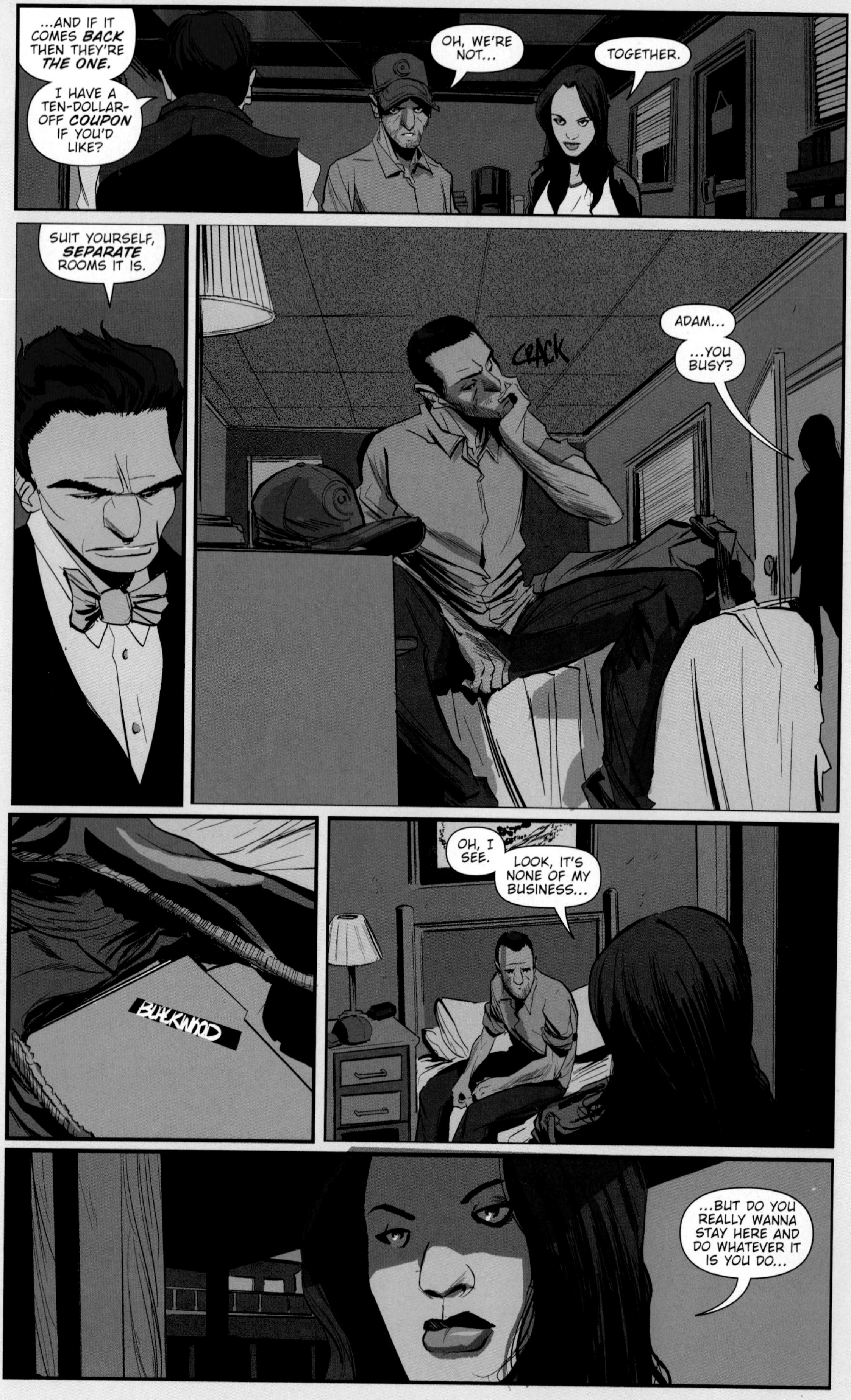
...AND IF IT COMES **BACK** THEN THEY'RE ***THE ONE.***
I HAVE A TEN-DOLLAR-OFF **COUPON** IF YOU'D LIKE?
OH, WE'RE NOT...
TOGETHER.
SUIT YOURSELF, ***SEPARATE*** ROOMS IT IS.
CRACK
ADAM...
...YOU BUSY?
BLACKWOOD
OH, I SEE.
LOOK, IT'S NONE OF MY BUSINESS...
...BUT DO YOU REALLY WANNA STAY HERE AND DO WHATEVER IT IS YOU DO...

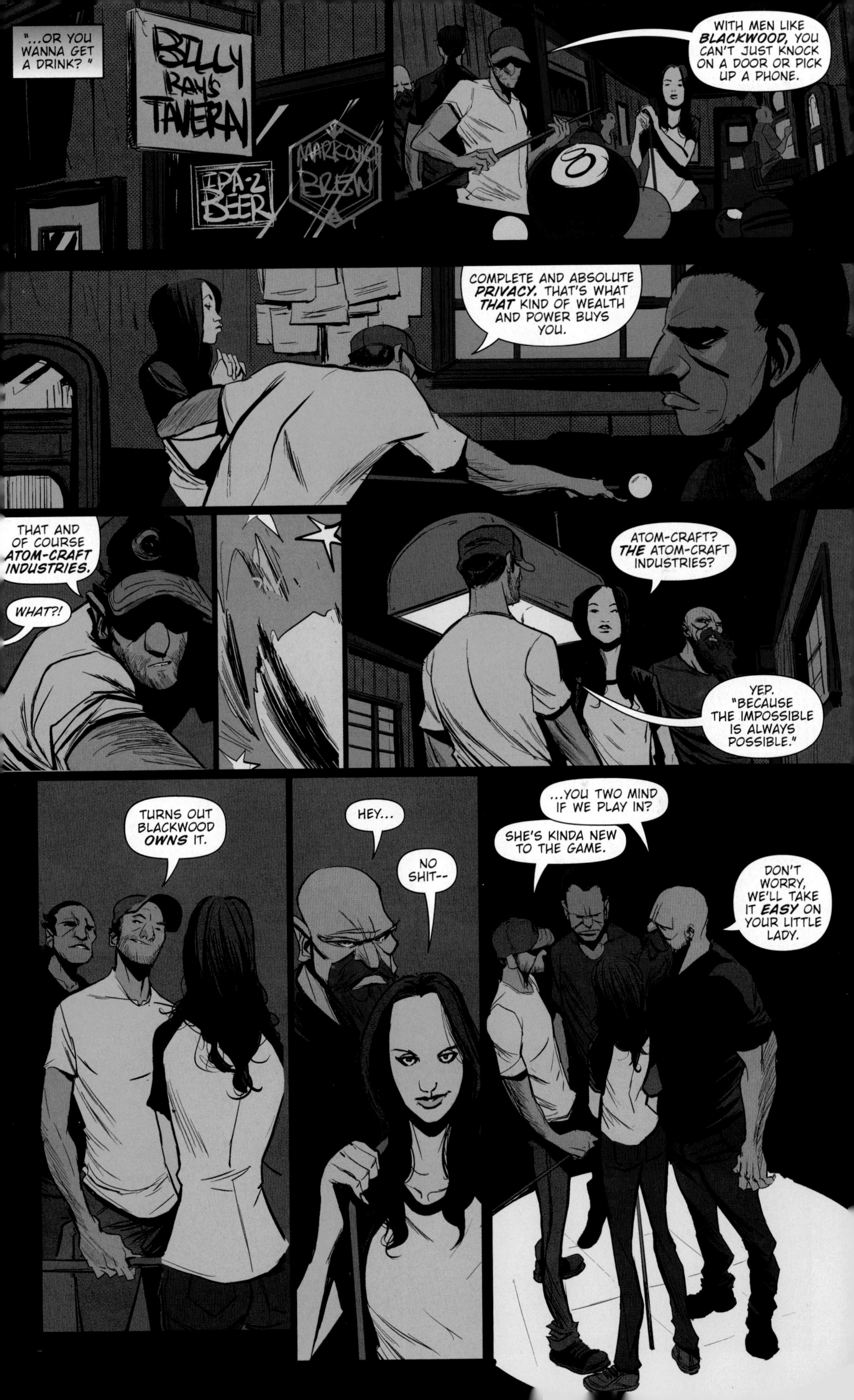
"...OR YOU WANNA GET A DRINK?"
BILLY RAY'S TAVERN
IPA-2 BEER
MARKOVIC BREW
WITH MEN LIKE BLACKWOOD, YOU CAN'T JUST KNOCK ON A DOOR OR PICK UP A PHONE.
COMPLETE AND ABSOLUTE PRIVACY. THAT'S WHAT THAT KIND OF WEALTH AND POWER BUYS YOU.
THAT AND OF COURSE ATOM-CRAFT INDUSTRIES.
WHAT?!
ATOM-CRAFT? THE ATOM-CRAFT INDUSTRIES?
YEP. "BECAUSE THE IMPOSSIBLE IS ALWAYS POSSIBLE."
TURNS OUT BLACKWOOD OWNS IT.
HEY...
NO SHIT--
...YOU TWO MIND IF WE PLAY IN?
SHE'S KINDA NEW TO THE GAME.
DON'T WORRY, WE'LL TAKE IT EASY ON YOUR LITTLE LADY.

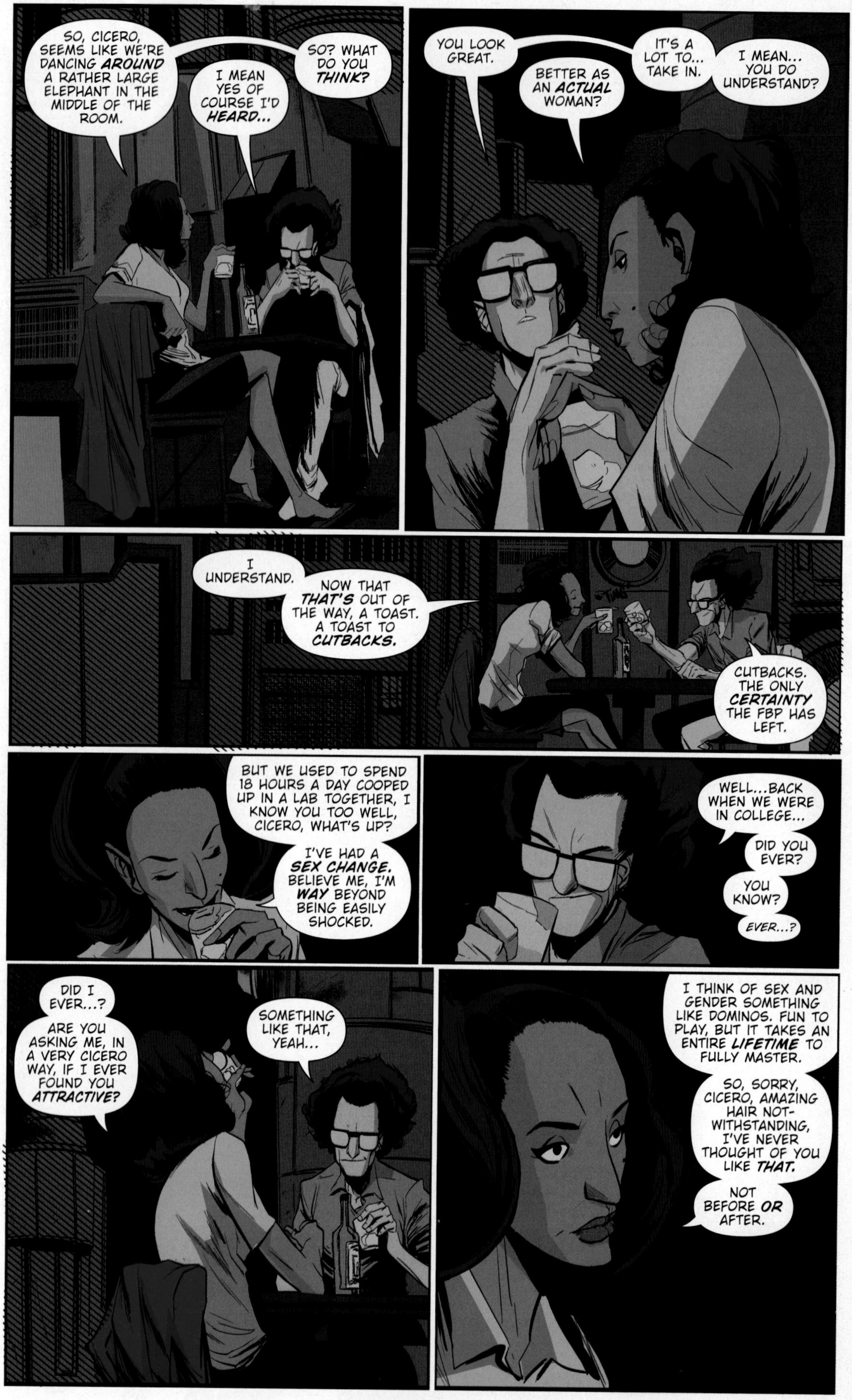

SO, CICERO, SEEMS LIKE WE'RE DANCING AROUND A RATHER LARGE ELEPHANT IN THE MIDDLE OF THE ROOM.
SO? WHAT DO YOU THINK?
I MEAN YES OF COURSE I'D HEARD...
YOU LOOK GREAT.
IT'S A LOT TO... TAKE IN.
BETTER AS AN ACTUAL WOMAN?
I MEAN... YOU DO UNDERSTAND?
I UNDERSTAND.
NOW THAT THAT'S OUT OF THE WAY, A TOAST. A TOAST TO CUTBACKS.
CUTBACKS. THE ONLY CERTAINTY THE FBP HAS LEFT.
BUT WE USED TO SPEND 18 HOURS A DAY COOPED UP IN A LAB TOGETHER, I KNOW YOU TOO WELL, CICERO, WHAT'S UP?
I'VE HAD A SEX CHANGE. BELIEVE ME, I'M WAY BEYOND BEING EASILY SHOCKED.
WELL...BACK WHEN WE WERE IN COLLEGE...
DID YOU EVER?
YOU KNOW?
EVER...?
DID I EVER...?
ARE YOU ASKING ME, IN A VERY CICERO WAY, IF I EVER FOUND YOU ATTRACTIVE?
SOMETHING LIKE THAT, YEAH...
I THINK OF SEX AND GENDER SOMETHING LIKE DOMINOS. FUN TO PLAY, BUT IT TAKES AN ENTIRE LIFETIME TO FULLY MASTER.
SO, SORRY, CICERO, AMAZING HAIR NOT-WITHSTANDING, I'VE NEVER THOUGHT OF YOU LIKE THAT.
NOT BEFORE OR AFTER.

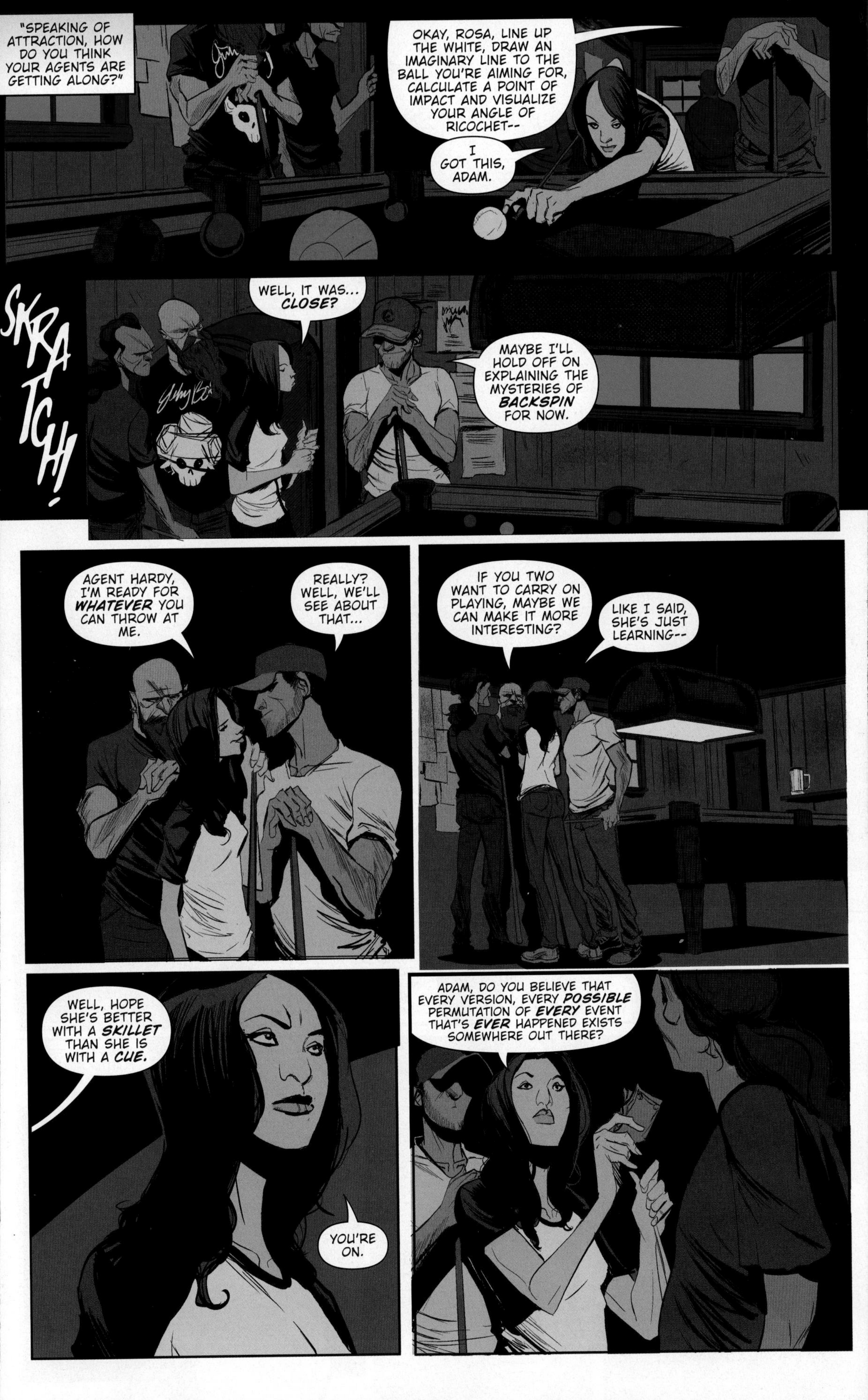
"SPEAKING OF ATTRACTION, HOW DO YOU THINK YOUR AGENTS ARE GETTING ALONG?"
OKAY, ROSA, LINE UP THE WHITE, DRAW AN IMAGINARY LINE TO THE BALL YOU'RE AIMING FOR, CALCULATE A POINT OF IMPACT AND VISUALIZE YOUR ANGLE OF RICOCHET--
I GOT THIS, ADAM.
SKRATCH!
WELL, IT WAS... CLOSE?
MAYBE I'LL HOLD OFF ON EXPLAINING THE MYSTERIES OF BACKSPIN FOR NOW.
AGENT HARDY, I'M READY FOR WHATEVER YOU CAN THROW AT ME.
REALLY? WELL, WE'LL SEE ABOUT THAT...
IF YOU TWO WANT TO CARRY ON PLAYING, MAYBE WE CAN MAKE IT MORE INTERESTING?
LIKE I SAID, SHE'S JUST LEARNING--
WELL, HOPE SHE'S BETTER WITH A SKILLET THAN SHE IS WITH A CUE.
YOU'RE ON.
ADAM, DO YOU BELIEVE THAT EVERY VERSION, EVERY POSSIBLE PERMUTATION OF EVERY EVENT THAT'S EVER HAPPENED EXISTS SOMEWHERE OUT THERE?

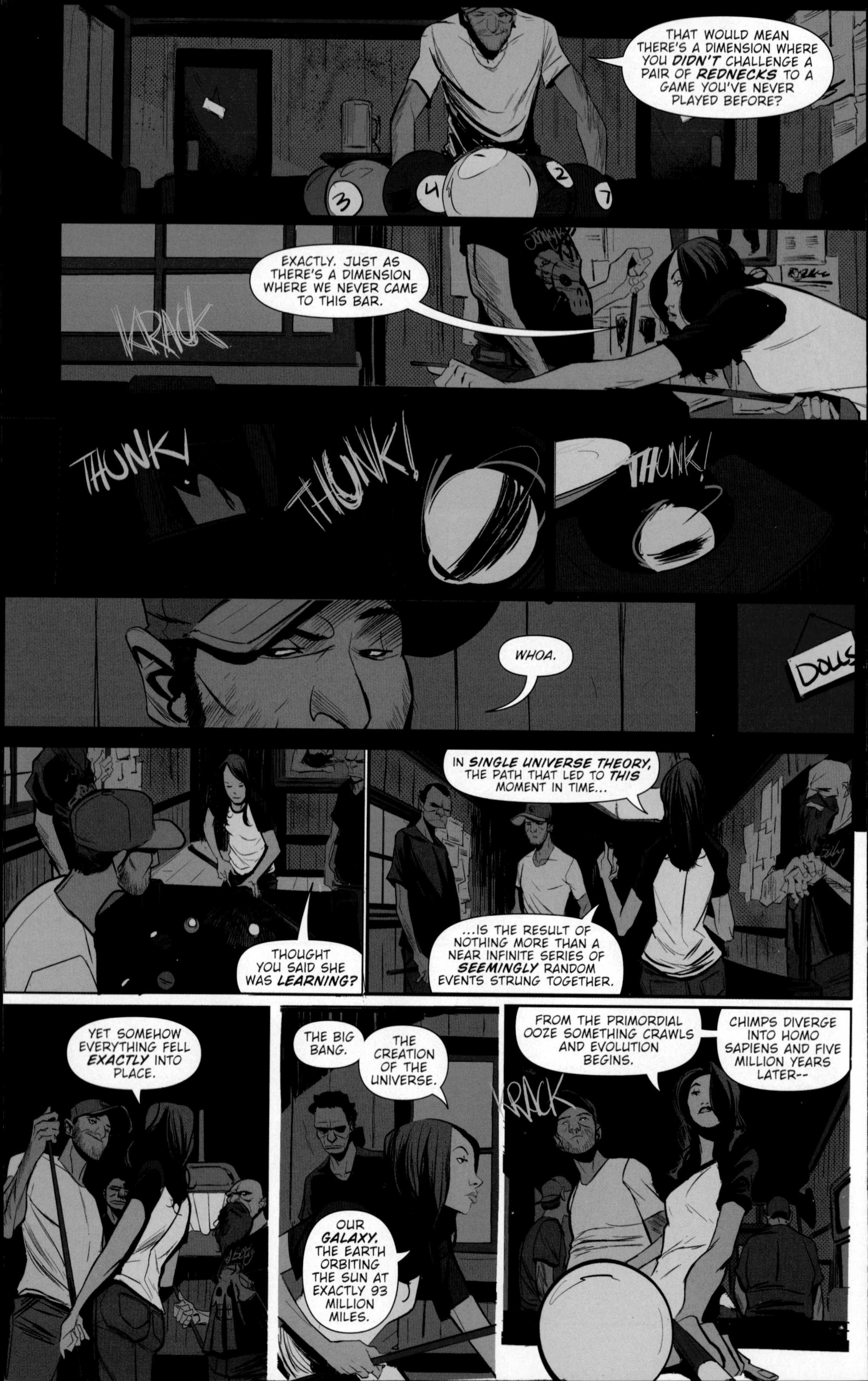
THAT WOULD MEAN THERE'S A DIMENSION WHERE YOU DIDN'T CHALLENGE A PAIR OF REDNECKS TO A GAME YOU'VE NEVER PLAYED BEFORE?
EXACTLY. JUST AS THERE'S A DIMENSION WHERE WE NEVER CAME TO THIS BAR.
KRACK
THUNK!
THUNK!
THUNK!
WHOA.
DOLLS
THOUGHT YOU SAID SHE WAS LEARNING?
IN SINGLE UNIVERSE THEORY, THE PATH THAT LED TO THIS MOMENT IN TIME...
...IS THE RESULT OF NOTHING MORE THAN A NEAR INFINITE SERIES OF SEEMINGLY RANDOM EVENTS STRUNG TOGETHER.
YET SOMEHOW EVERYTHING FELL EXACTLY INTO PLACE.
THE BIG BANG.
THE CREATION OF THE UNIVERSE.
OUR GALAXY. THE EARTH ORBITING THE SUN AT EXACTLY 93 MILLION MILES.
FROM THE PRIMORDIAL OOZE SOMETHING CRAWLS AND EVOLUTION BEGINS.
CHIMPS DIVERGE INTO HOMO SAPIENS AND FIVE MILLION YEARS LATER--
KRACK

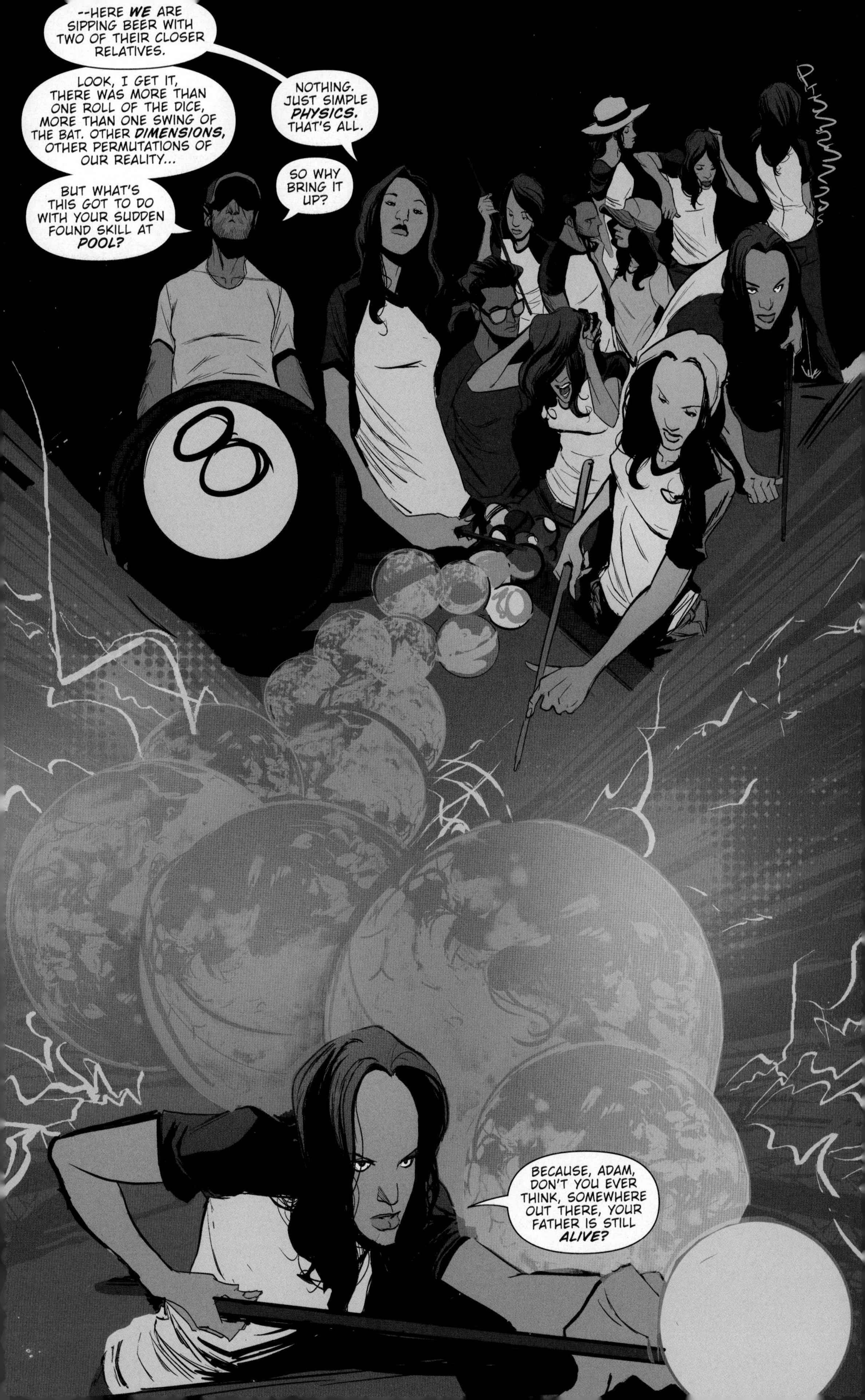

--HERE WE ARE SIPPING BEER WITH TWO OF THEIR CLOSER RELATIVES.
LOOK, I GET IT, THERE WAS MORE THAN ONE ROLL OF THE DICE, MORE THAN ONE SWING OF THE BAT. OTHER DIMENSIONS, OTHER PERMUTATIONS OF OUR REALITY...
BUT WHAT'S THIS GOT TO DO WITH YOUR SUDDEN FOUND SKILL AT POOL?
NOTHING. JUST SIMPLE PHYSICS. THAT'S ALL.
SO WHY BRING IT UP?
BECAUSE, ADAM, DON'T YOU EVER THINK, SOMEWHERE OUT THERE, YOUR FATHER IS STILL ALIVE?

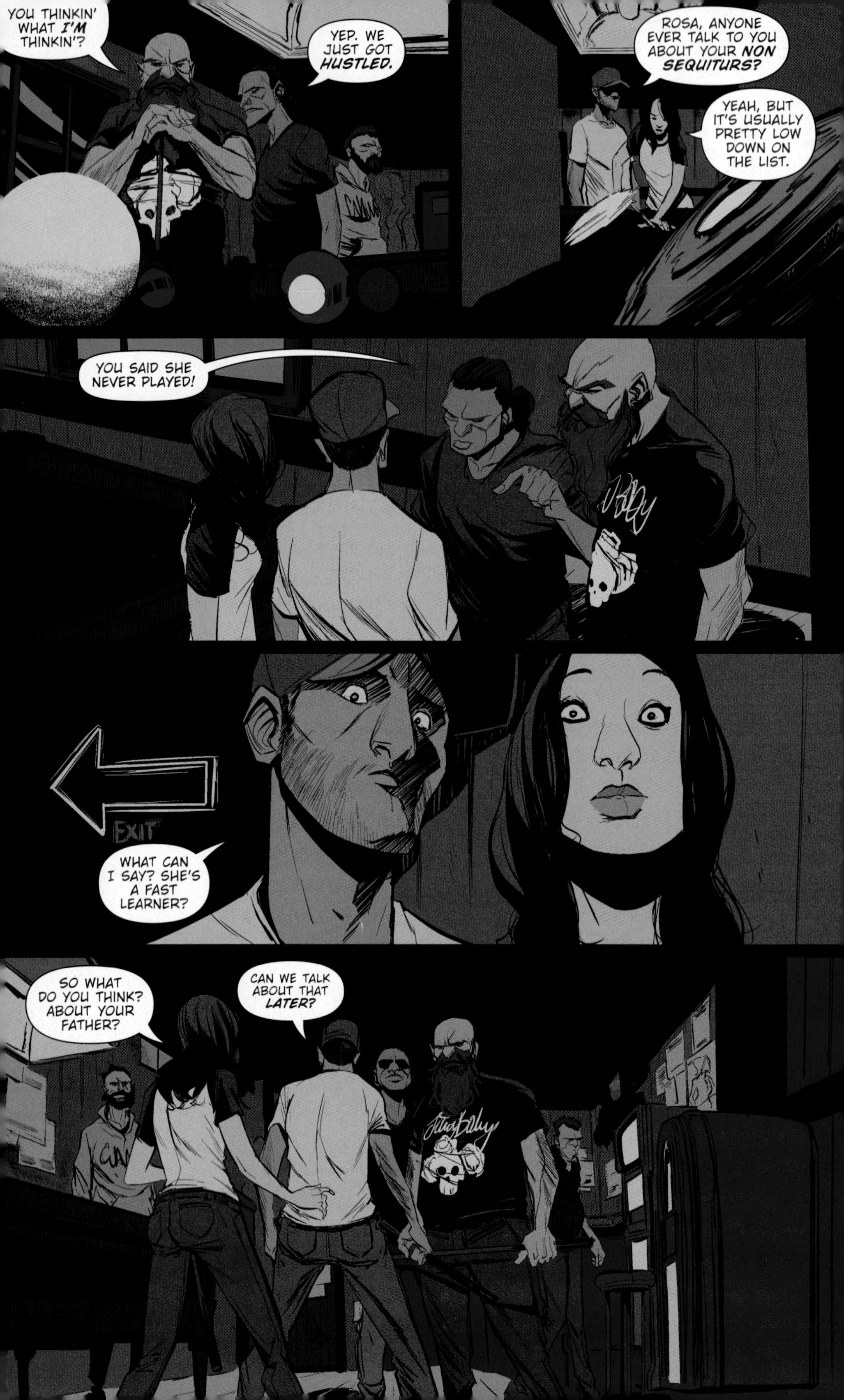
YOU THINKIN' WHAT *I'M* THINKIN'?
YEP. WE JUST GOT *HUSTLED.*
ROSA, ANYONE EVER TALK TO YOU ABOUT YOUR *NON SEQUITURS?*
YEAH, BUT IT'S USUALLY PRETTY LOW DOWN ON THE LIST.
YOU SAID SHE NEVER PLAYED!
EXIT
WHAT CAN I SAY? SHE'S A FAST LEARNER?
SO WHAT DO YOU THINK? ABOUT YOUR FATHER?
CAN WE TALK ABOUT THAT *LATER?*

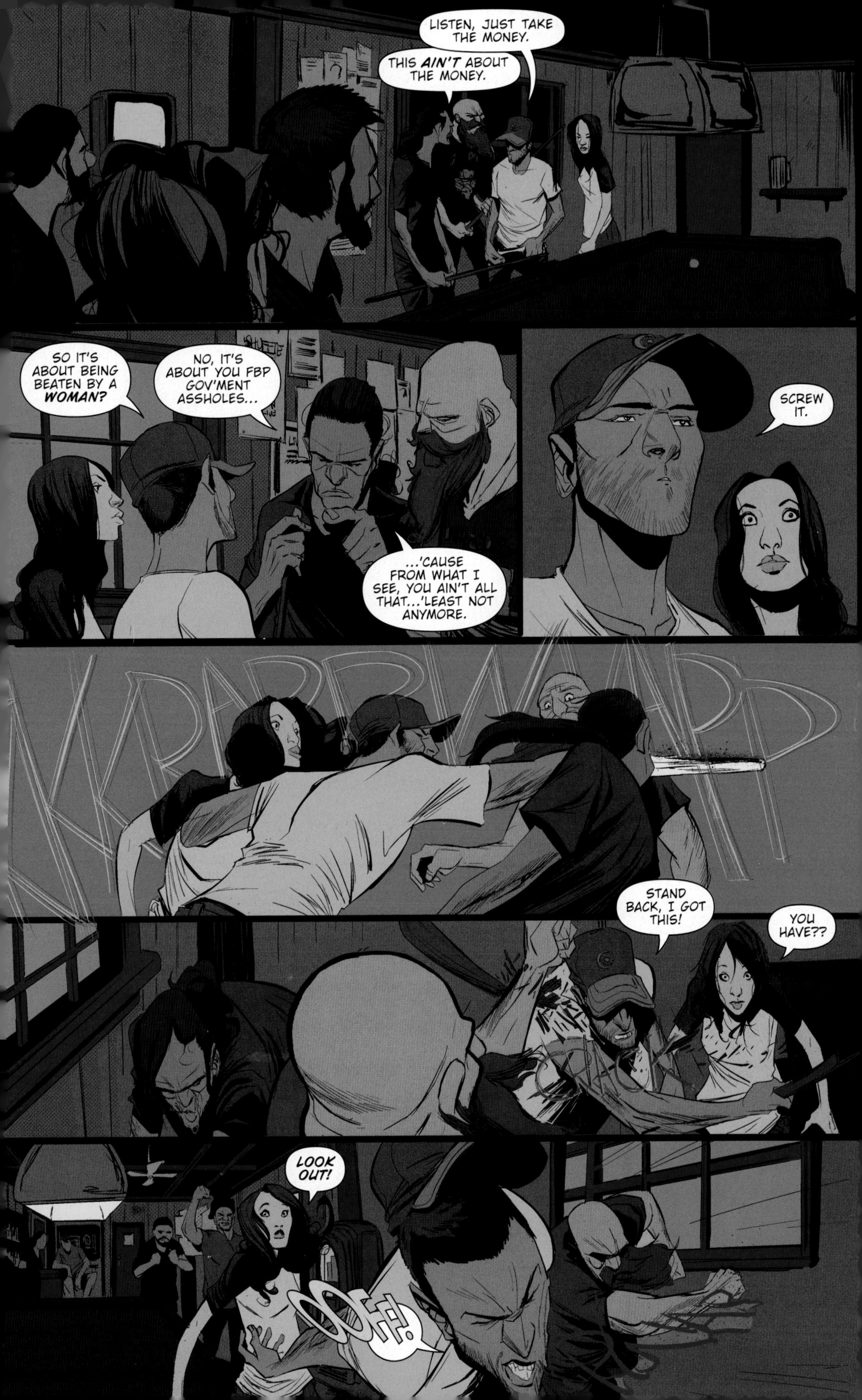
LISTEN, JUST TAKE THE MONEY.
THIS AIN'T ABOUT THE MONEY.
SO IT'S ABOUT BEING BEATEN BY A WOMAN?
NO, IT'S ABOUT YOU FBP GOV'MENT ASSHOLES...
...'CAUSE FROM WHAT I SEE, YOU AIN'T ALL THAT...'LEAST NOT ANYMORE.
SCREW IT.
KRAPPWAPP
STAND BACK, I GOT THIS!
YOU HAVE??
LOOK OUT!
OOF!

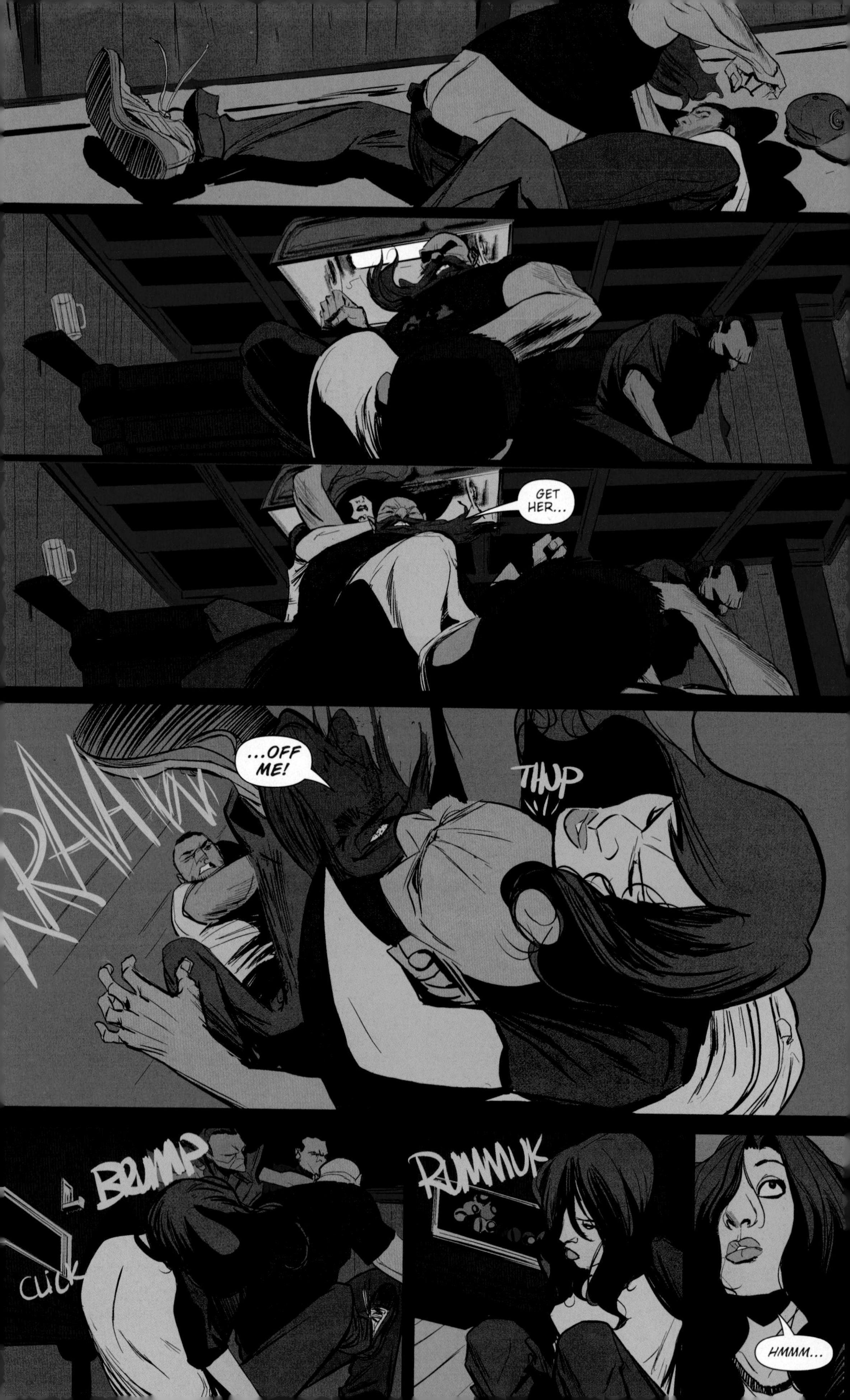

GET HER...
...OFF ME!
THUP
BRUMP
CLICK
RUMMUK
HMMM...

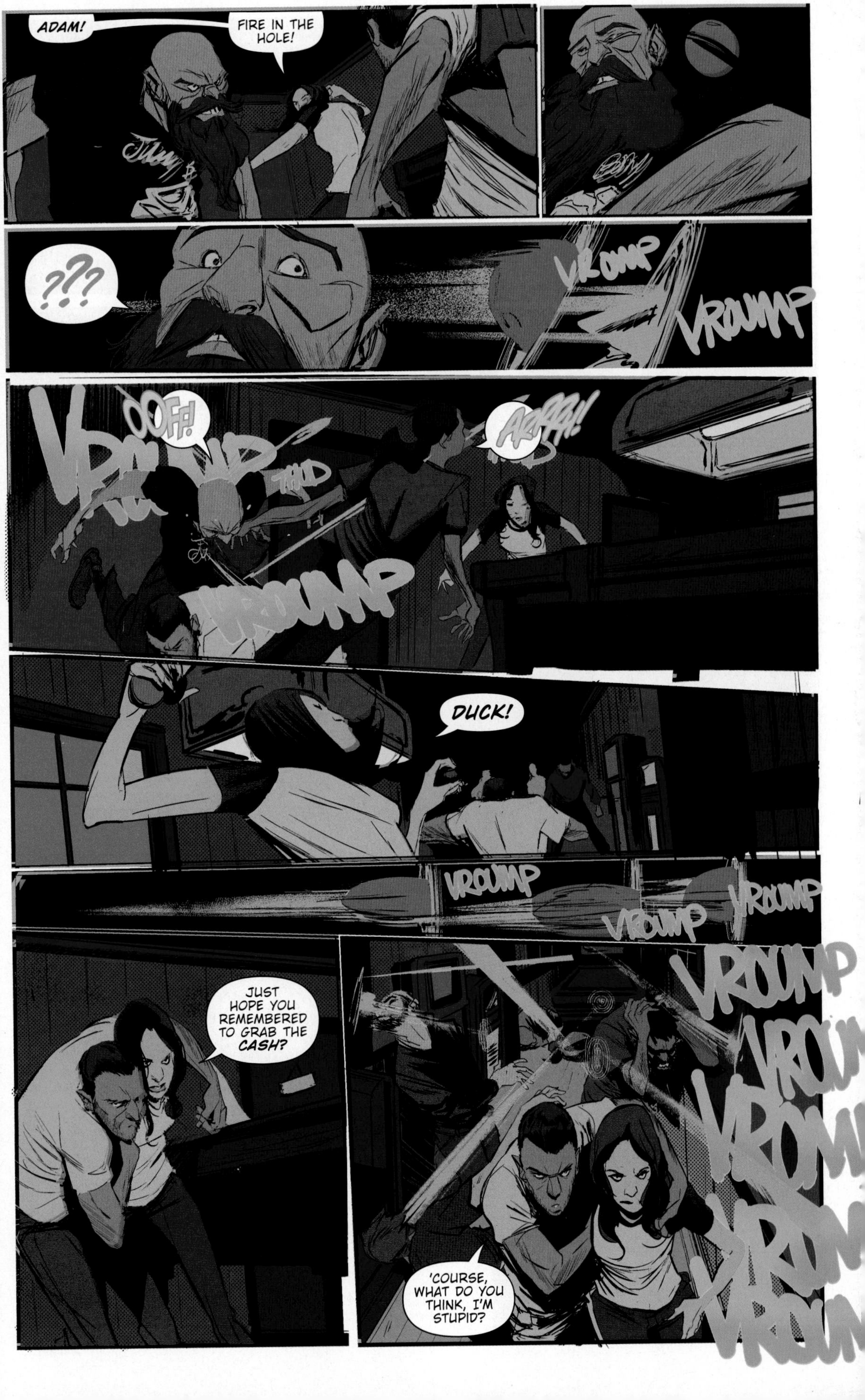
ADAM!
FIRE IN THE HOLE!
???
VROUMP
VROUMP
OOFF!
THUD
VROUMP
DUCK!
VROUMP
VROUMP
VROUMP
JUST HOPE YOU REMEMBERED TO GRAB THE CASH?
VROUMP
'COURSE, WHAT DO YOU THINK, I'M STUPID?

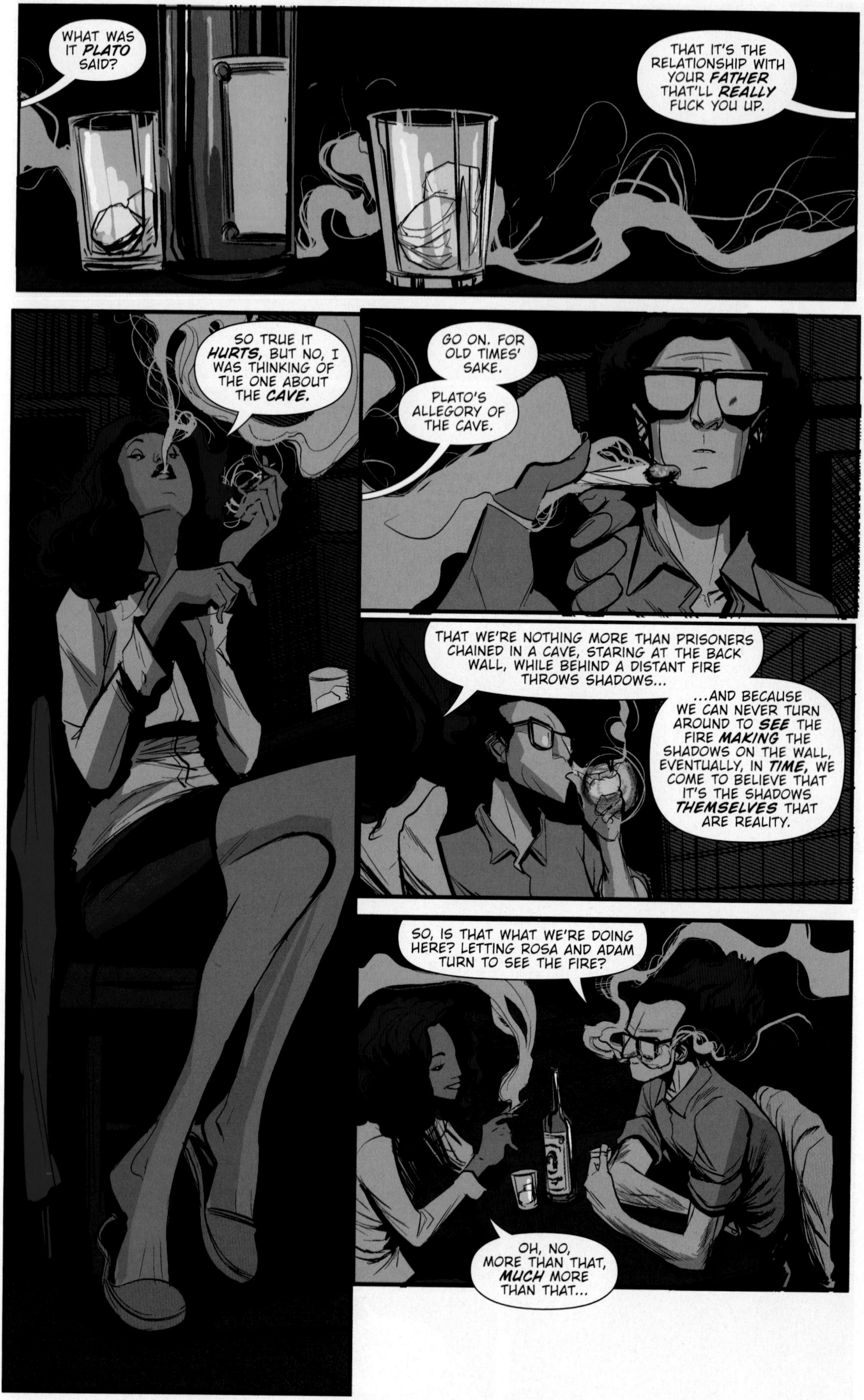
WHAT WAS IT PLATO SAID?
THAT IT'S THE RELATIONSHIP WITH YOUR FATHER THAT'LL REALLY FUCK YOU UP.
SO TRUE IT HURTS, BUT NO, I WAS THINKING OF THE ONE ABOUT THE CAVE.
GO ON. FOR OLD TIMES' SAKE.
PLATO'S ALLEGORY OF THE CAVE.
THAT WE'RE NOTHING MORE THAN PRISONERS CHAINED IN A CAVE, STARING AT THE BACK WALL, WHILE BEHIND A DISTANT FIRE THROWS SHADOWS...
...AND BECAUSE WE CAN NEVER TURN AROUND TO SEE THE FIRE MAKING THE SHADOWS ON THE WALL, EVENTUALLY, IN TIME, WE COME TO BELIEVE THAT IT'S THE SHADOWS THEMSELVES THAT ARE REALITY.
SO, IS THAT WHAT WE'RE DOING HERE? LETTING ROSA AND ADAM TURN TO SEE THE FIRE?
OH, NO, MORE THAN THAT, MUCH MORE THAN THAT...

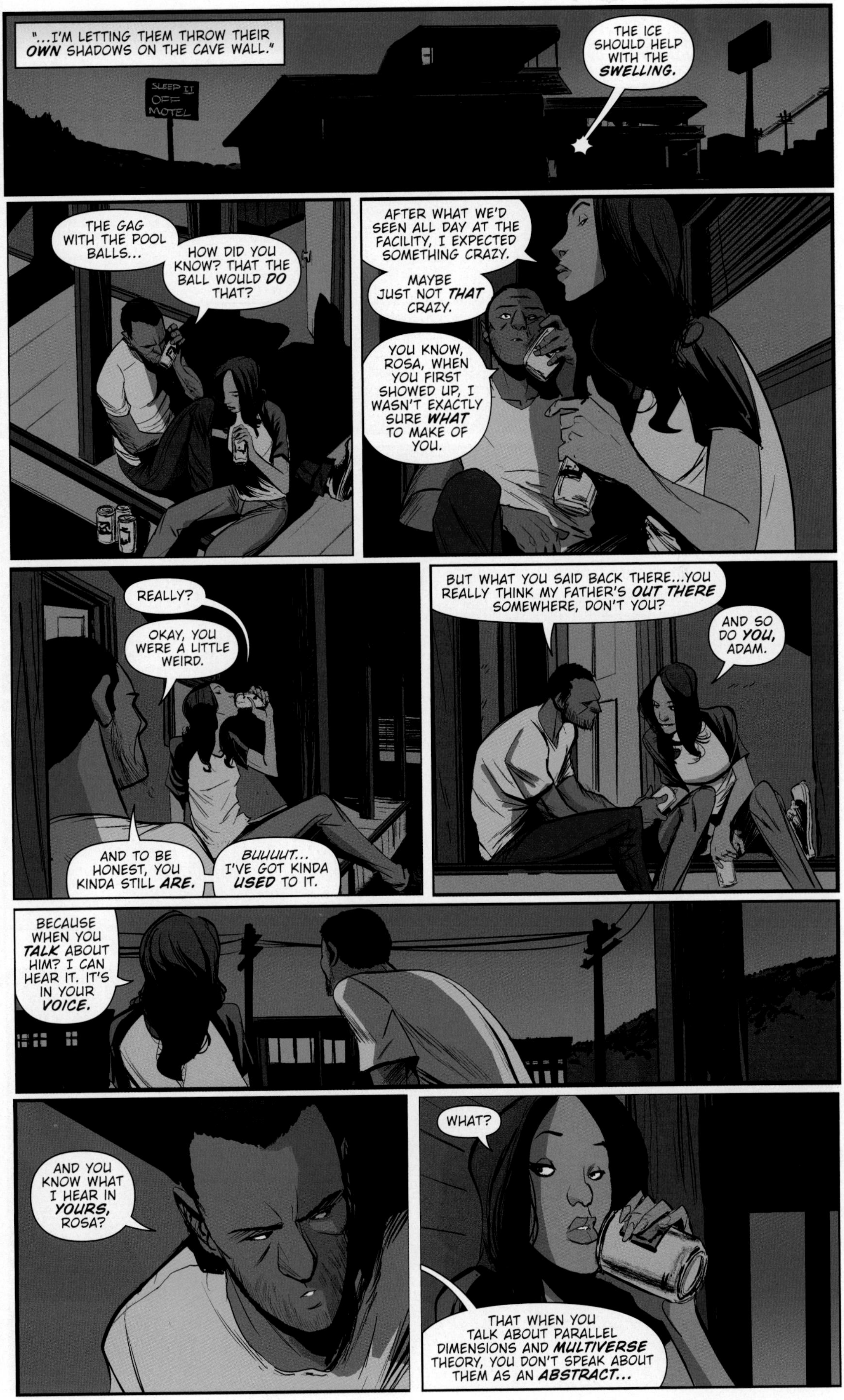
"...I'M LETTING THEM THROW THEIR OWN SHADOWS ON THE CAVE WALL."
SLEEP IT OFF MOTEL
THE ICE SHOULD HELP WITH THE SWELLING.
THE GAG WITH THE POOL BALLS...
HOW DID YOU KNOW? THAT THE BALL WOULD DO THAT?
AFTER WHAT WE'D SEEN ALL DAY AT THE FACILITY, I EXPECTED SOMETHING CRAZY.
MAYBE JUST NOT THAT CRAZY.
YOU KNOW, ROSA, WHEN YOU FIRST SHOWED UP, I WASN'T EXACTLY SURE WHAT TO MAKE OF YOU.
REALLY?
OKAY, YOU WERE A LITTLE WEIRD.
AND TO BE HONEST, YOU KINDA STILL ARE.
BUUUUT... I'VE GOT KINDA USED TO IT.
BUT WHAT YOU SAID BACK THERE...YOU REALLY THINK MY FATHER'S OUT THERE SOMEWHERE, DON'T YOU?
AND SO DO YOU, ADAM.
BECAUSE WHEN YOU TALK ABOUT HIM? I CAN HEAR IT. IT'S IN YOUR VOICE.
AND YOU KNOW WHAT I HEAR IN YOURS, ROSA?
WHAT?
THAT WHEN YOU TALK ABOUT PARALLEL DIMENSIONS AND MULTIVERSE THEORY, YOU DON'T SPEAK ABOUT THEM AS AN ABSTRACT...

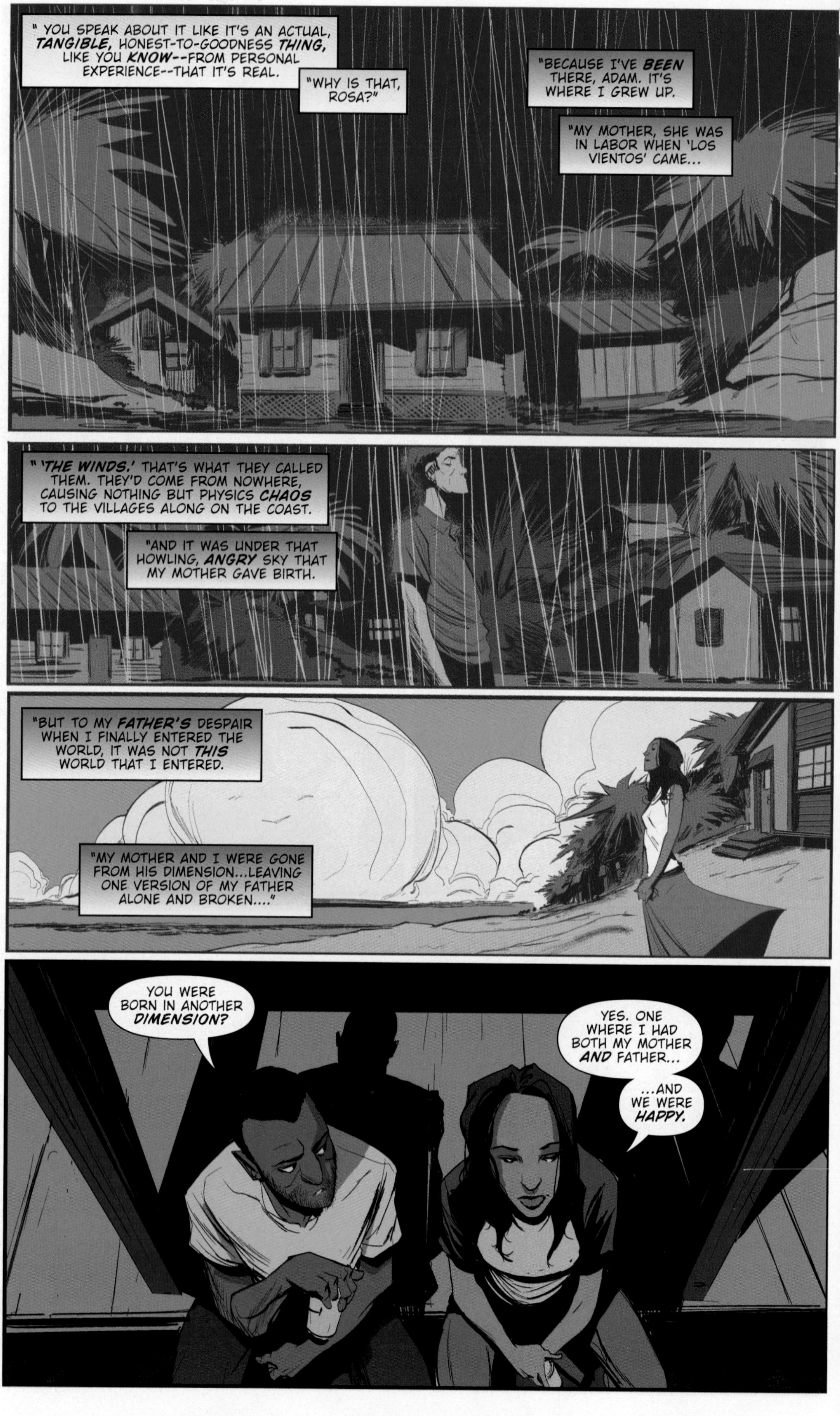
" YOU SPEAK ABOUT IT LIKE IT'S AN ACTUAL, TANGIBLE, HONEST-TO-GOODNESS THING, LIKE YOU KNOW--FROM PERSONAL EXPERIENCE--THAT IT'S REAL.
"WHY IS THAT, ROSA?"
"BECAUSE I'VE BEEN THERE, ADAM. IT'S WHERE I GREW UP.
"MY MOTHER, SHE WAS IN LABOR WHEN 'LOS VIENTOS' CAME...
" 'THE WINDS.' THAT'S WHAT THEY CALLED THEM. THEY'D COME FROM NOWHERE, CAUSING NOTHING BUT PHYSICS CHAOS TO THE VILLAGES ALONG ON THE COAST.
"AND IT WAS UNDER THAT HOWLING, ANGRY SKY THAT MY MOTHER GAVE BIRTH.
"BUT TO MY FATHER'S DESPAIR WHEN I FINALLY ENTERED THE WORLD, IT WAS NOT THIS WORLD THAT I ENTERED.
"MY MOTHER AND I WERE GONE FROM HIS DIMENSION...LEAVING ONE VERSION OF MY FATHER ALONE AND BROKEN...."
YOU WERE BORN IN ANOTHER DIMENSION?
YES. ONE WHERE I HAD BOTH MY MOTHER AND FATHER...
...AND WE WERE HAPPY.

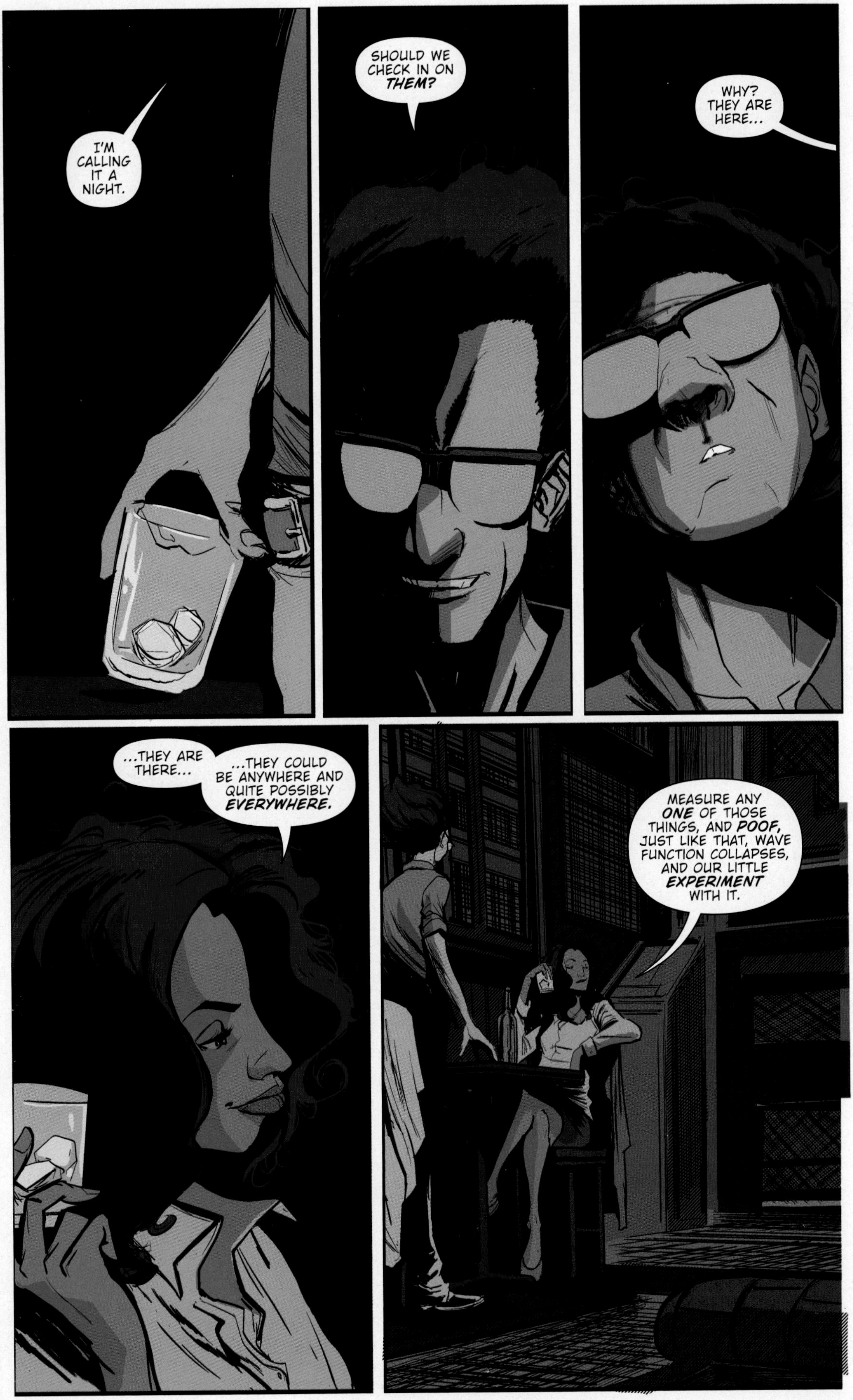
I'M CALLING IT A NIGHT.
SHOULD WE CHECK IN ON *THEM?*
WHY? THEY ARE HERE...
...THEY ARE THERE...
...THEY COULD BE ANYWHERE AND QUITE POSSIBLY *EVERYWHERE.*
MEASURE ANY *ONE* OF THOSE THINGS, AND *POOF,* JUST LIKE THAT, WAVE FUNCTION COLLAPSES, AND OUR LITTLE *EXPERIMENT* WITH IT.

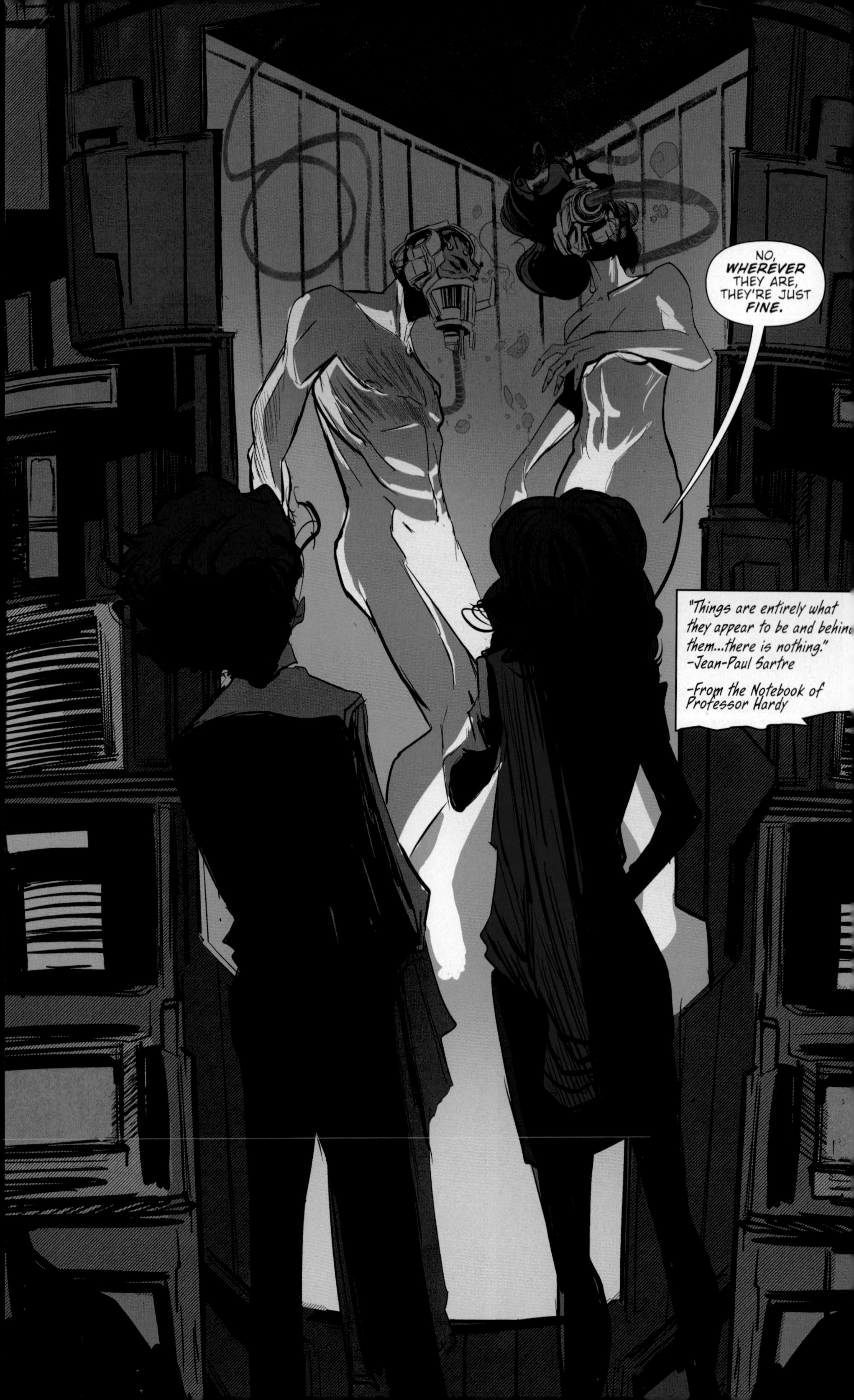
NO, *WHEREVER* THEY ARE, THEY'RE JUST *FINE.*
"Things are entirely what they appear to be and behind them...there is nothing." -Jean-Paul Sartre
-From the Notebook of Professor Hardy

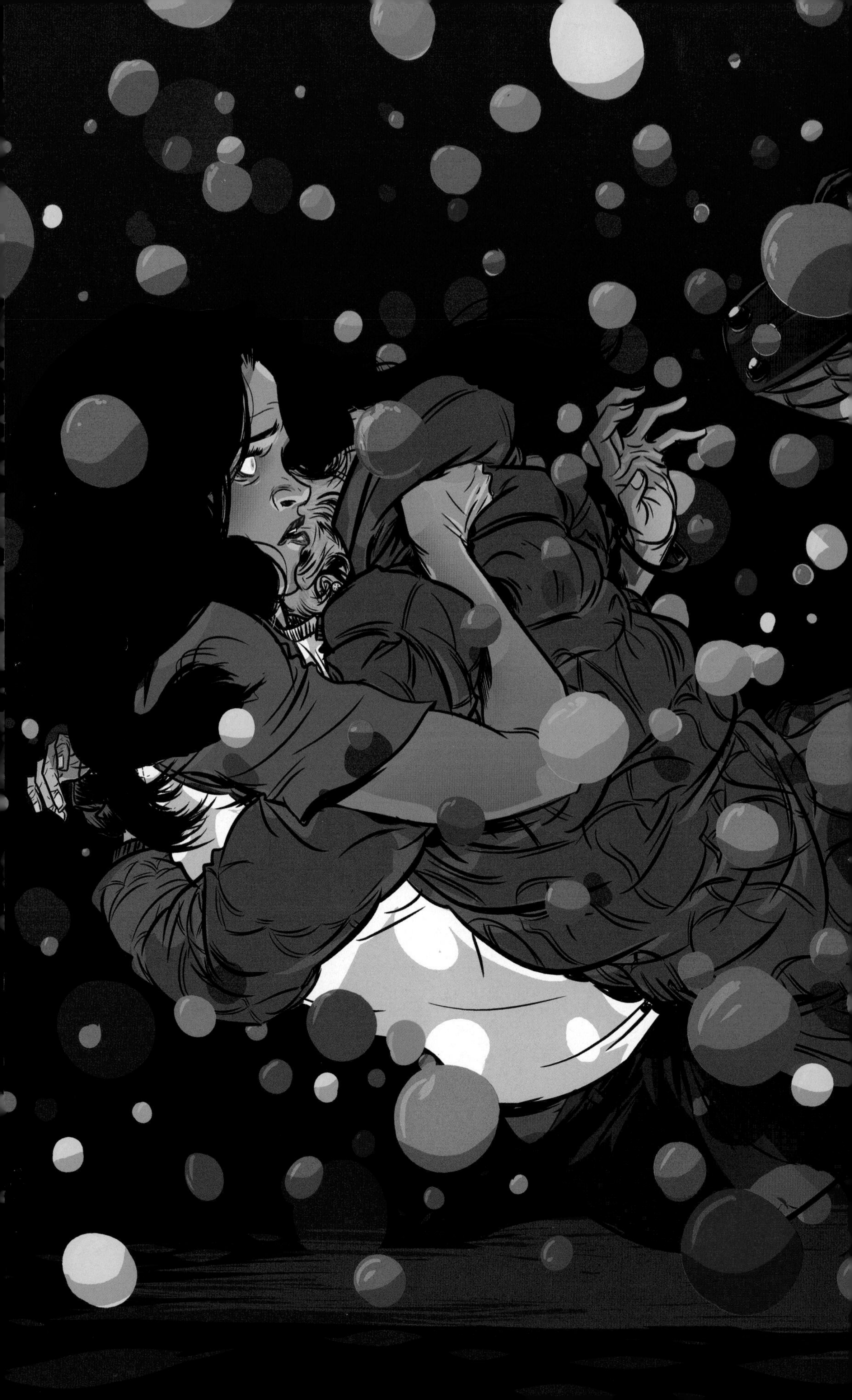

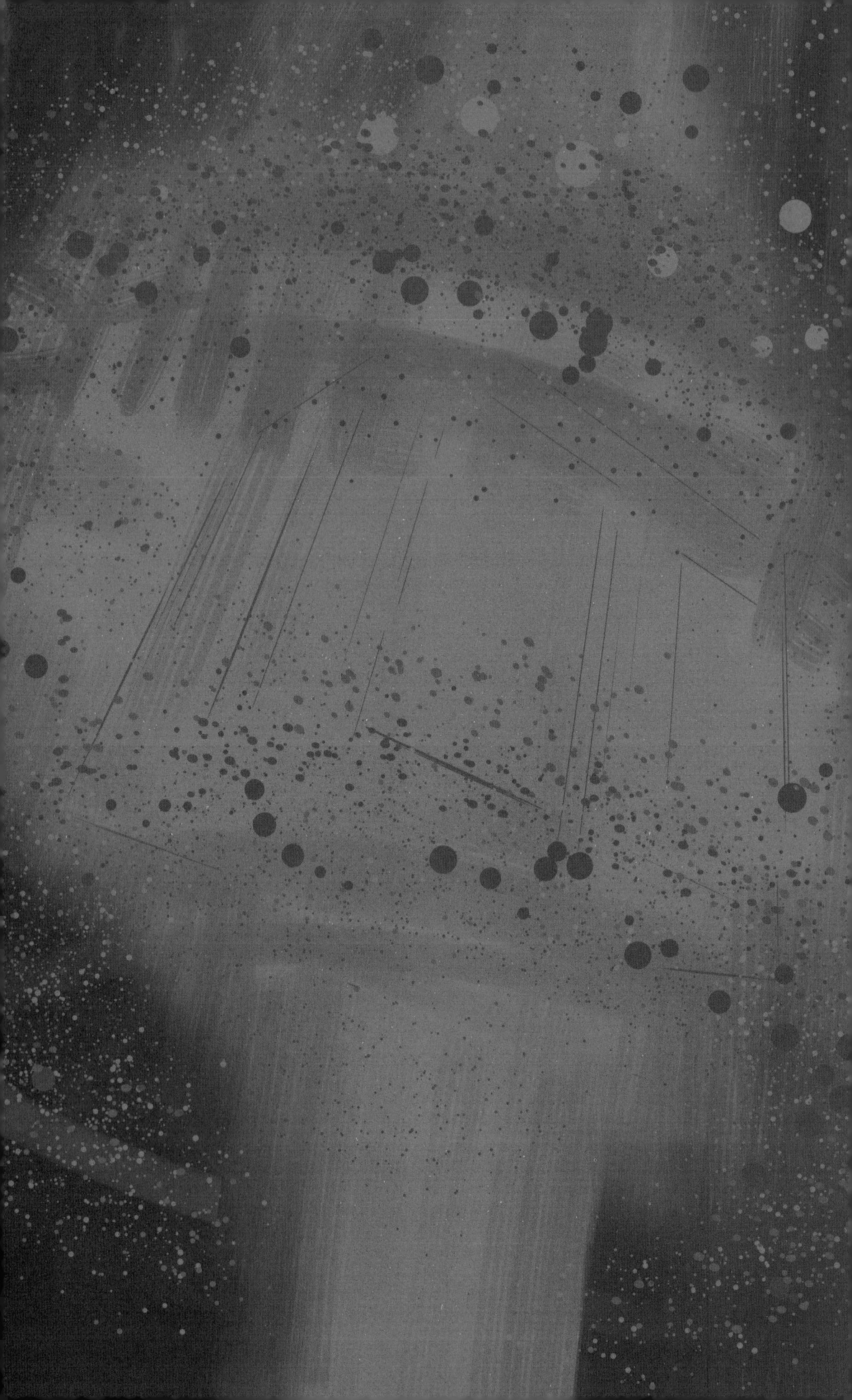

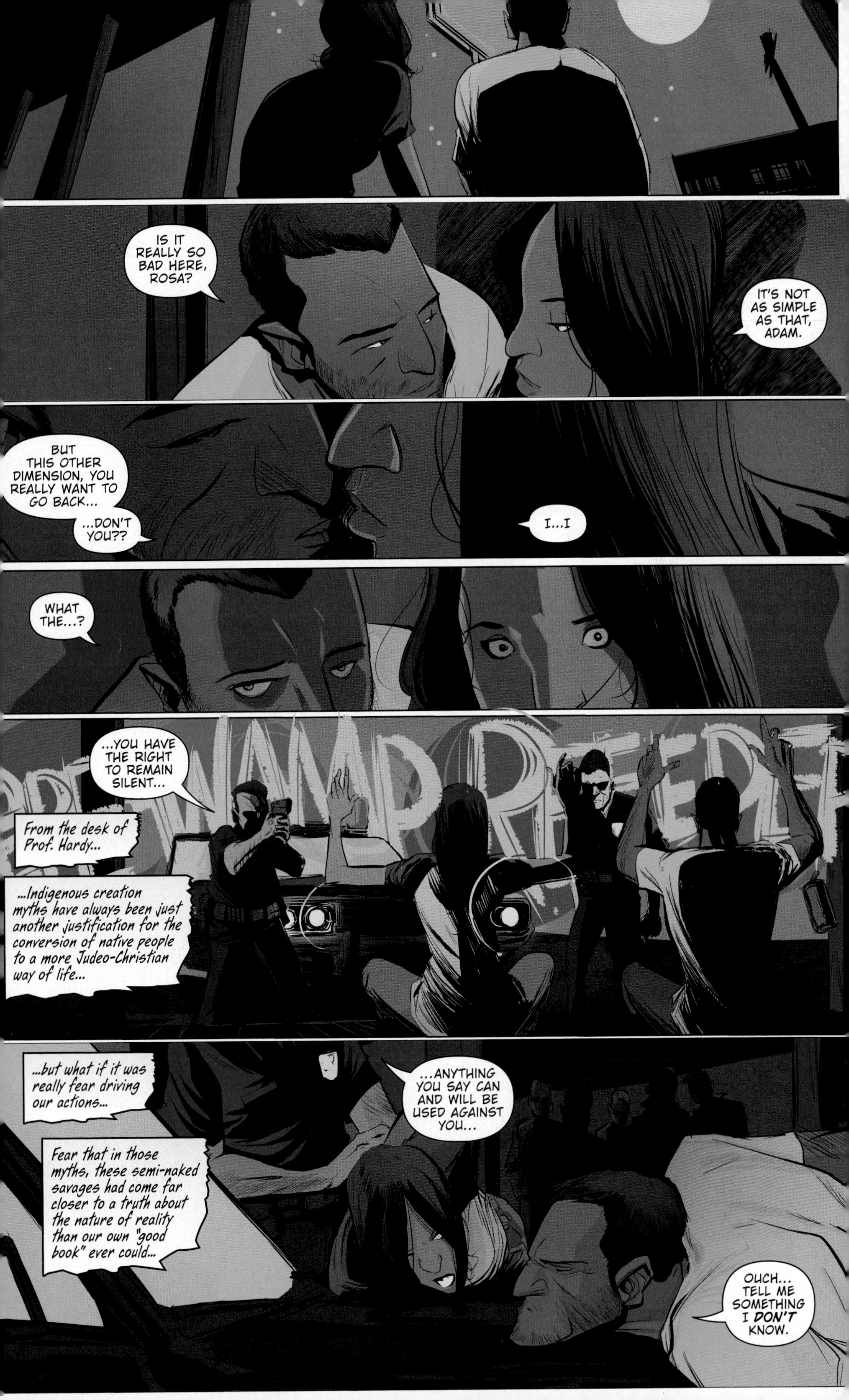
IS IT REALLY SO BAD HERE, ROSA?
IT'S NOT AS SIMPLE AS THAT, ADAM.
BUT THIS OTHER DIMENSION, YOU REALLY WANT TO GO BACK...
...DON'T YOU??
I...I
WHAT THE...?
...YOU HAVE THE RIGHT TO REMAIN SILENT...
From the desk of Prof. Hardy...
...Indigenous creation myths have always been just another justification for the conversion of native people to a more Judeo-Christian way of life...
...but what if it was really fear driving our actions...
...ANYTHING YOU SAY CAN AND WILL BE USED AGAINST YOU...
Fear that in those myths, these semi-naked savages had come far closer to a truth about the nature of reality than our own "good book" ever could...
OUCH... TELL ME SOMETHING I **DON'T** KNOW.

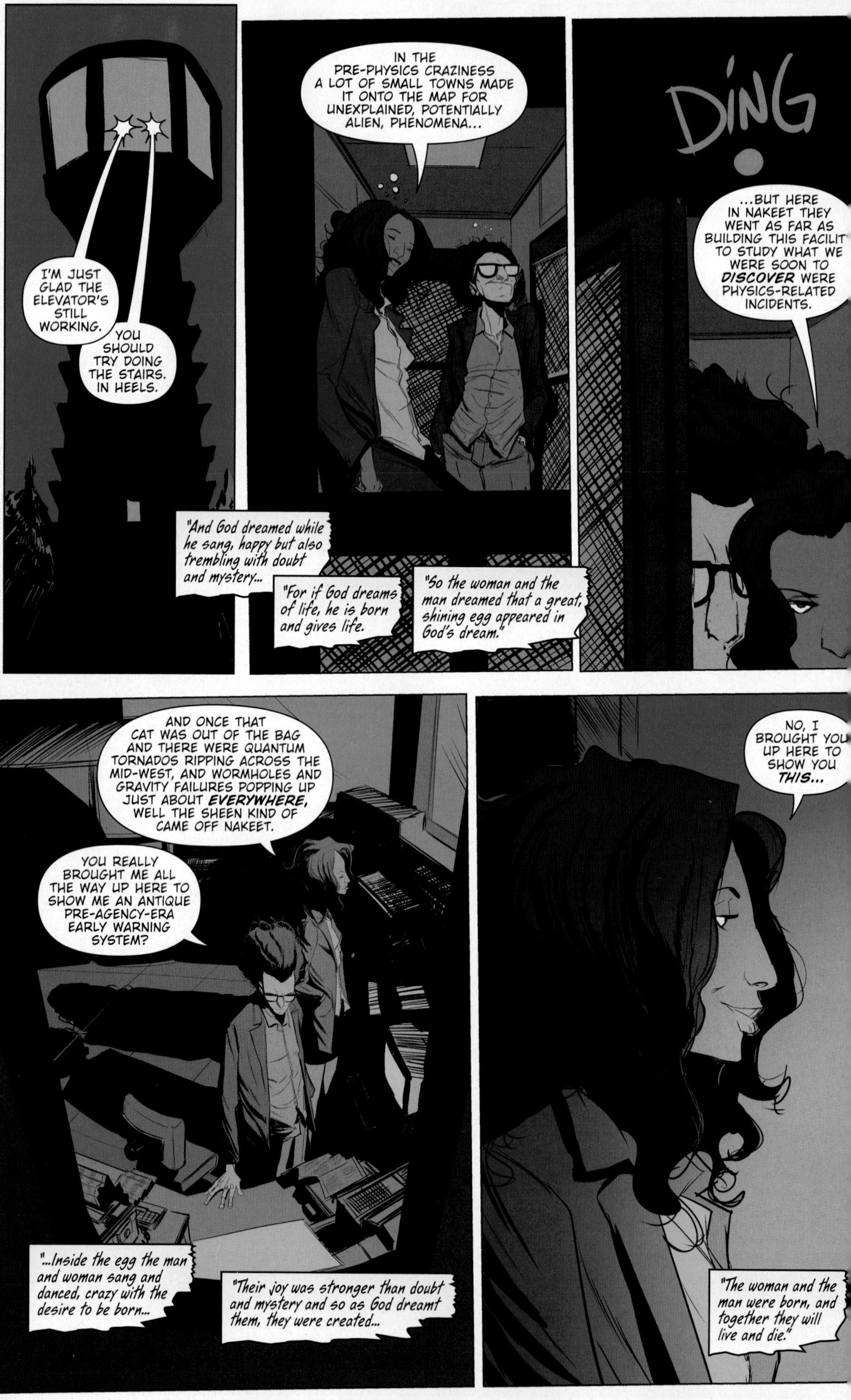
I'M JUST GLAD THE ELEVATOR'S STILL WORKING.
YOU SHOULD TRY DOING THE STAIRS. IN HEELS.
IN THE PRE-PHYSICS CRAZINESS A LOT OF SMALL TOWNS MADE IT ONTO THE MAP FOR UNEXPLAINED, POTENTIALLY ALIEN, PHENOMENA...
"And God dreamed while he sang, happy but also trembling with doubt and mystery...
"For if God dreams of life, he is born and gives life.
"So the woman and the man dreamed that a great, shining egg appeared in God's dream."
DING
...BUT HERE IN NAKEET THEY WENT AS FAR AS BUILDING THIS FACILIT TO STUDY WHAT WE WERE SOON TO DISCOVER WERE PHYSICS-RELATED INCIDENTS.
AND ONCE THAT CAT WAS OUT OF THE BAG AND THERE WERE QUANTUM TORNADOS RIPPING ACROSS THE MID-WEST, AND WORMHOLES AND GRAVITY FAILURES POPPING UP JUST ABOUT EVERYWHERE, WELL THE SHEEN KIND OF CAME OFF NAKEET.
YOU REALLY BROUGHT ME ALL THE WAY UP HERE TO SHOW ME AN ANTIQUE PRE-AGENCY-ERA EARLY WARNING SYSTEM?
"...Inside the egg the man and woman sang and danced, crazy with the desire to be born...
"Their joy was stronger than doubt and mystery and so as God dreamt them, they were created...
NO, I BROUGHT YOU UP HERE TO SHOW YOU THIS...
"The woman and the man were born, and together they will live and die."

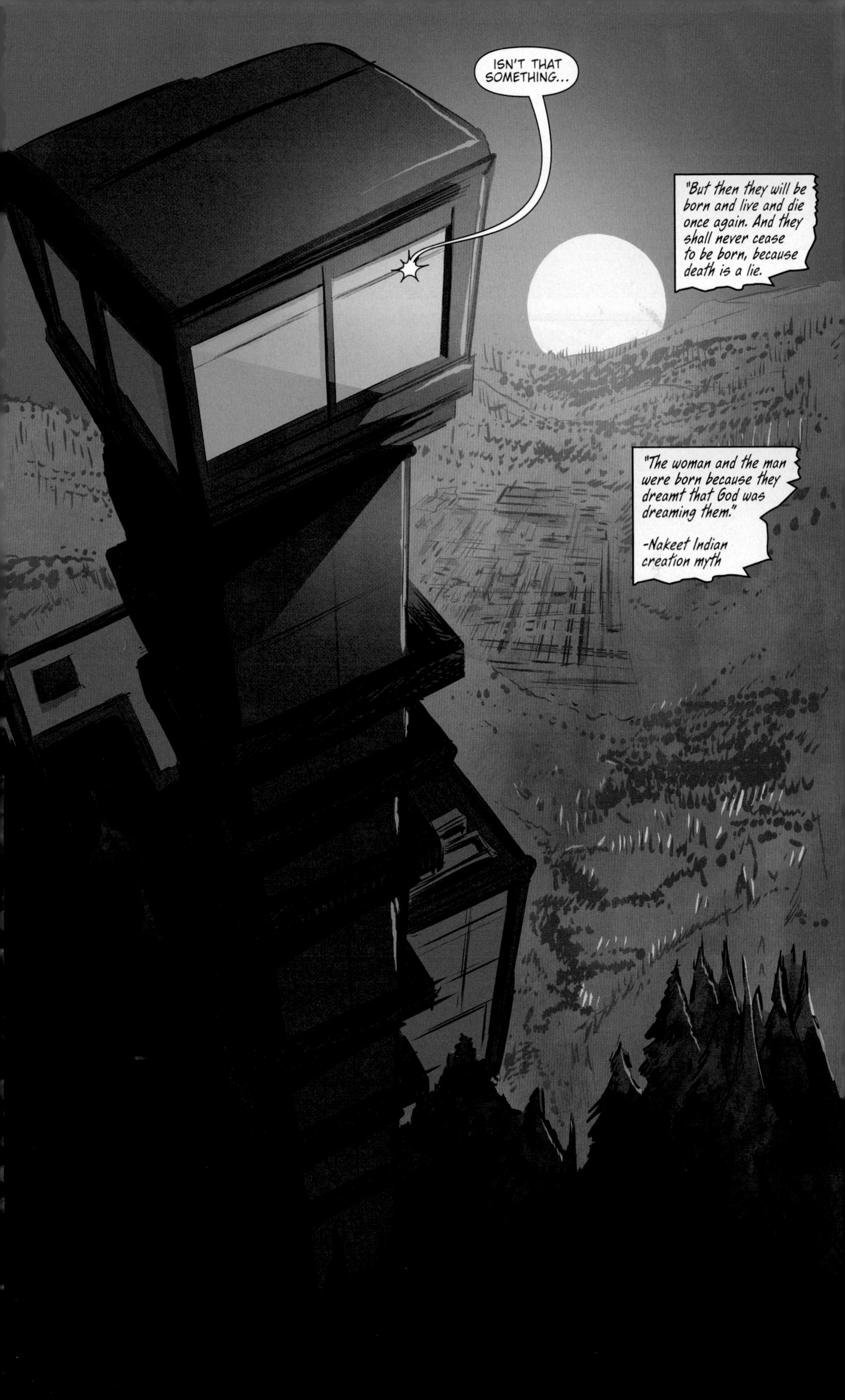
ISN'T THAT SOMETHING...
"But then they will be born and live and die once again. And they shall never cease to be born, because death is a lie.
"The woman and the man were born because they dreamt that God was dreaming them."
-Nakeet Indian creation myth

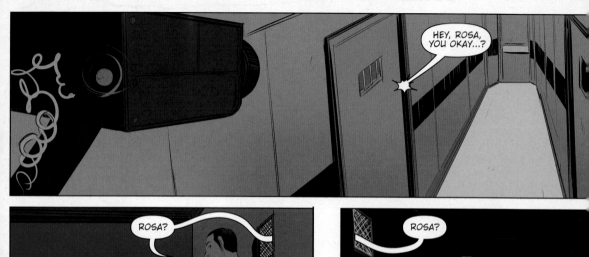

HEY, ROSA, YOU OKAY...?

ROSA?

ROSA?

YEAH, I'M OKAY...

GOOD, 'CAUSE I WAS STARTING TO WORRY...

GET UP, BOSS WANTS TO SEE YOU...

DON'T WORRY ABOUT ME.

DON'T SWEAT IT, IT'S A MISUNDERSTAND-ING, HAPPENS ALL THE TIME TO ME.

I'LL WORK A LITTLE MAGIC, HAVE US OUT IN NO TIME.

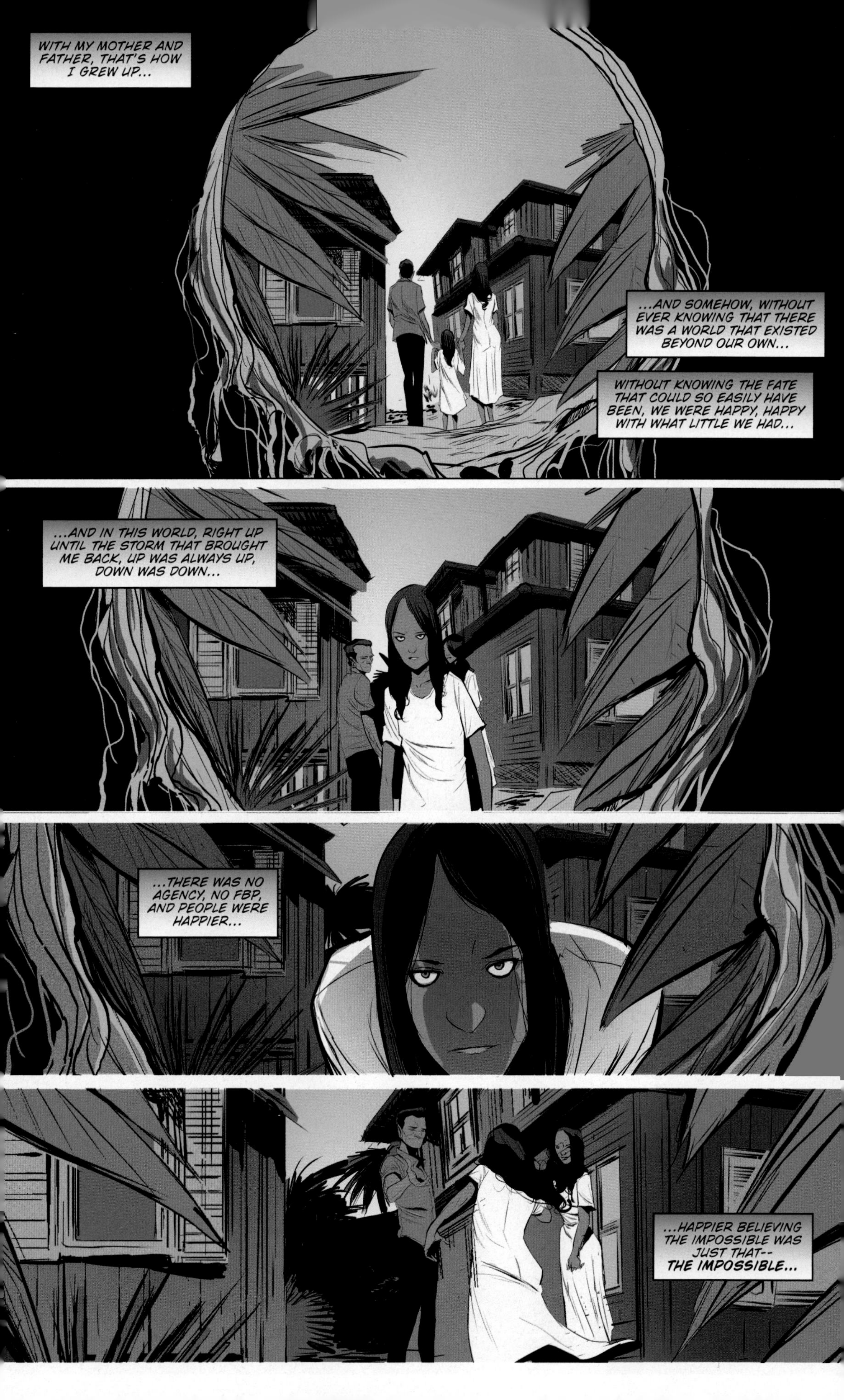
WITH MY MOTHER AND FATHER, THAT'S HOW I GREW UP...
...AND SOMEHOW, WITHOUT EVER KNOWING THAT THERE WAS A WORLD THAT EXISTED BEYOND OUR OWN...
WITHOUT KNOWING THE FATE THAT COULD SO EASILY HAVE BEEN, WE WERE HAPPY, HAPPY WITH WHAT LITTLE WE HAD...
...AND IN THIS WORLD, RIGHT UP UNTIL THE STORM THAT BROUGHT ME BACK, UP WAS ALWAYS UP, DOWN WAS DOWN...
...THERE WAS NO AGENCY, NO FBP, AND PEOPLE WERE HAPPIER...
...HAPPIER BELIEVING THE IMPOSSIBLE WAS JUST THAT-- THE IMPOSSIBLE...

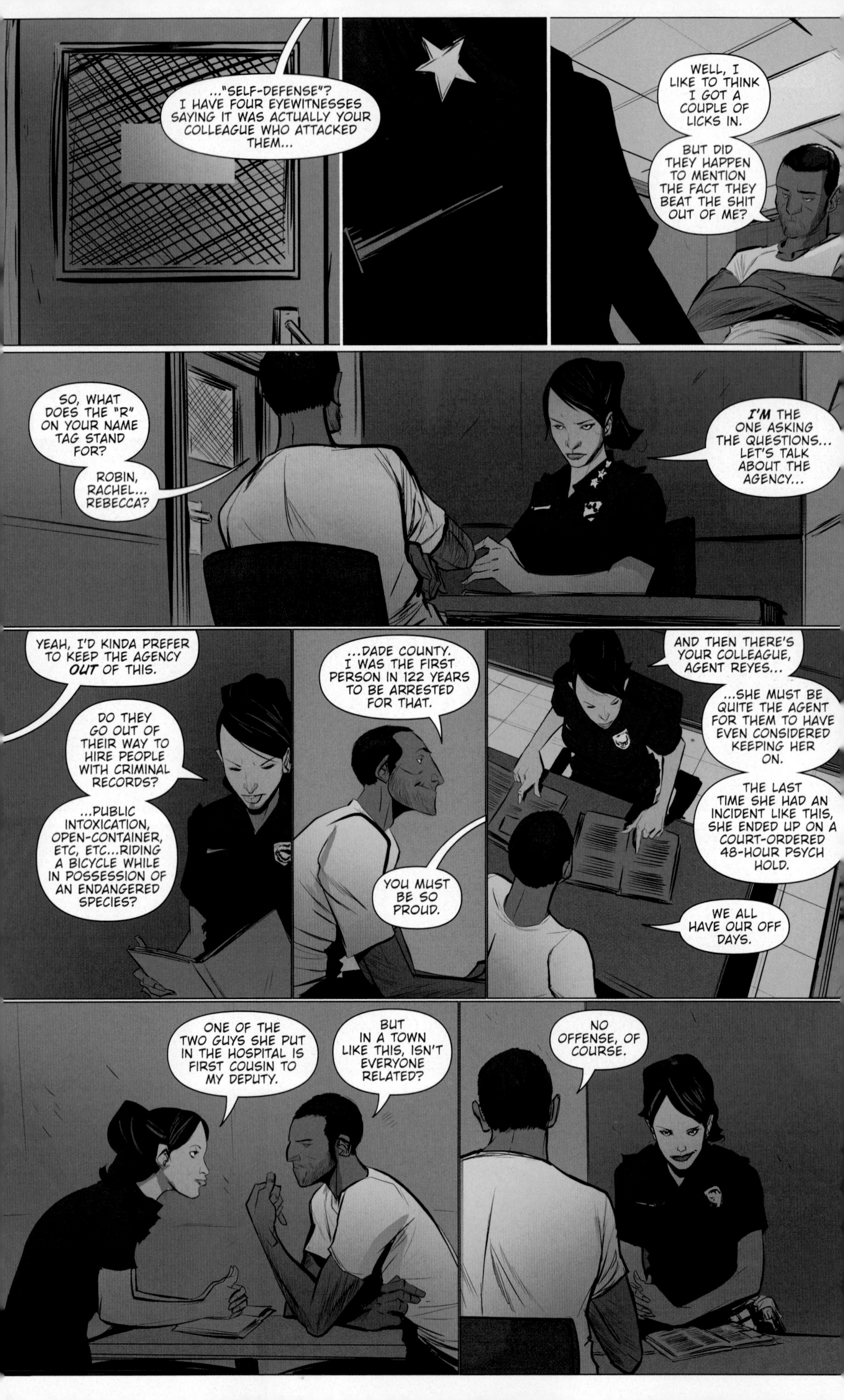
..."SELF-DEFENSE"? I HAVE FOUR EYEWITNESSES SAYING IT WAS ACTUALLY YOUR COLLEAGUE WHO ATTACKED THEM...
WELL, I LIKE TO THINK I GOT A COUPLE OF LICKS IN.
BUT DID THEY HAPPEN TO MENTION THE FACT THEY BEAT THE SHIT OUT OF ME?
SO, WHAT DOES THE "R" ON YOUR NAME TAG STAND FOR?
ROBIN, RACHEL... REBECCA?
I'M THE ONE ASKING THE QUESTIONS... LET'S TALK ABOUT THE AGENCY...
YEAH, I'D KINDA PREFER TO KEEP THE AGENCY *OUT* OF THIS.
DO THEY GO OUT OF THEIR WAY TO HIRE PEOPLE WITH CRIMINAL RECORDS?
...PUBLIC INTOXICATION, OPEN-CONTAINER, ETC, ETC...RIDING A BICYCLE WHILE IN POSSESSION OF AN ENDANGERED SPECIES?
...DADE COUNTY. I WAS THE FIRST PERSON IN 122 YEARS TO BE ARRESTED FOR THAT.
YOU MUST BE SO PROUD.
AND THEN THERE'S YOUR COLLEAGUE, AGENT REYES...
...SHE MUST BE QUITE THE AGENT FOR THEM TO HAVE EVEN CONSIDERED KEEPING HER ON.
THE LAST TIME SHE HAD AN INCIDENT LIKE THIS, SHE ENDED UP ON A COURT-ORDERED 48-HOUR PSYCH HOLD.
WE ALL HAVE OUR OFF DAYS.
ONE OF THE TWO GUYS SHE PUT IN THE HOSPITAL IS FIRST COUSIN TO MY DEPUTY.
BUT IN A TOWN LIKE THIS, ISN'T EVERYONE RELATED?
NO OFFENSE, OF COURSE.

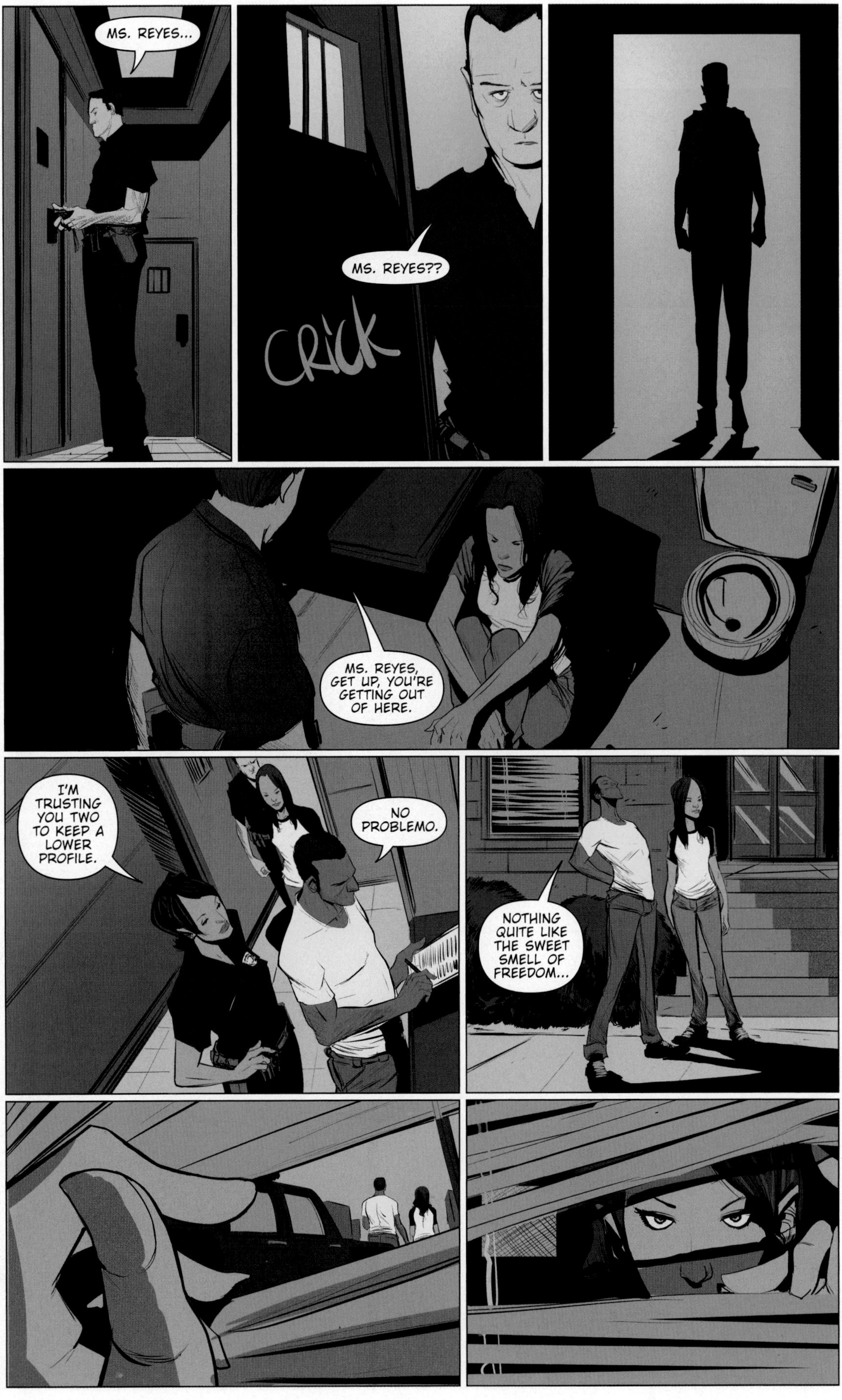

MS. REYES...
MS. REYES??
CRICK
MS. REYES, GET UP, YOU'RE GETTING OUT OF HERE.
I'M TRUSTING YOU TWO TO KEEP A LOWER PROFILE.
NO PROBLEMO.
NOTHING QUITE LIKE THE SWEET SMELL OF FREEDOM...

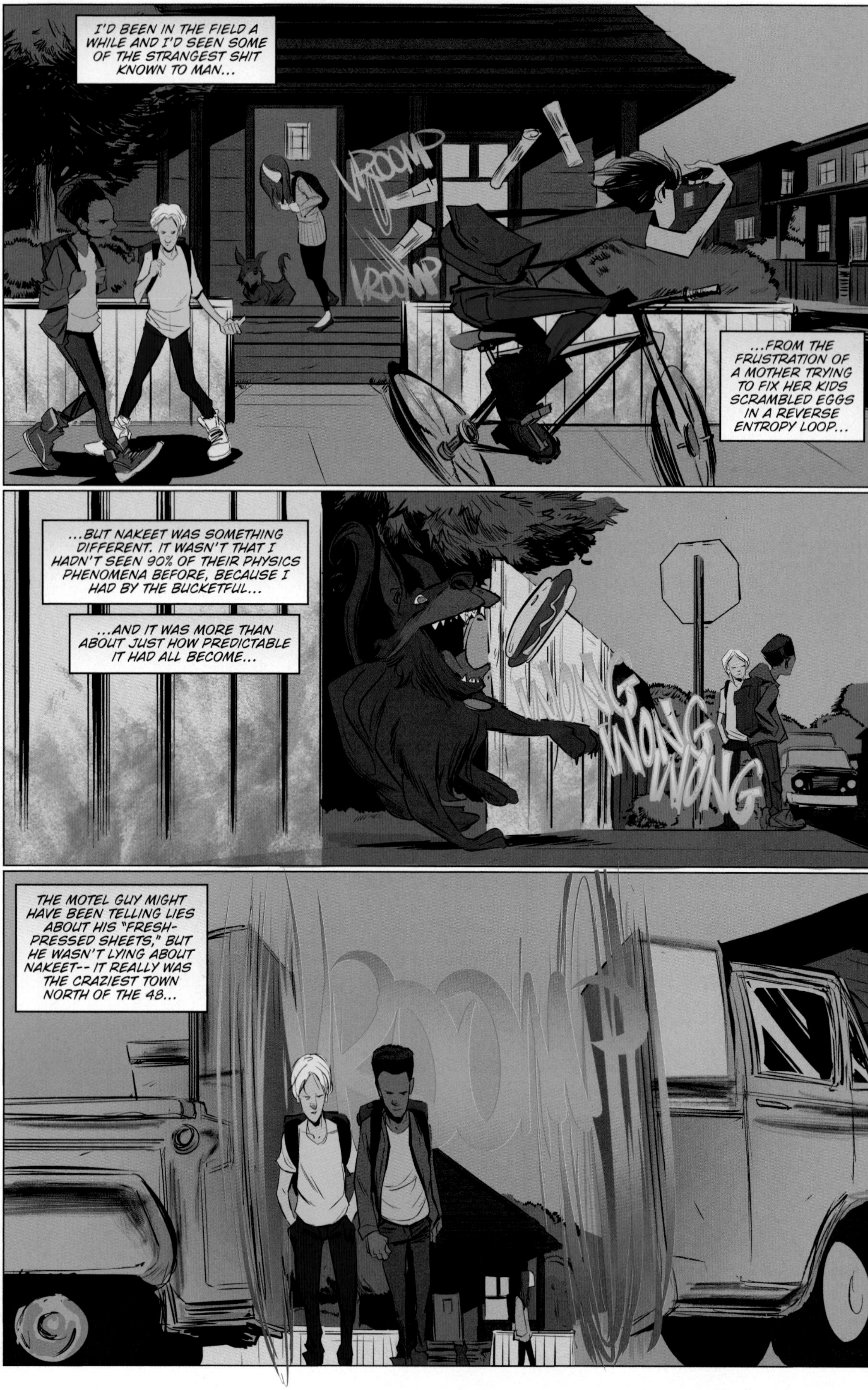
I'D BEEN IN THE FIELD A WHILE AND I'D SEEN SOME OF THE STRANGEST SHIT KNOWN TO MAN...
VROOMP
VROOMP
...FROM THE FRUSTRATION OF A MOTHER TRYING TO FIX HER KIDS SCRAMBLED EGGS IN A REVERSE ENTROPY LOOP...
...BUT NAKEET WAS SOMETHING DIFFERENT. IT WASN'T THAT I HADN'T SEEN 90% OF THEIR PHYSICS PHENOMENA BEFORE, BECAUSE I HAD BY THE BUCKETFUL...
...AND IT WAS MORE THAN ABOUT JUST HOW PREDICTABLE IT HAD ALL BECOME...
WONG
WONG
WONG
THE MOTEL GUY MIGHT HAVE BEEN TELLING LIES ABOUT HIS "FRESH-PRESSED SHEETS," BUT HE WASN'T LYING ABOUT NAKEET-- IT REALLY WAS THE CRAZIEST TOWN NORTH OF THE 48...
VROOMP

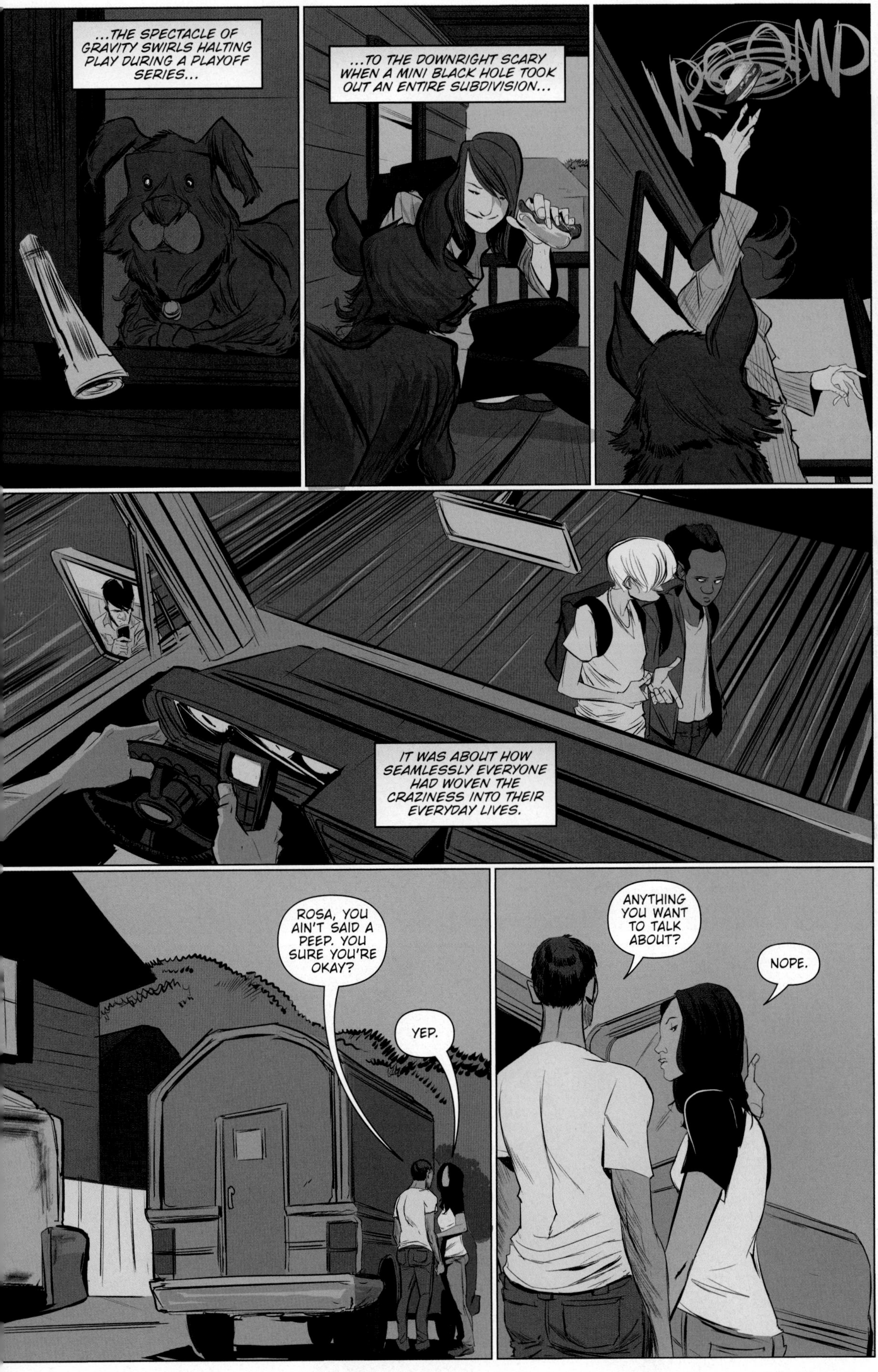
...THE SPECTACLE OF GRAVITY SWIRLS HALTING PLAY DURING A PLAYOFF SERIES...
...TO THE DOWNRIGHT SCARY WHEN A MINI BLACK HOLE TOOK OUT AN ENTIRE SUBDIVISION...
IT WAS ABOUT HOW SEAMLESSLY EVERYONE HAD WOVEN THE CRAZINESS INTO THEIR EVERYDAY LIVES.
ROSA, YOU AIN'T SAID A PEEP. YOU SURE YOU'RE OKAY?
YEP.
ANYTHING YOU WANT TO TALK ABOUT?
NOPE.

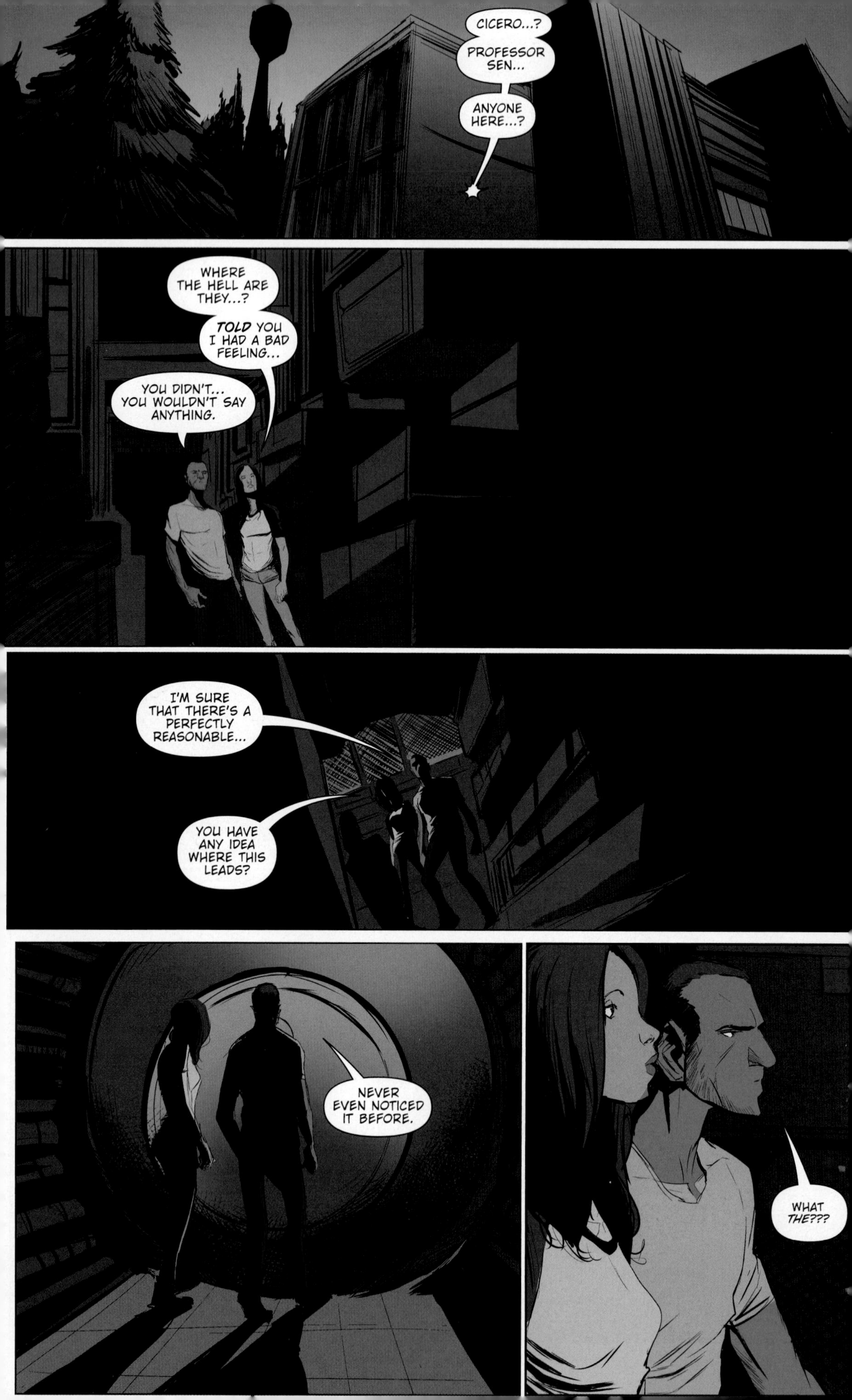
CICERO...?
PROFESSOR SEN...
ANYONE HERE...?
WHERE THE HELL ARE THEY...?
TOLD YOU I HAD A BAD FEELING...
YOU DIDN'T... YOU WOULDN'T SAY ANYTHING.
I'M SURE THAT THERE'S A PERFECTLY REASONABLE...
YOU HAVE ANY IDEA WHERE THIS LEADS?
NEVER EVEN NOTICED IT BEFORE.
WHAT *THE*???

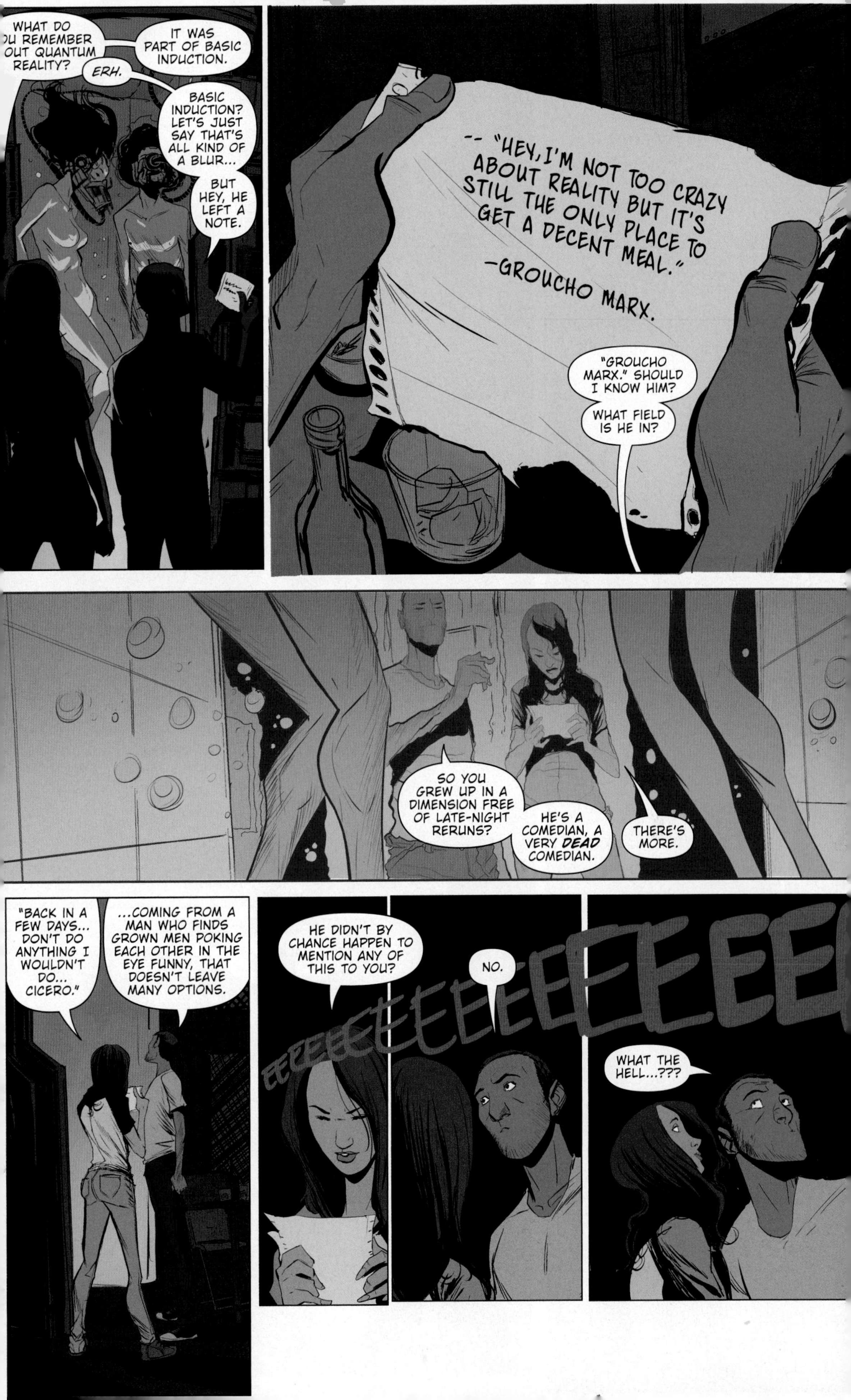
WHAT DO
OU REMEMBER
OUT QUANTUM
REALITY?
IT WAS PART OF BASIC INDUCTION.
ERH.
BASIC INDUCTION? LET'S JUST SAY THAT'S ALL KIND OF A BLUR...
BUT HEY, HE LEFT A NOTE.
-- "HEY, I'M NOT TOO CRAZY ABOUT REALITY BUT IT'S STILL THE ONLY PLACE TO GET A DECENT MEAL."
-GROUCHO MARX.
"GROUCHO MARX." SHOULD I KNOW HIM?
WHAT FIELD IS HE IN?
SO YOU GREW UP IN A DIMENSION FREE OF LATE-NIGHT RERUNS?
HE'S A COMEDIAN, A VERY DEAD COMEDIAN.
THERE'S MORE.
"BACK IN A FEW DAYS... DON'T DO ANYTHING I WOULDN'T DO... CICERO."
...COMING FROM A MAN WHO FINDS GROWN MEN POKING EACH OTHER IN THE EYE FUNNY, THAT DOESN'T LEAVE MANY OPTIONS.
HE DIDN'T BY CHANCE HAPPEN TO MENTION ANY OF THIS TO YOU?
NO.
EEEEEEEEEEEEEEEEEEE
WHAT THE HELL...???

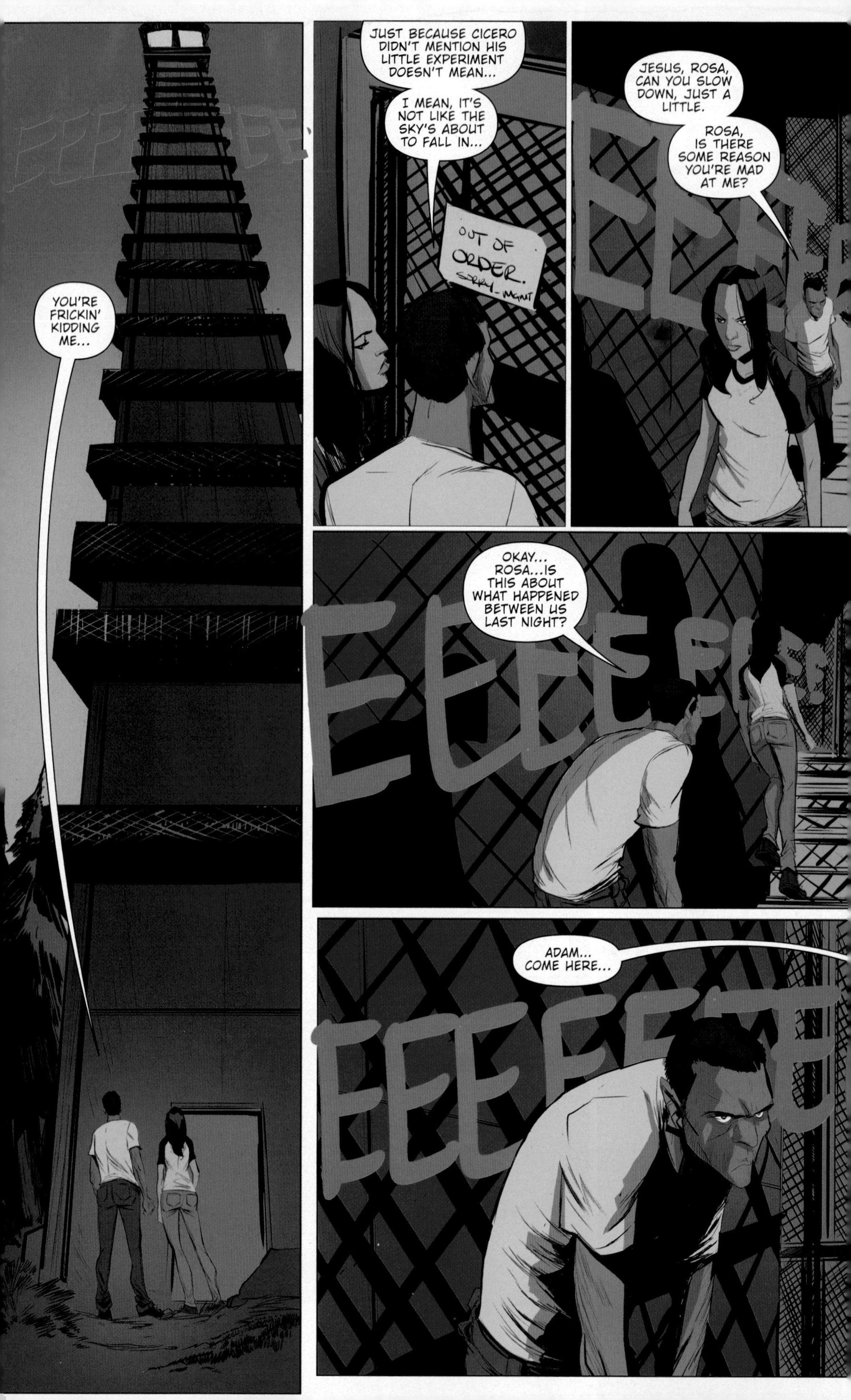
YOU'RE FRICKIN' KIDDING ME...
JUST BECAUSE CICERO DIDN'T MENTION HIS LITTLE EXPERIMENT DOESN'T MEAN...
I MEAN, IT'S NOT LIKE THE SKY'S ABOUT TO FALL IN...
OUT OF ORDER.
JESUS, ROSA, CAN YOU SLOW DOWN, JUST A LITTLE.
ROSA, IS THERE SOME REASON YOU'RE MAD AT ME?
OKAY... ROSA...IS THIS ABOUT WHAT HAPPENED BETWEEN US LAST NIGHT?
ADAM... COME HERE...

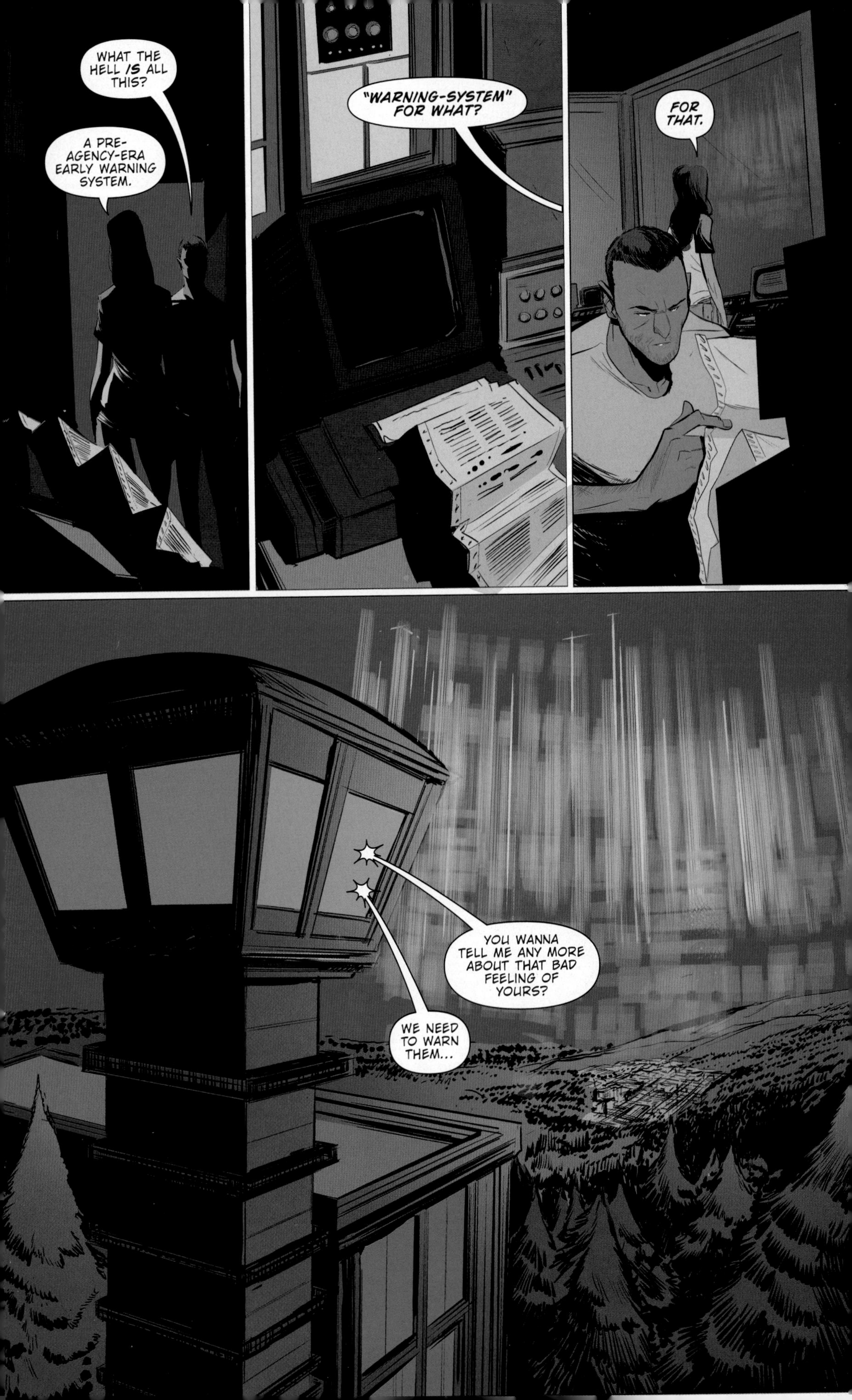
WHAT THE HELL *IS* ALL THIS?
A PRE-AGENCY-ERA EARLY WARNING SYSTEM.
"WARNING-SYSTEM" FOR WHAT?
FOR THAT.
YOU WANNA TELL ME ANY MORE ABOUT THAT BAD FEELING OF YOURS?
WE NEED TO WARN THEM...

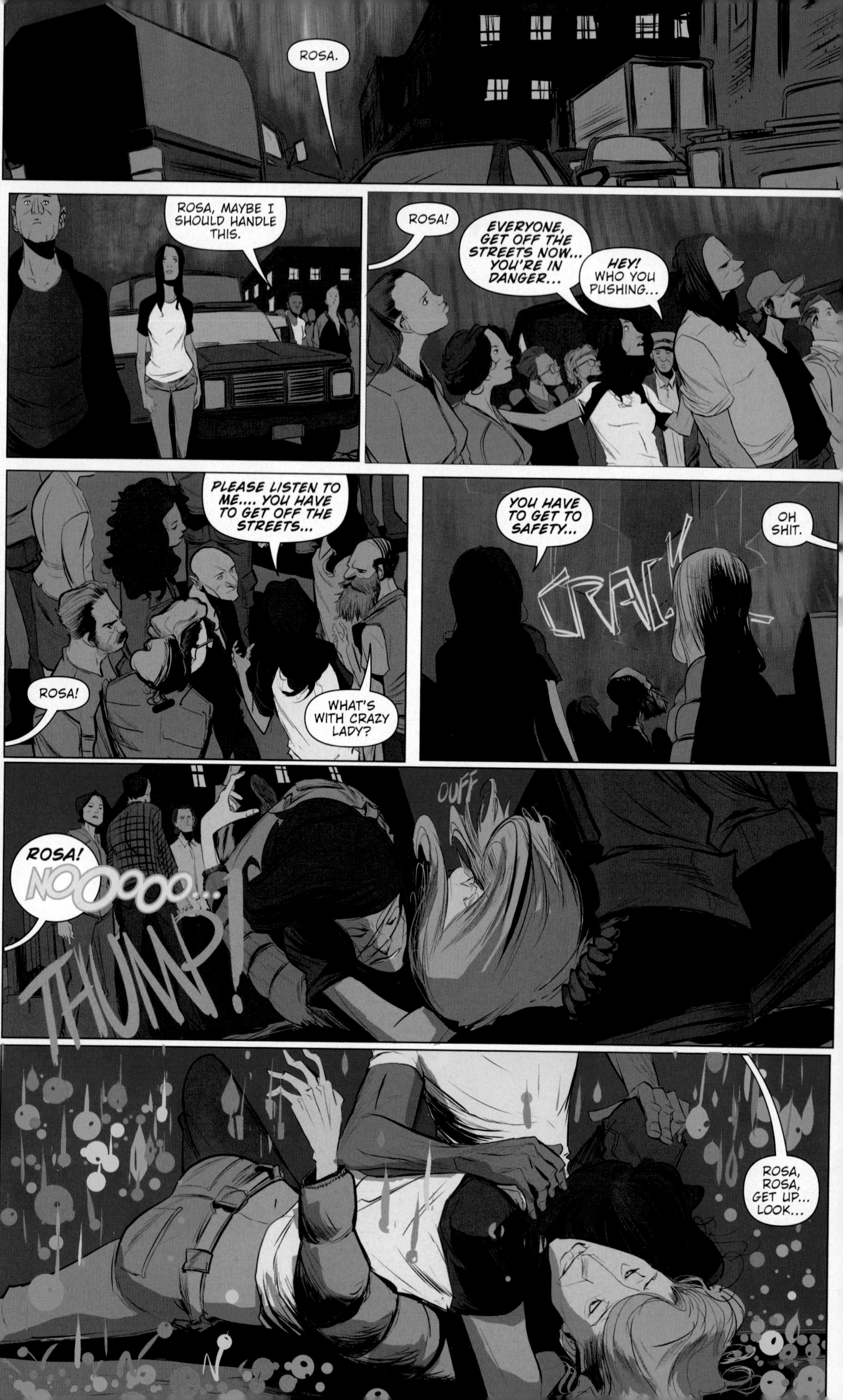
ROSA.
ROSA, MAYBE I SHOULD HANDLE THIS.
ROSA!
EVERYONE, GET OFF THE STREETS NOW... YOU'RE IN DANGER...
HEY! WHO YOU PUSHING...
PLEASE LISTEN TO ME.... YOU HAVE TO GET OFF THE STREETS...
ROSA!
WHAT'S WITH CRAZY LADY?
YOU HAVE TO GET TO SAFETY...
OH SHIT.
ROSA! NOOOOO...!
OUFF
THUMP!
ROSA, ROSA, GET UP... LOOK...

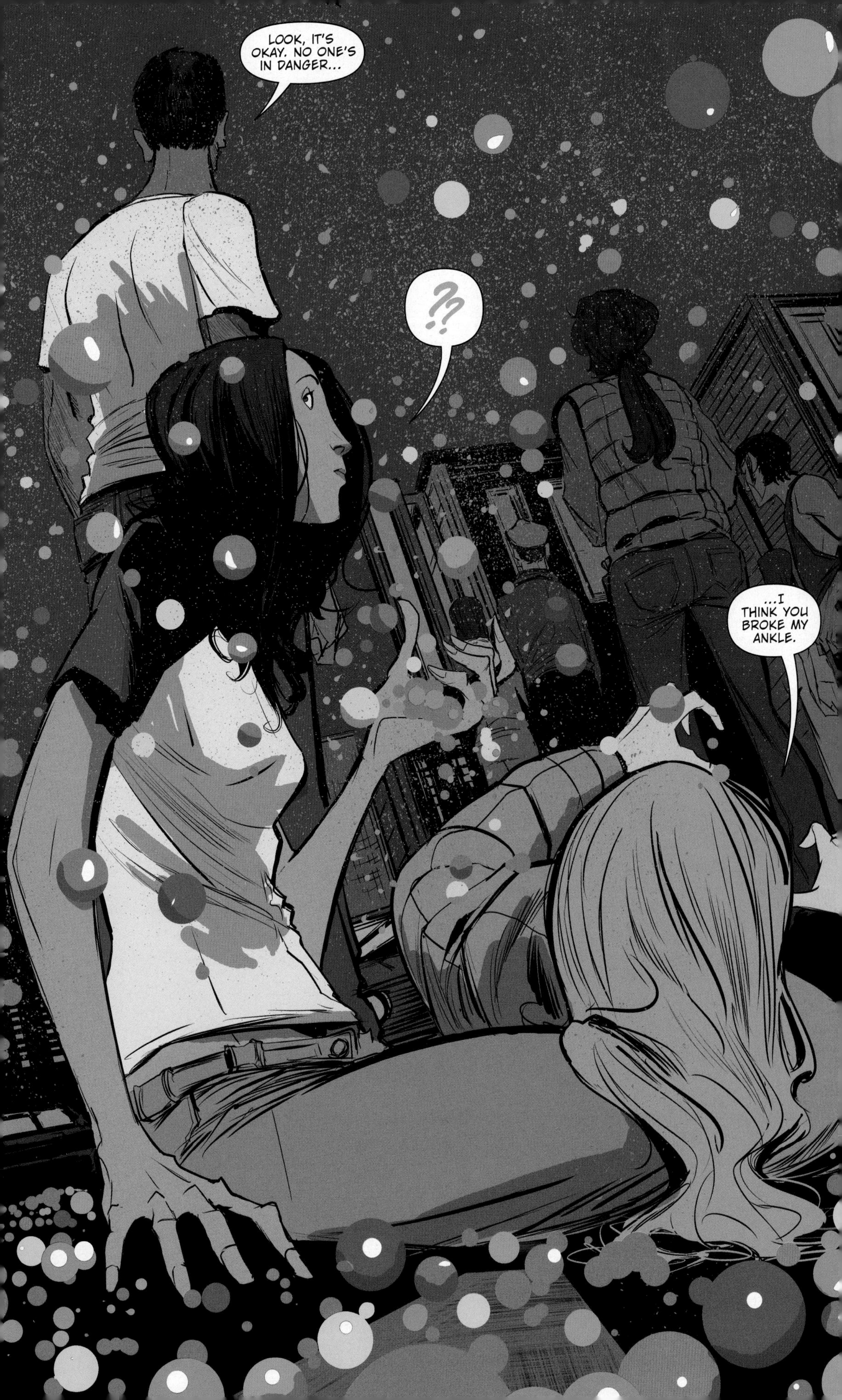
LOOK, IT'S OKAY. NO ONE'S IN DANGER...
??
...I THINK YOU BROKE MY ANKLE.

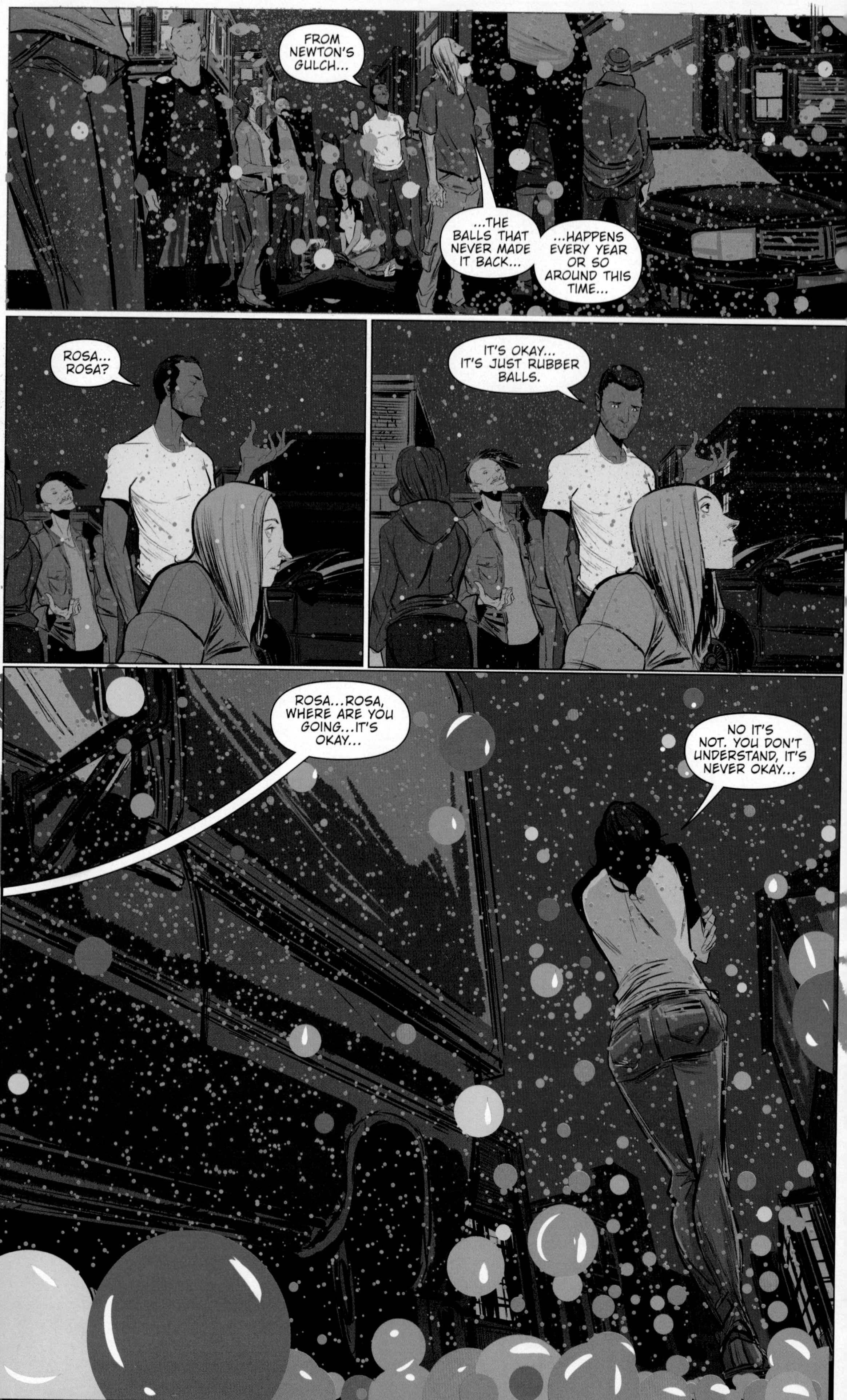
FROM NEWTON'S GULCH...
...THE BALLS THAT NEVER MADE IT BACK...
...HAPPENS EVERY YEAR OR SO AROUND THIS TIME...
ROSA... ROSA?
IT'S OKAY... IT'S JUST RUBBER BALLS.
ROSA...ROSA, WHERE ARE YOU GOING...IT'S OKAY...
NO IT'S NOT. YOU DON'T UNDERSTAND, IT'S NEVER OKAY...

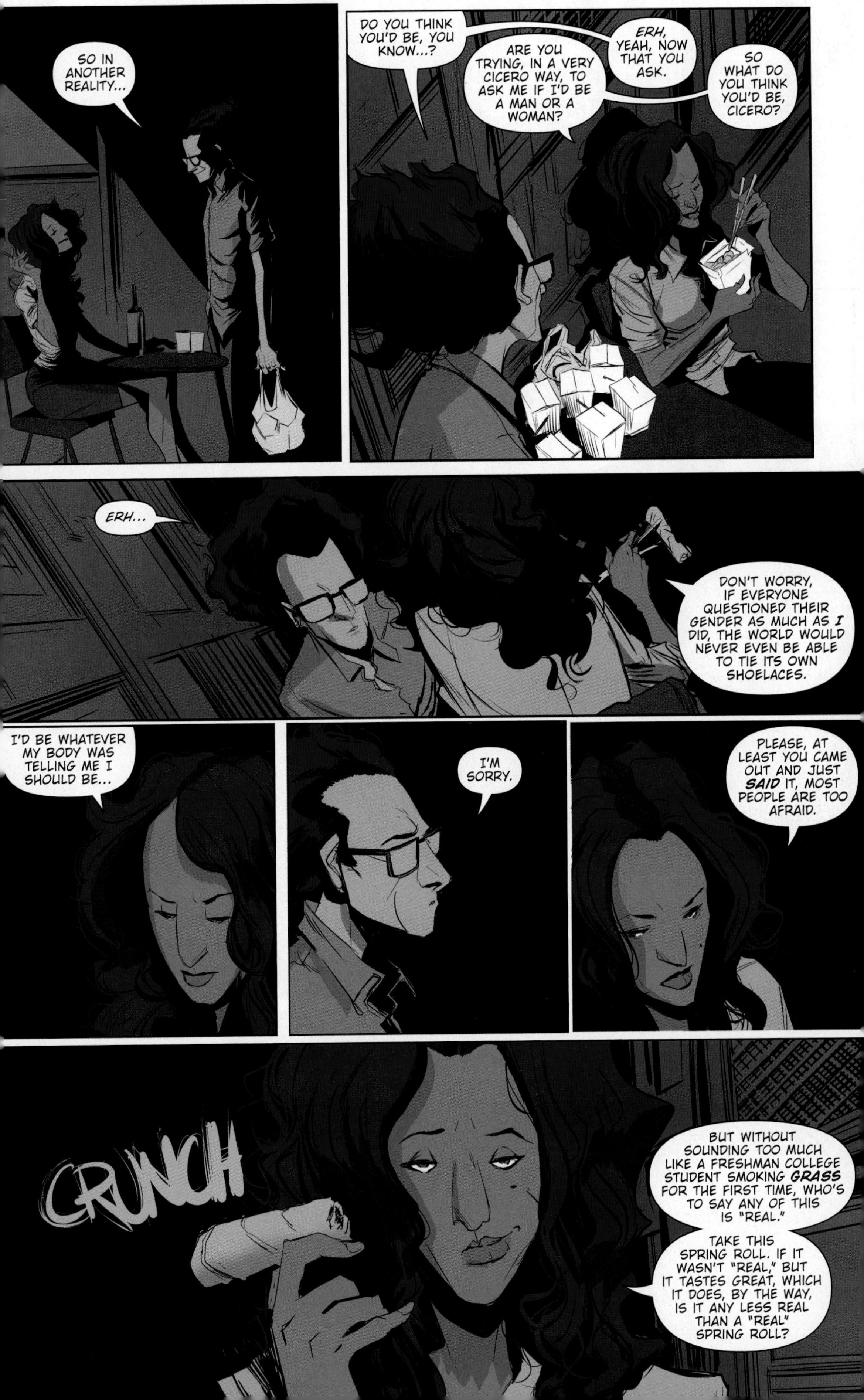
SO IN ANOTHER REALITY...
DO YOU THINK YOU'D BE, YOU KNOW...?
ARE YOU TRYING, IN A VERY CICERO WAY, TO ASK ME IF I'D BE A MAN OR A WOMAN?
ERH, YEAH, NOW THAT YOU ASK.
SO WHAT DO YOU THINK YOU'D BE, CICERO?
ERH...
DON'T WORRY, IF EVERYONE QUESTIONED THEIR GENDER AS MUCH AS I DID, THE WORLD WOULD NEVER EVEN BE ABLE TO TIE ITS OWN SHOELACES.
I'D BE WHATEVER MY BODY WAS TELLING ME I SHOULD BE...
I'M SORRY.
PLEASE, AT LEAST YOU CAME OUT AND JUST SAID IT, MOST PEOPLE ARE TOO AFRAID.
CRUNCH
BUT WITHOUT SOUNDING TOO MUCH LIKE A FRESHMAN COLLEGE STUDENT SMOKING GRASS FOR THE FIRST TIME, WHO'S TO SAY ANY OF THIS IS "REAL."
TAKE THIS SPRING ROLL. IF IT WASN'T "REAL," BUT IT TASTES GREAT, WHICH IT DOES, BY THE WAY, IS IT ANY LESS REAL THAN A "REAL" SPRING ROLL?

"...WITH ONLY OUR FIVE SENSES TO GUIDE US THROUGH WHAT WE PERCEIVE AS 'REALITY'..."

CLICK CLICK

CLICK CLICK CLICK

ROSA...

WHY DO I GET THE FEELING I'M GONNA *REGRET* THIS?

...YOU DIDN'T KNOW...

"...CHANCES ARE WE'LL NEVER KNOW FOR SURE IF IT'S REAL OR NOT."

...YOU WERE JUST DOING WHAT YOU THOUGHT WAS RIGHT.

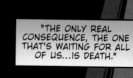

"THE ONLY REAL CONSEQUENCE, THE ONE THAT'S WAITING FOR ALL OF US...IS DEATH."

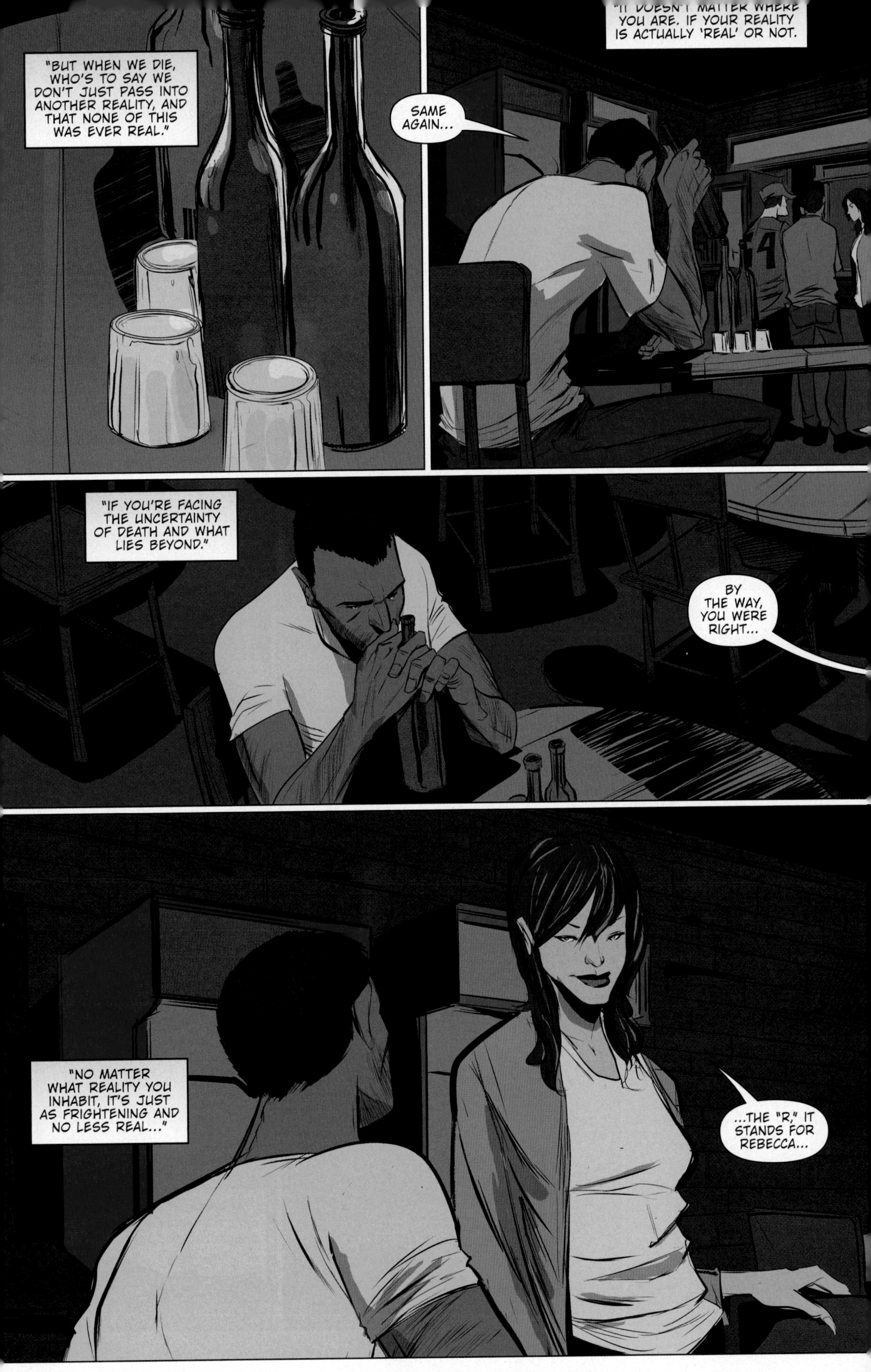
"BUT WHEN WE DIE, WHO'S TO SAY WE DON'T JUST PASS INTO ANOTHER REALITY, AND THAT NONE OF THIS WAS EVER REAL."
"IT DOESN'T MATTER WHERE YOU ARE. IF YOUR REALITY IS ACTUALLY 'REAL' OR NOT.
SAME AGAIN...
"IF YOU'RE FACING THE UNCERTAINTY OF DEATH AND WHAT LIES BEYOND."
BY THE WAY, YOU WERE RIGHT...
"NO MATTER WHAT REALITY YOU INHABIT, IT'S JUST AS FRIGHTENING AND NO LESS REAL..."
...THE "R," IT STANDS FOR REBECCA...

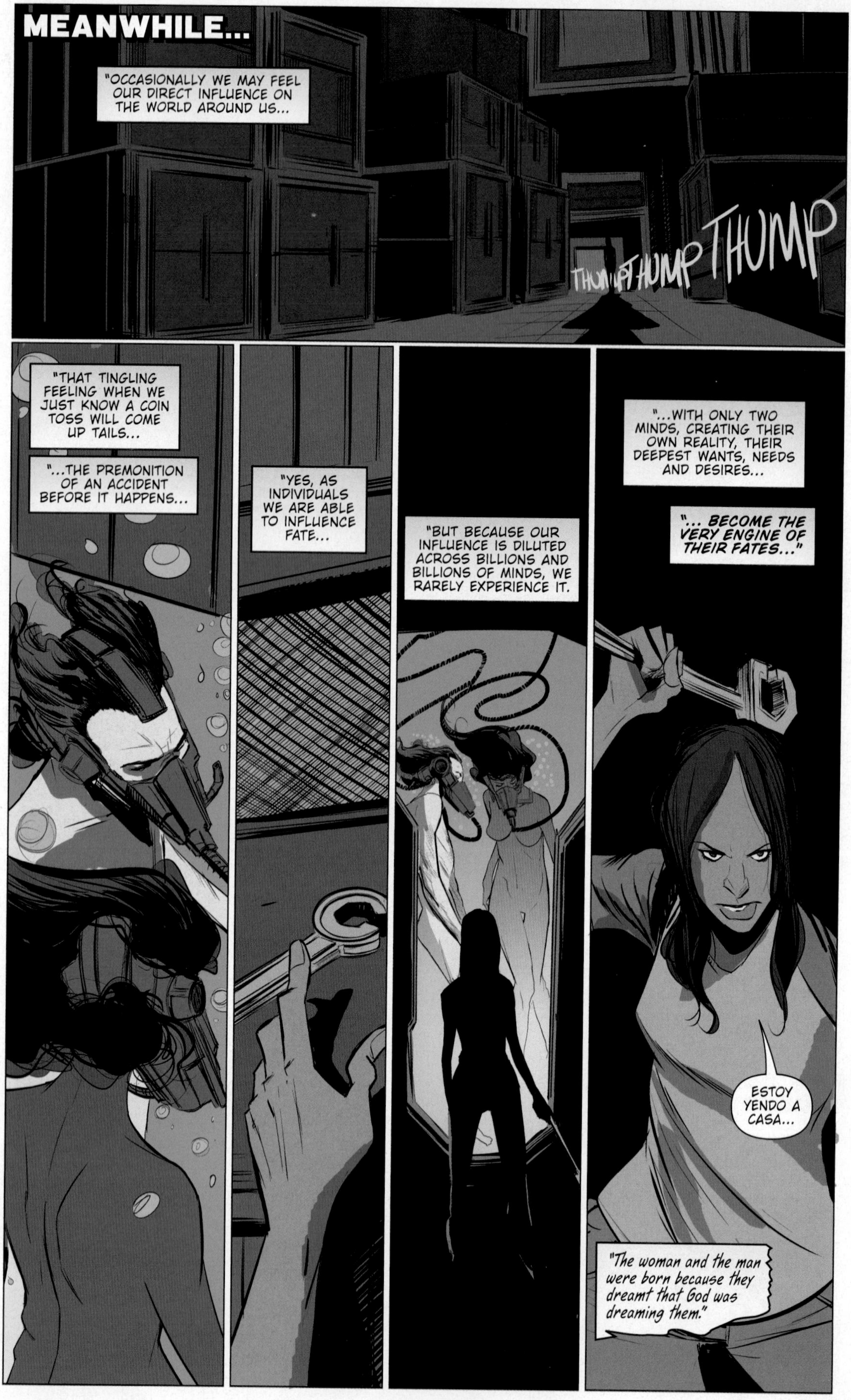
MEANWHILE...
"OCCASIONALLY WE MAY FEEL OUR DIRECT INFLUENCE ON THE WORLD AROUND US...
THUMP THUMP THUMP
"THAT TINGLING FEELING WHEN WE JUST KNOW A COIN TOSS WILL COME UP TAILS...
"...THE PREMONITION OF AN ACCIDENT BEFORE IT HAPPENS...
"YES, AS INDIVIDUALS WE ARE ABLE TO INFLUENCE FATE...
"BUT BECAUSE OUR INFLUENCE IS DILUTED ACROSS BILLIONS AND BILLIONS OF MINDS, WE RARELY EXPERIENCE IT.
"...WITH ONLY TWO MINDS, CREATING THEIR OWN REALITY, THEIR DEEPEST WANTS, NEEDS AND DESIRES...
"... BECOME THE VERY ENGINE OF THEIR FATES..."
ESTOY YENDO A CASA...
"The woman and the man were born because they dreamt that God was dreaming them."

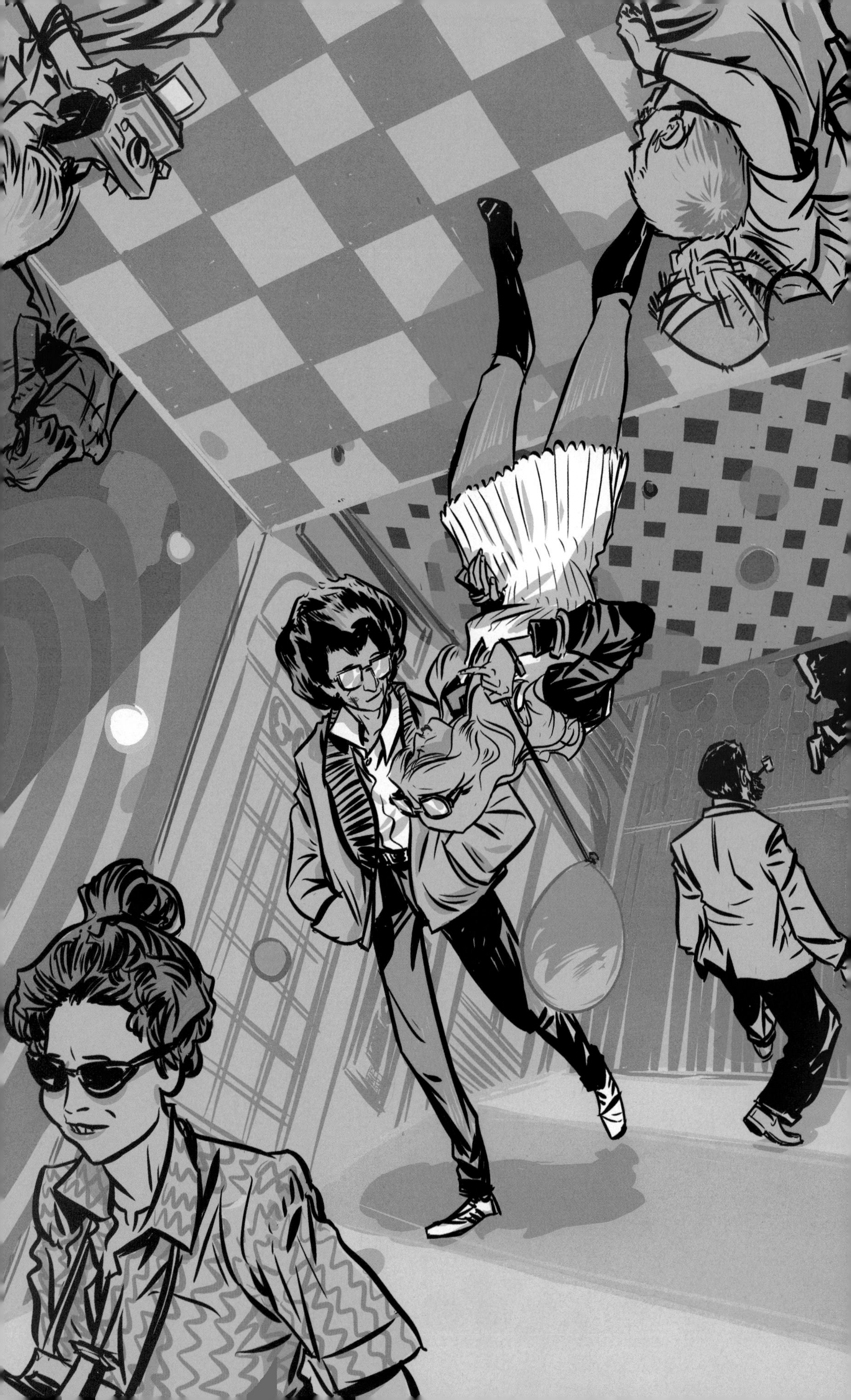

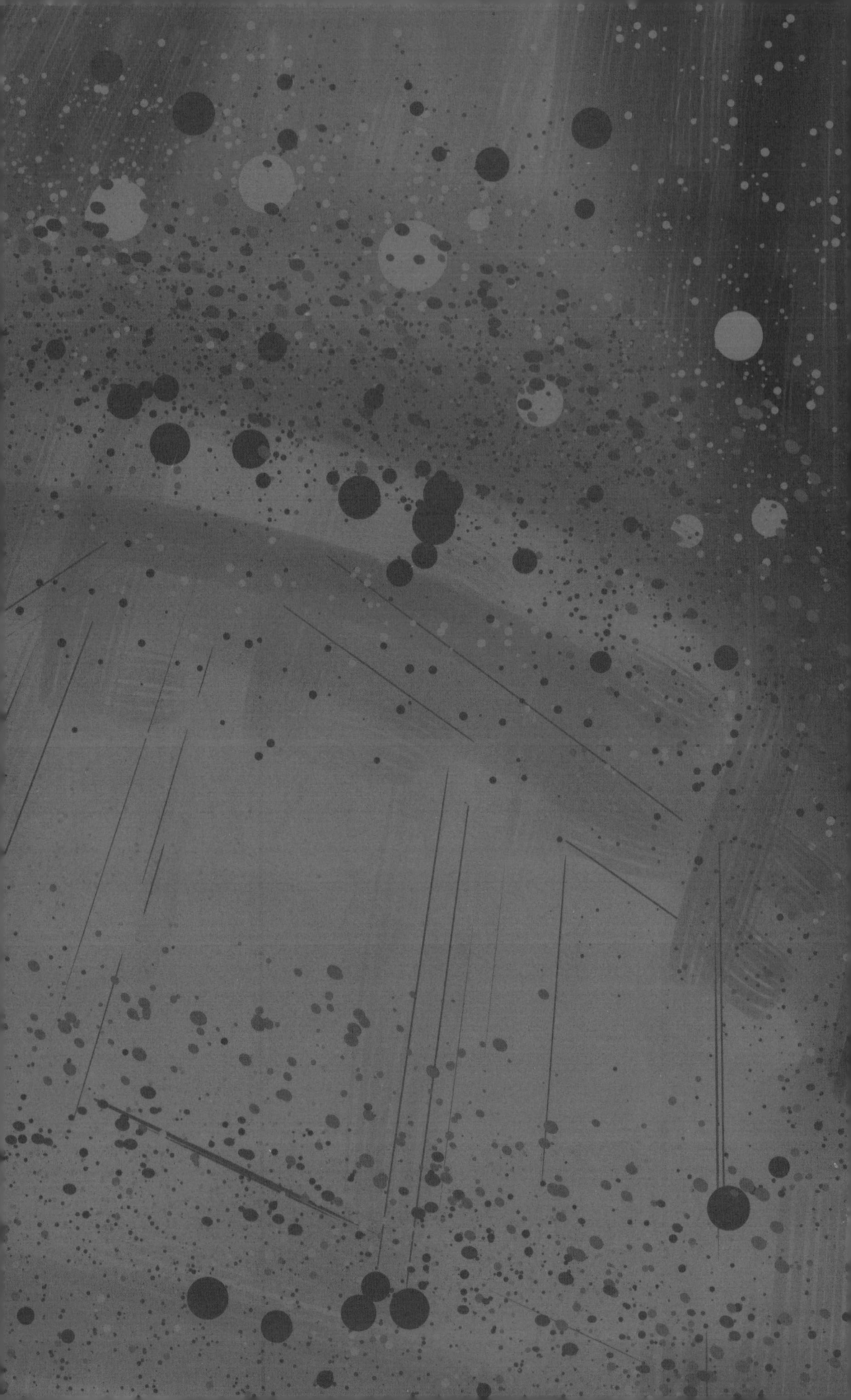

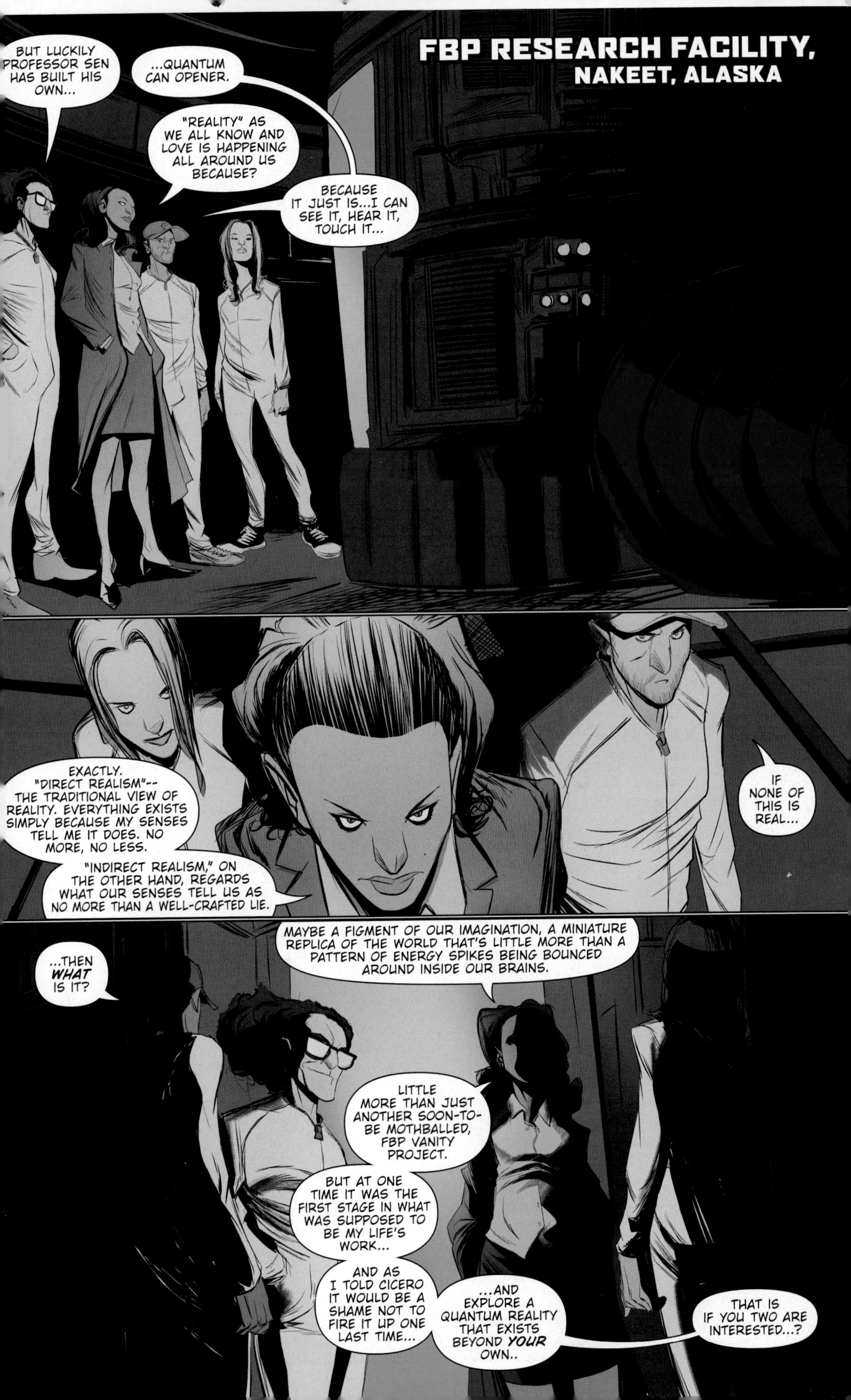
FBP RESEARCH FACILITY, NAKEET, ALASKA
BUT LUCKILY PROFESSOR SEN HAS BUILT HIS OWN...
...QUANTUM CAN OPENER.
"REALITY" AS WE ALL KNOW AND LOVE IS HAPPENING ALL AROUND US BECAUSE?
BECAUSE IT JUST IS...I CAN SEE IT, HEAR IT, TOUCH IT...
EXACTLY. "DIRECT REALISM"-- THE TRADITIONAL VIEW OF REALITY. EVERYTHING EXISTS SIMPLY BECAUSE MY SENSES TELL ME IT DOES. NO MORE, NO LESS.
"INDIRECT REALISM," ON THE OTHER HAND, REGARDS WHAT OUR SENSES TELL US AS NO MORE THAN A WELL-CRAFTED LIE.
IF NONE OF THIS IS REAL...
...THEN WHAT IS IT?
MAYBE A FIGMENT OF OUR IMAGINATION, A MINIATURE REPLICA OF THE WORLD THAT'S LITTLE MORE THAN A PATTERN OF ENERGY SPIKES BEING BOUNCED AROUND INSIDE OUR BRAINS.
LITTLE MORE THAN JUST ANOTHER SOON-TO-BE MOTHBALLED, FBP VANITY PROJECT.
BUT AT ONE TIME IT WAS THE FIRST STAGE IN WHAT WAS SUPPOSED TO BE MY LIFE'S WORK...
AND AS I TOLD CICERO IT WOULD BE A SHAME NOT TO FIRE IT UP ONE LAST TIME...
...AND EXPLORE A QUANTUM REALITY THAT EXISTS BEYOND YOUR OWN..
THAT IS IF YOU TWO ARE INTERESTED...?

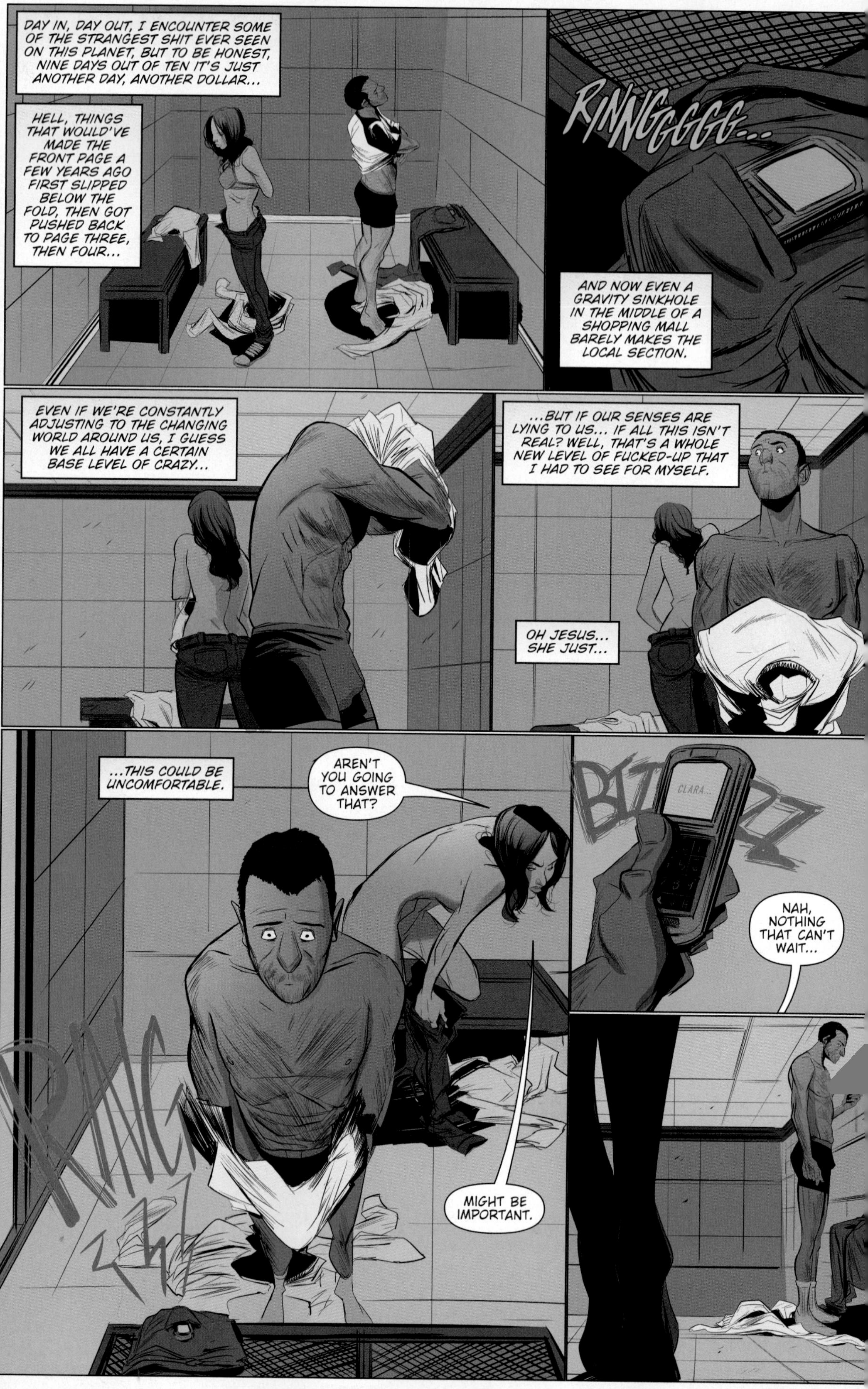
DAY IN, DAY OUT, I ENCOUNTER SOME OF THE STRANGEST SHIT EVER SEEN ON THIS PLANET, BUT TO BE HONEST, NINE DAYS OUT OF TEN IT'S JUST ANOTHER DAY, ANOTHER DOLLAR...
HELL, THINGS THAT WOULD'VE MADE THE FRONT PAGE A FEW YEARS AGO FIRST SLIPPED BELOW THE FOLD, THEN GOT PUSHED BACK TO PAGE THREE, THEN FOUR...
RINNGGGGG...
AND NOW EVEN A GRAVITY SINKHOLE IN THE MIDDLE OF A SHOPPING MALL BARELY MAKES THE LOCAL SECTION.
EVEN IF WE'RE CONSTANTLY ADJUSTING TO THE CHANGING WORLD AROUND US, I GUESS WE ALL HAVE A CERTAIN BASE LEVEL OF CRAZY...
...BUT IF OUR SENSES ARE LYING TO US... IF ALL THIS ISN'T REAL? WELL, THAT'S A WHOLE NEW LEVEL OF FUCKED-UP THAT I HAD TO SEE FOR MYSELF.
OH JESUS... SHE JUST...
...THIS COULD BE UNCOMFORTABLE.
AREN'T YOU GOING TO ANSWER THAT?
MIGHT BE IMPORTANT.
CLARA...
NAH, NOTHING THAT CAN'T WAIT...

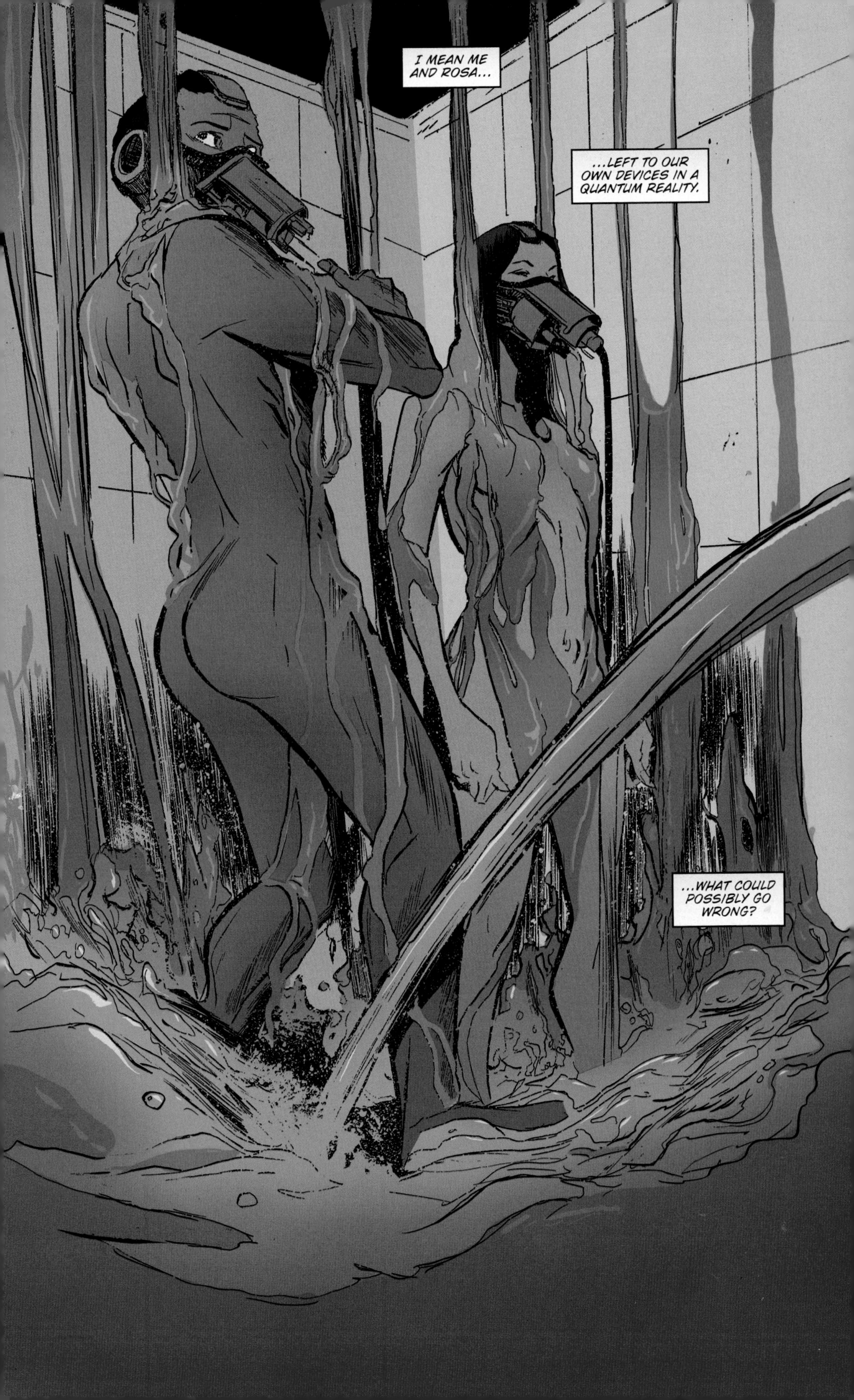
I MEAN ME AND ROSA...
...LEFT TO OUR OWN DEVICES IN A QUANTUM REALITY.
...WHAT COULD POSSIBLY GO WRONG?

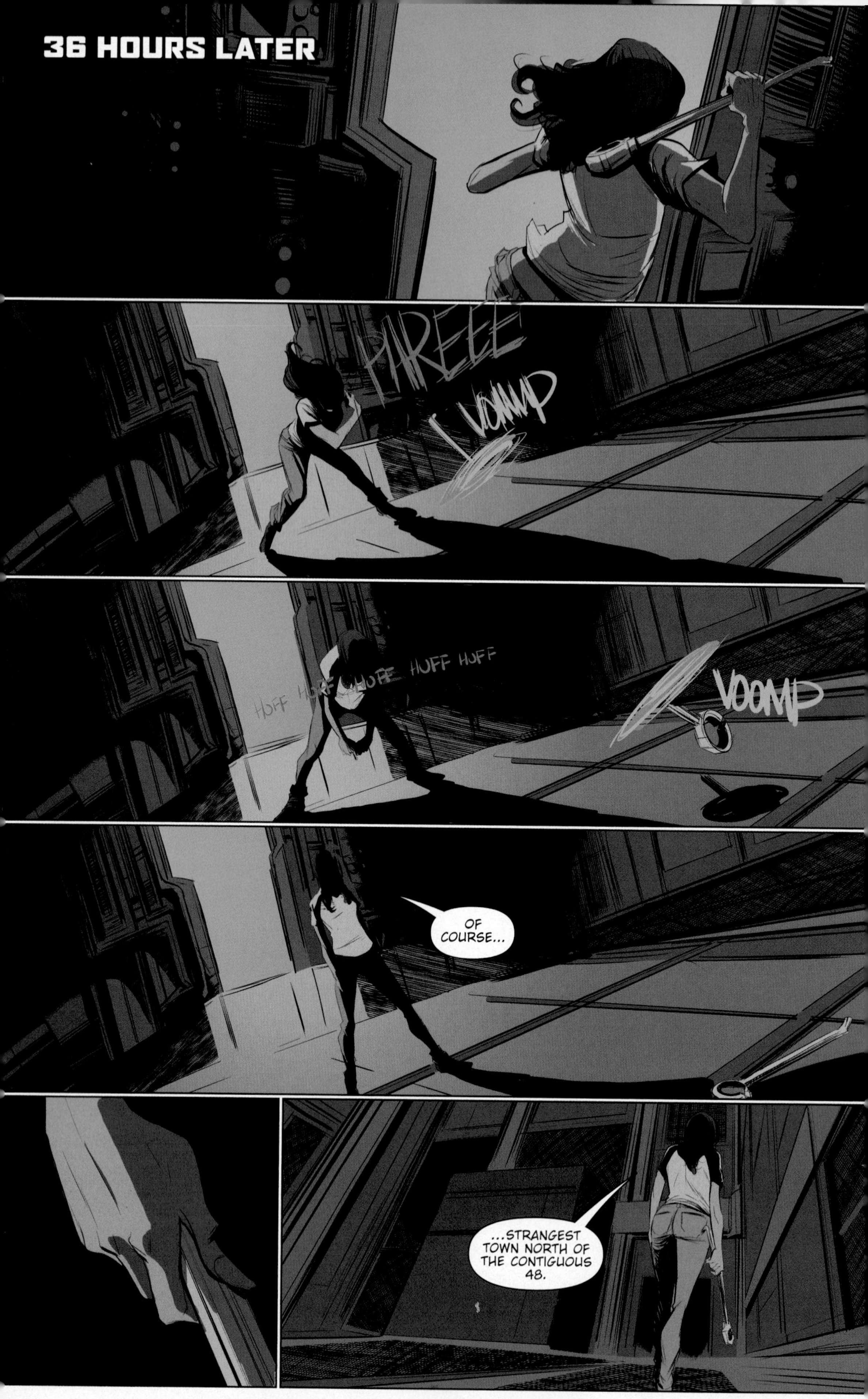
36 HOURS LATER
PHREEE
VOOMP
HUFF HUFF HUFF HUFF HUFF
VOOMP
OF COURSE...
...STRANGEST TOWN NORTH OF THE CONTIGUOUS 48.

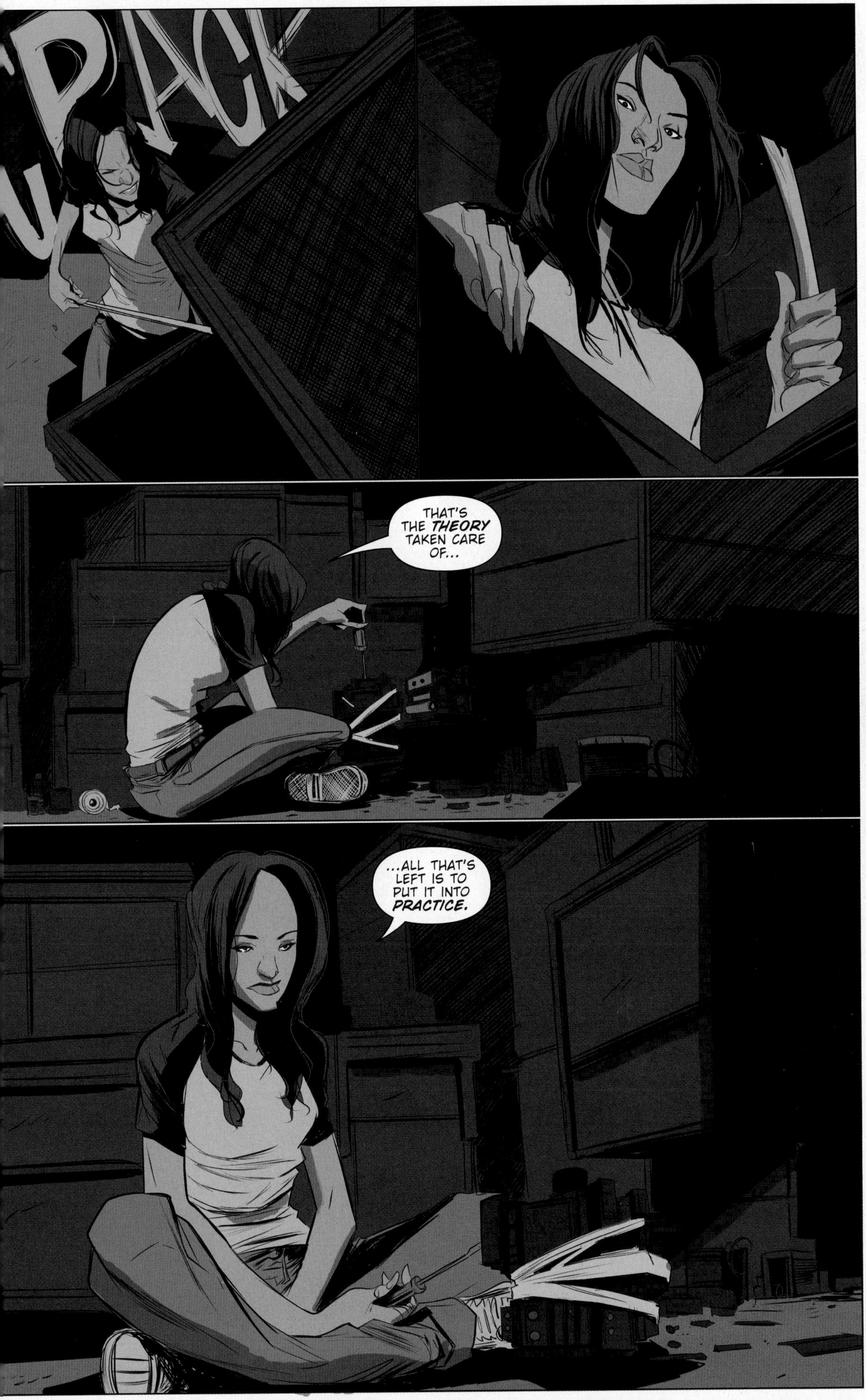
CRACK
THAT'S THE THEORY TAKEN CARE OF...
...ALL THAT'S LEFT IS TO PUT IT INTO PRACTICE.

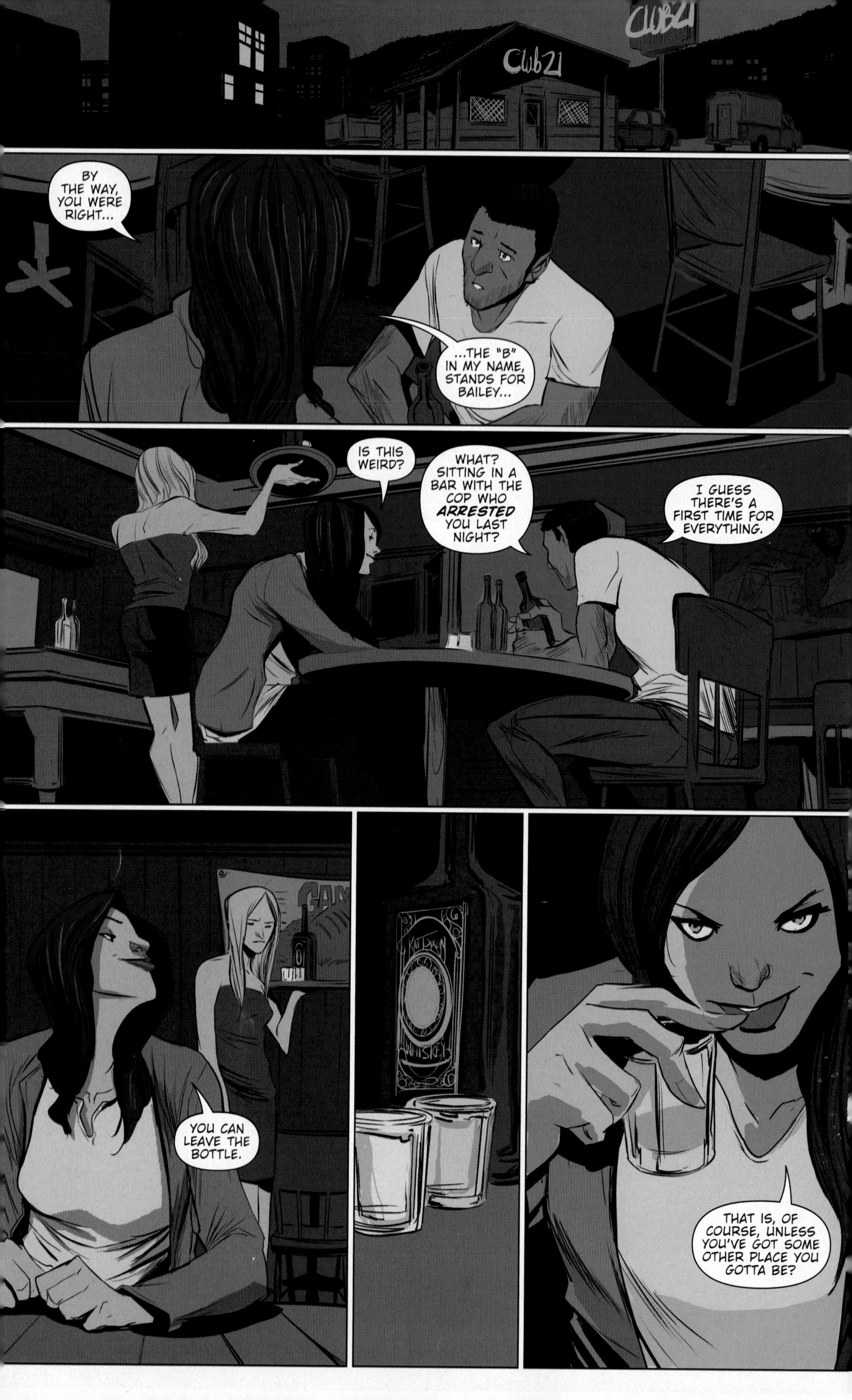
CLUB 21
Club 21
BY THE WAY, YOU WERE RIGHT...
...THE "B" IN MY NAME, STANDS FOR BAILEY...
IS THIS WEIRD?
WHAT? SITTING IN A BAR WITH THE COP WHO ARRESTED YOU LAST NIGHT?
I GUESS THERE'S A FIRST TIME FOR EVERYTHING.
YOU CAN LEAVE THE BOTTLE.
WHISKEY
THAT IS, OF COURSE, UNLESS YOU'VE GOT SOME OTHER PLACE YOU GOTTA BE?

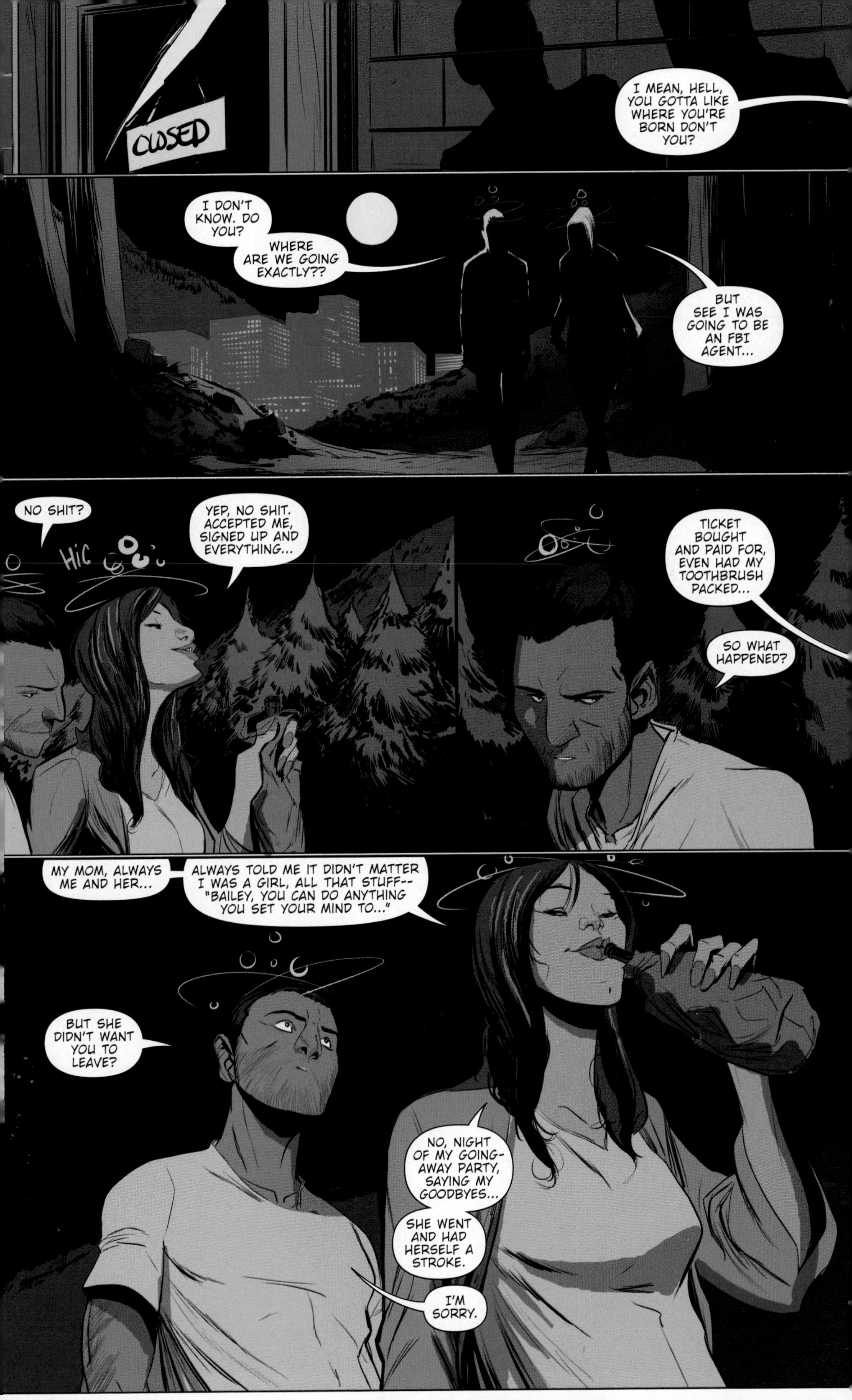
CLOSED
I MEAN, HELL, YOU GOTTA LIKE WHERE YOU'RE BORN DON'T YOU?
I DON'T KNOW. DO YOU?
WHERE ARE WE GOING EXACTLY??
BUT SEE I WAS GOING TO BE AN FBI AGENT...
NO SHIT?
HIC
YEP, NO SHIT. ACCEPTED ME, SIGNED UP AND EVERYTHING...
TICKET BOUGHT AND PAID FOR, EVEN HAD MY TOOTHBRUSH PACKED...
SO WHAT HAPPENED?
MY MOM, ALWAYS ME AND HER...
ALWAYS TOLD ME IT DIDN'T MATTER I WAS A GIRL, ALL THAT STUFF-- "BAILEY, YOU CAN DO ANYTHING YOU SET YOUR MIND TO..."
BUT SHE DIDN'T WANT YOU TO LEAVE?
NO, NIGHT OF MY GOING-AWAY PARTY, SAYING MY GOODBYES...
SHE WENT AND HAD HERSELF A STROKE.
I'M SORRY.

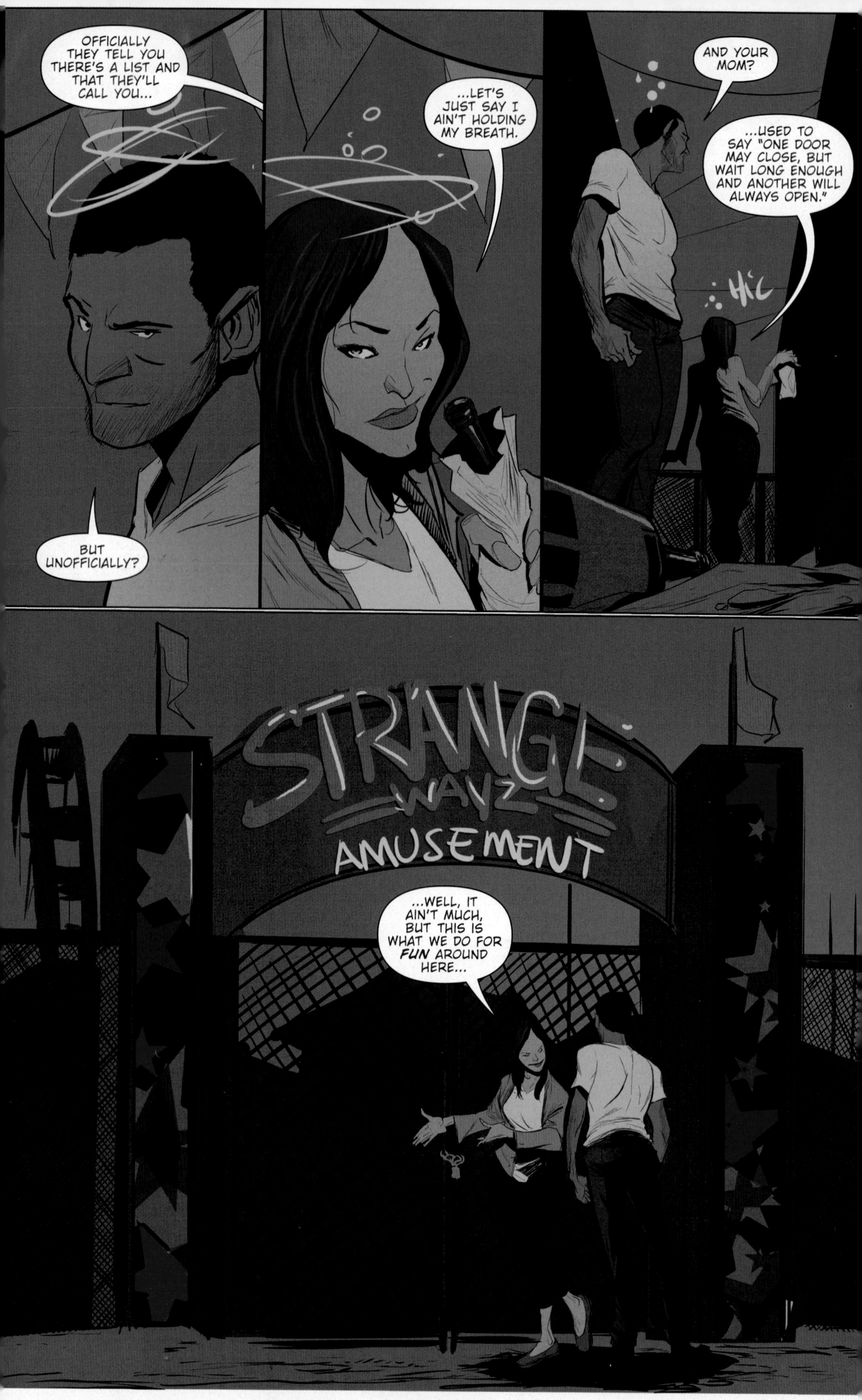
OFFICIALLY THEY TELL YOU THERE'S A LIST AND THAT THEY'LL CALL YOU...
BUT UNOFFICIALLY?
...LET'S JUST SAY I AIN'T HOLDING MY BREATH.
AND YOUR MOM?
...USED TO SAY "ONE DOOR MAY CLOSE, BUT WAIT LONG ENOUGH AND ANOTHER WILL ALWAYS OPEN."
HIC
STRANGE WAYZ AMUSEMENT
...WELL, IT AIN'T MUCH, BUT THIS IS WHAT WE DO FOR FUN AROUND HERE...

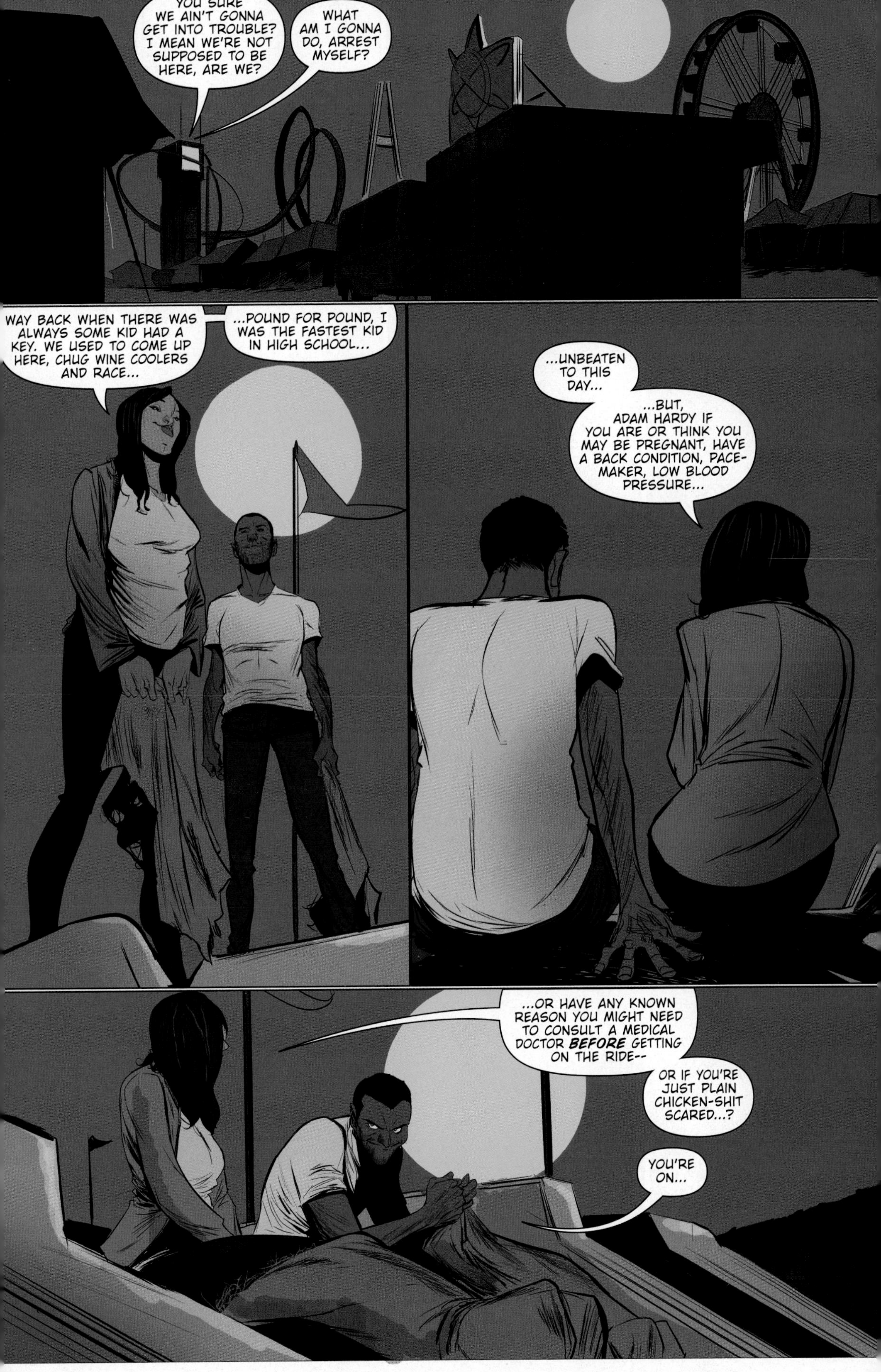
YOU SURE WE AIN'T GONNA GET INTO TROUBLE? I MEAN WE'RE NOT SUPPOSED TO BE HERE, ARE WE?
WHAT AM I GONNA DO, ARREST MYSELF?
WAY BACK WHEN THERE WAS ALWAYS SOME KID HAD A KEY. WE USED TO COME UP HERE, CHUG WINE COOLERS AND RACE...
...POUND FOR POUND, I WAS THE FASTEST KID IN HIGH SCHOOL...
...UNBEATEN TO THIS DAY...
...BUT, ADAM HARDY IF YOU ARE OR THINK YOU MAY BE PREGNANT, HAVE A BACK CONDITION, PACE-MAKER, LOW BLOOD PRESSURE...
...OR HAVE ANY KNOWN REASON YOU MIGHT NEED TO CONSULT A MEDICAL DOCTOR ***BEFORE*** GETTING ON THE RIDE--
OR IF YOU'RE JUST PLAIN CHICKEN-SHIT SCARED...?
YOU'RE ON...

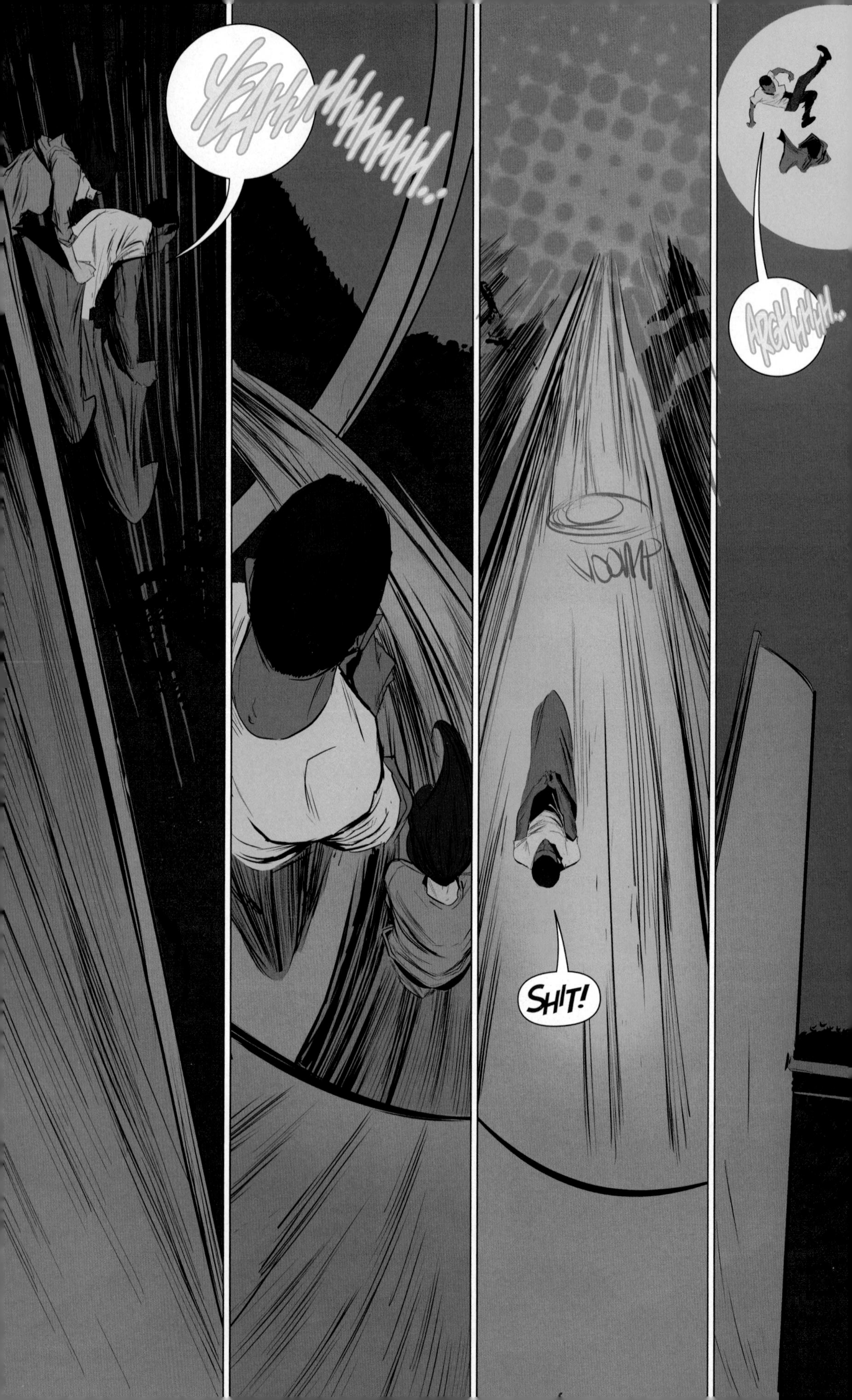
YEAAHHHHHHHHHH...
VOOMP
SHIT!
ARGHHHH...

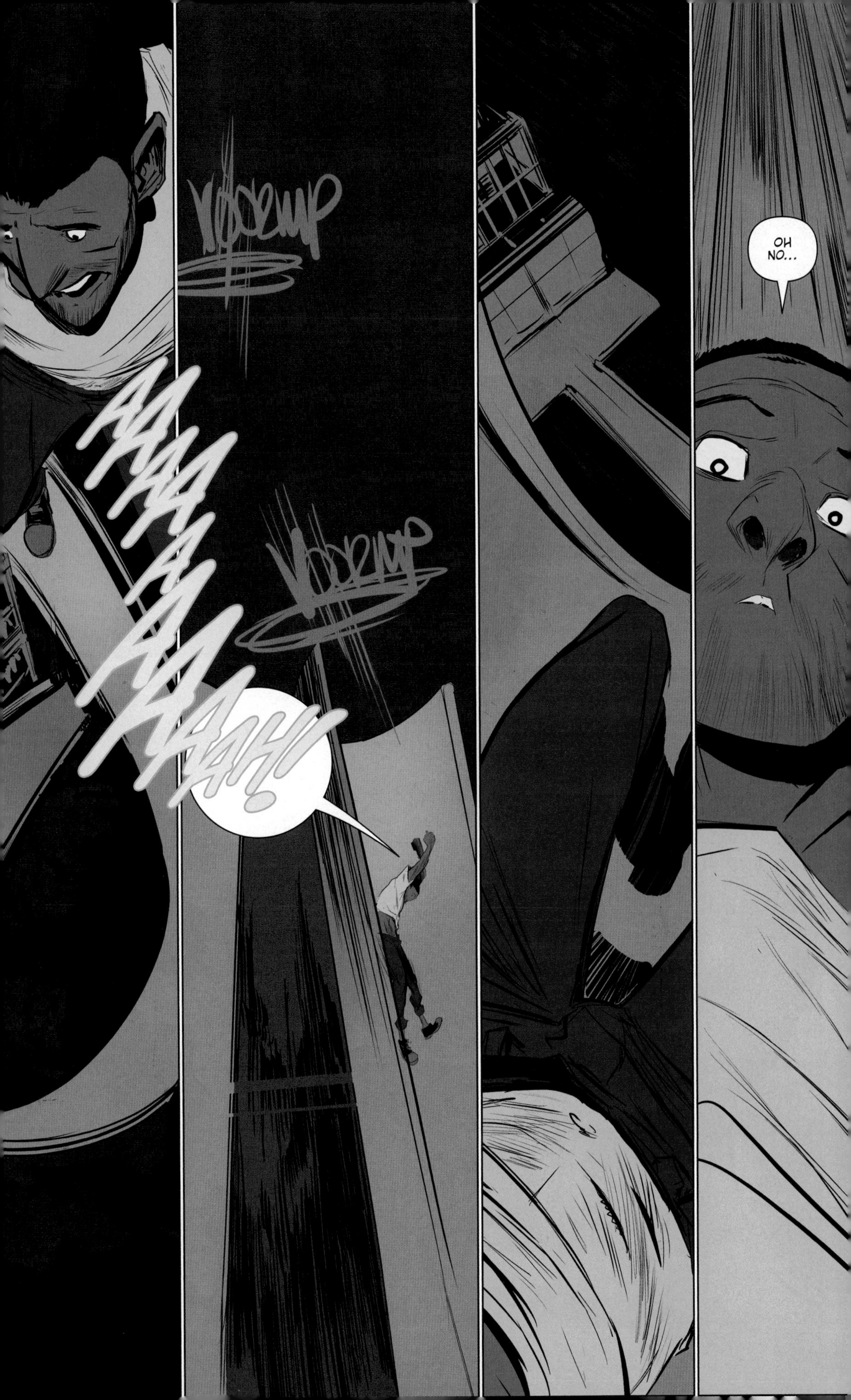
OH NO...

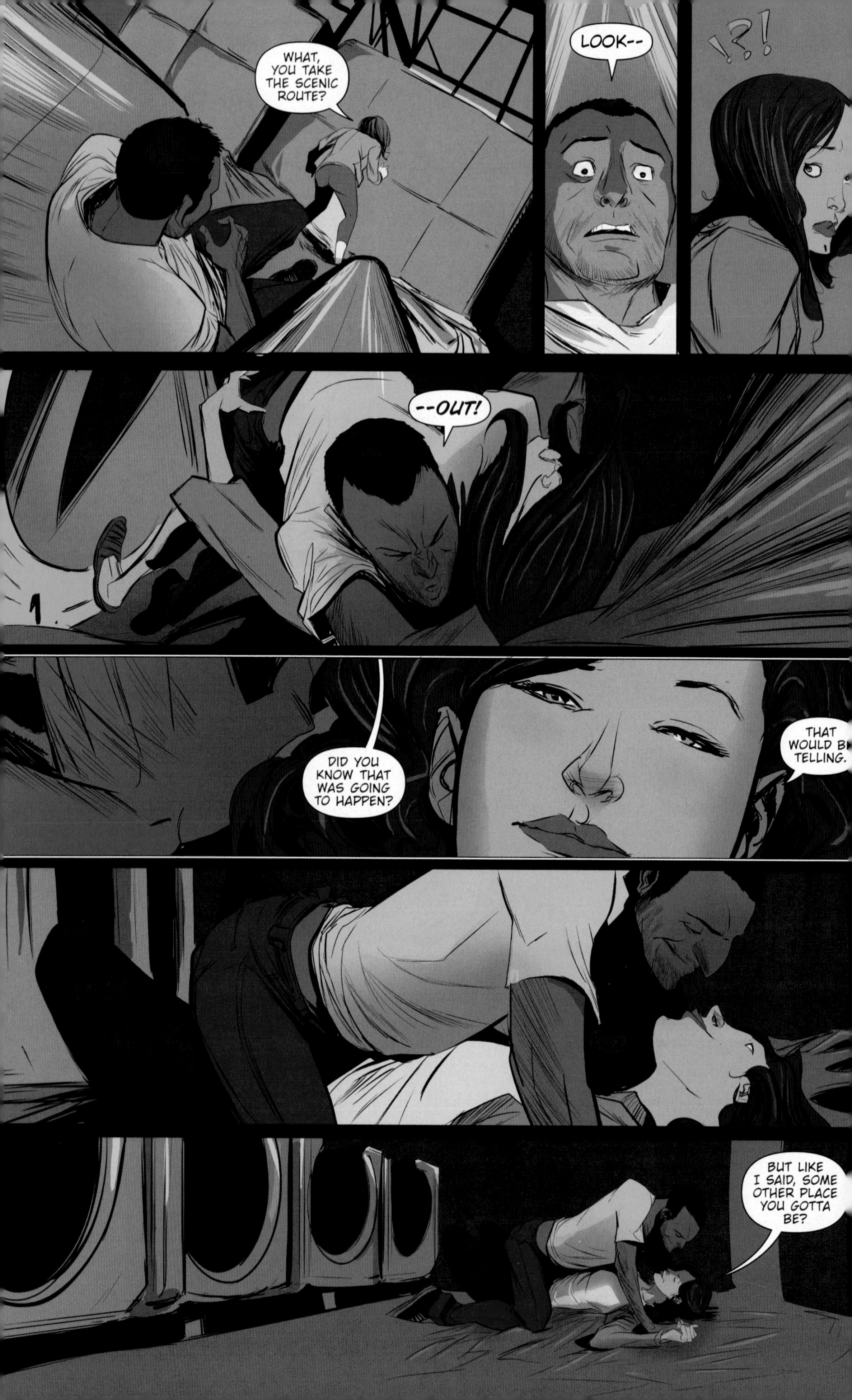
WHAT, YOU TAKE THE SCENIC ROUTE?
LOOK--
!?!
--OUT!
DID YOU KNOW THAT WAS GOING TO HAPPEN?
THAT WOULD B TELLING.
BUT LIKE I SAID, SOME OTHER PLACE YOU GOTTA BE?

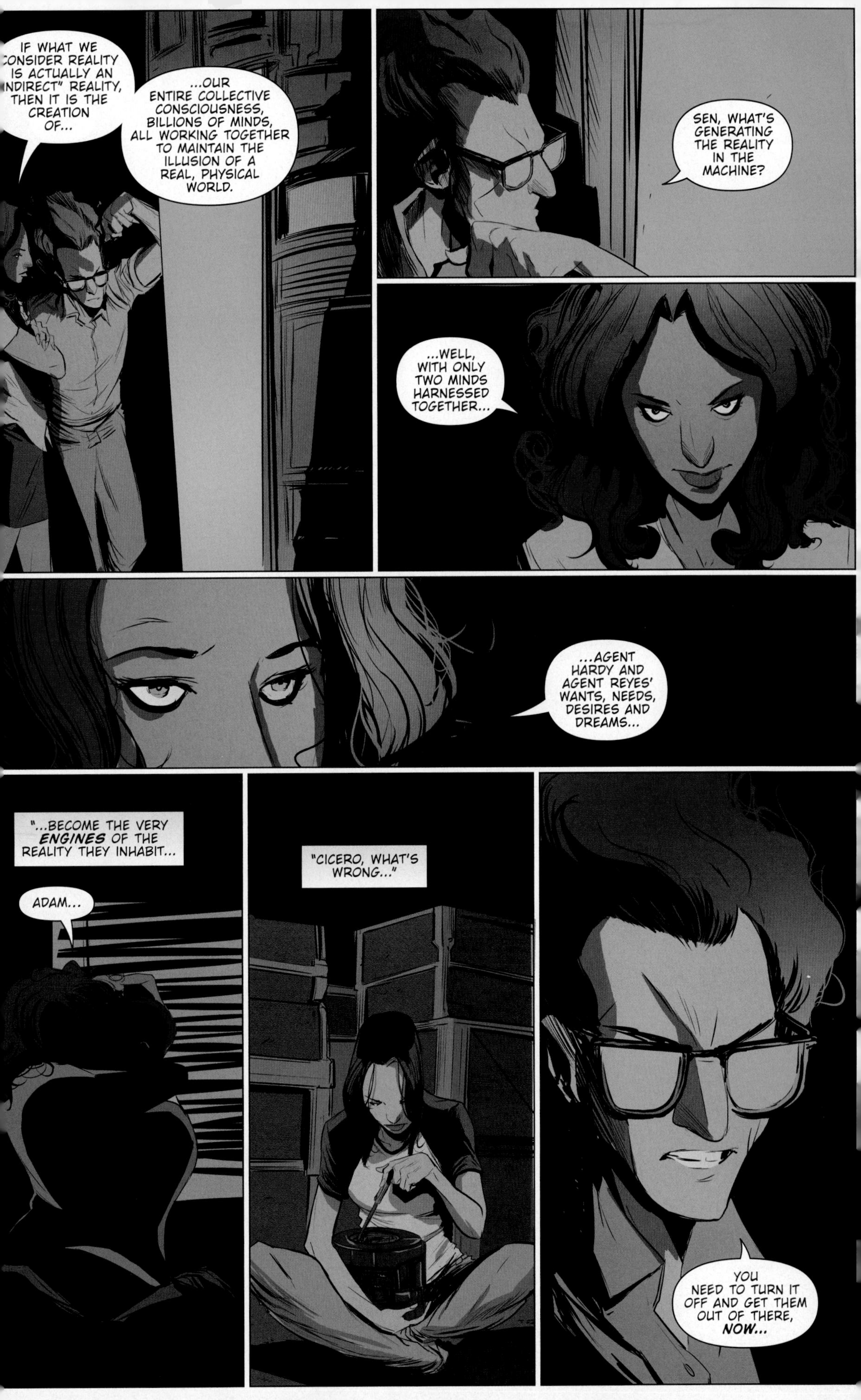
IF WHAT WE CONSIDER REALITY IS ACTUALLY AN "INDIRECT" REALITY, THEN IT IS THE CREATION OF...
...OUR ENTIRE COLLECTIVE CONSCIOUSNESS, BILLIONS OF MINDS, ALL WORKING TOGETHER TO MAINTAIN THE ILLUSION OF A REAL, PHYSICAL WORLD.
SEN, WHAT'S GENERATING THE REALITY IN THE MACHINE?
...WELL, WITH ONLY TWO MINDS HARNESSED TOGETHER...
...AGENT HARDY AND AGENT REYES' WANTS, NEEDS, DESIRES AND DREAMS...
"...BECOME THE VERY ENGINES OF THE REALITY THEY INHABIT...
ADAM...
"CICERO, WHAT'S WRONG..."
YOU NEED TO TURN IT OFF AND GET THEM OUT OF THERE, NOW...

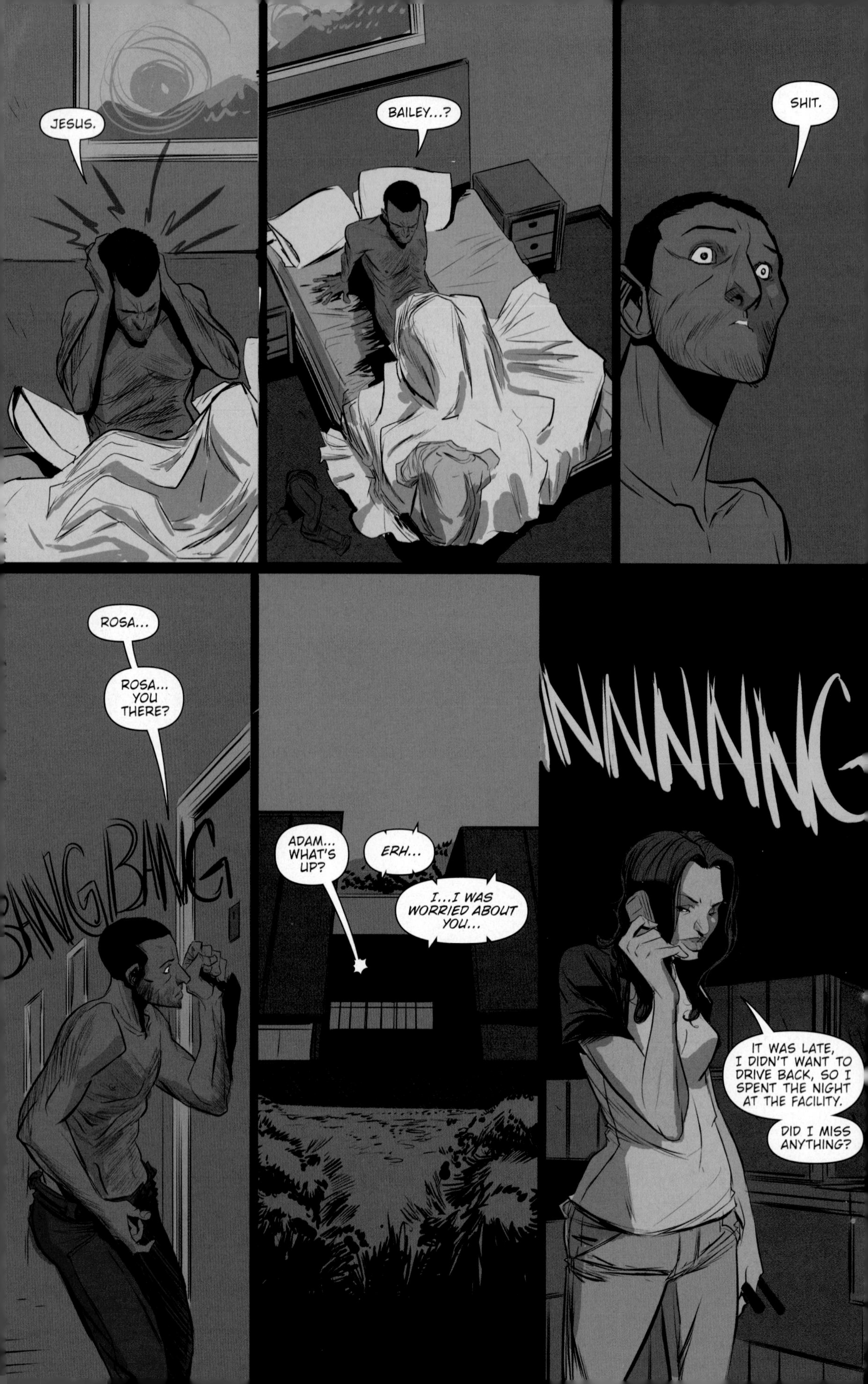
JESUS.
BAILEY...?
SHIT.
ROSA...
ROSA... YOU THERE?
BANG BANG
NNNNNNG
ADAM... WHAT'S UP?
ERH...
I...I WAS WORRIED ABOUT YOU...
IT WAS LATE, I DIDN'T WANT TO DRIVE BACK, SO I SPENT THE NIGHT AT THE FACILITY.
DID I MISS ANYTHING?

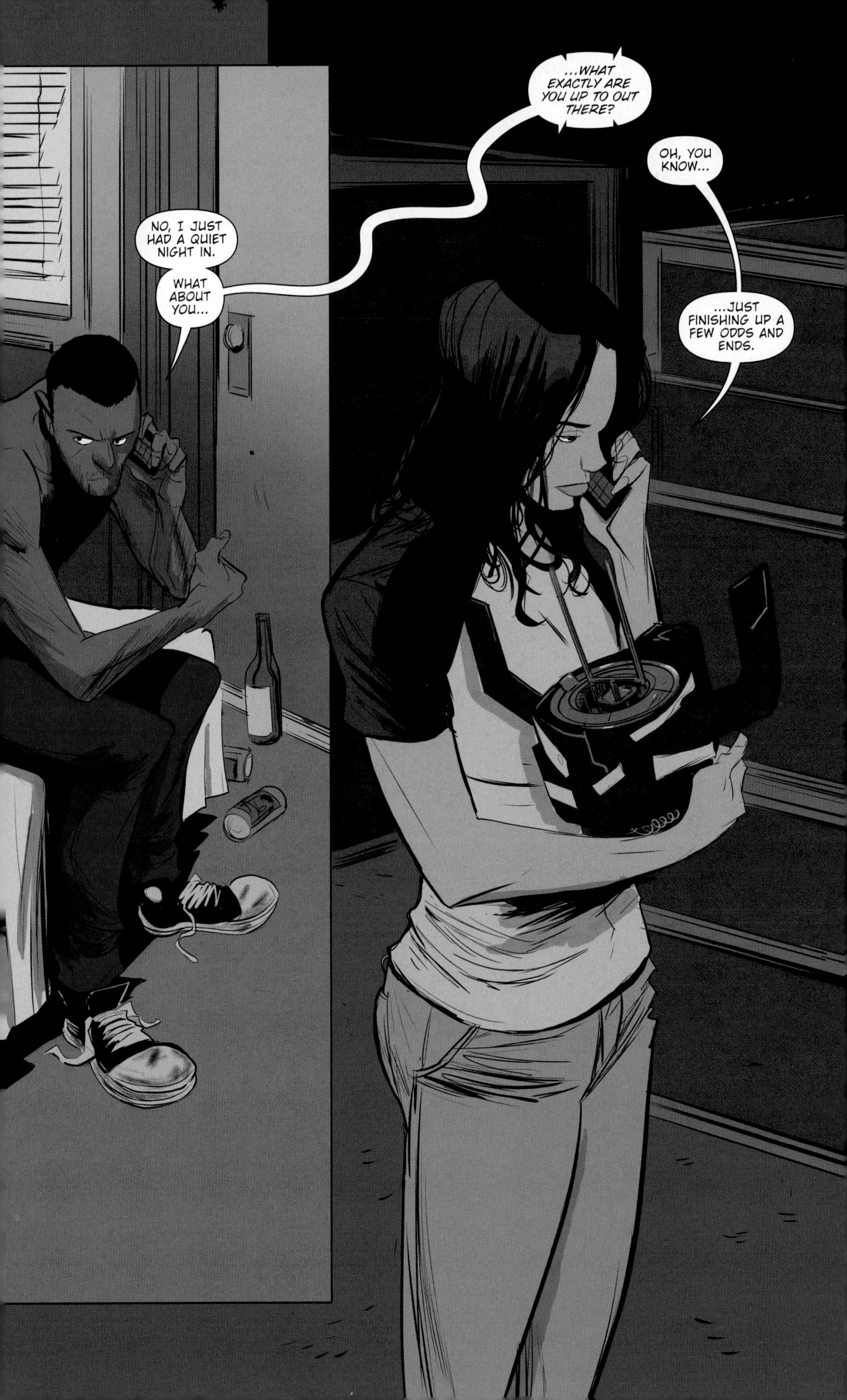
NO, I JUST HAD A QUIET NIGHT IN.
WHAT ABOUT YOU...
...WHAT EXACTLY ARE YOU UP TO OUT THERE?
OH, YOU KNOW...
...JUST FINISHING UP A FEW ODDS AND ENDS.

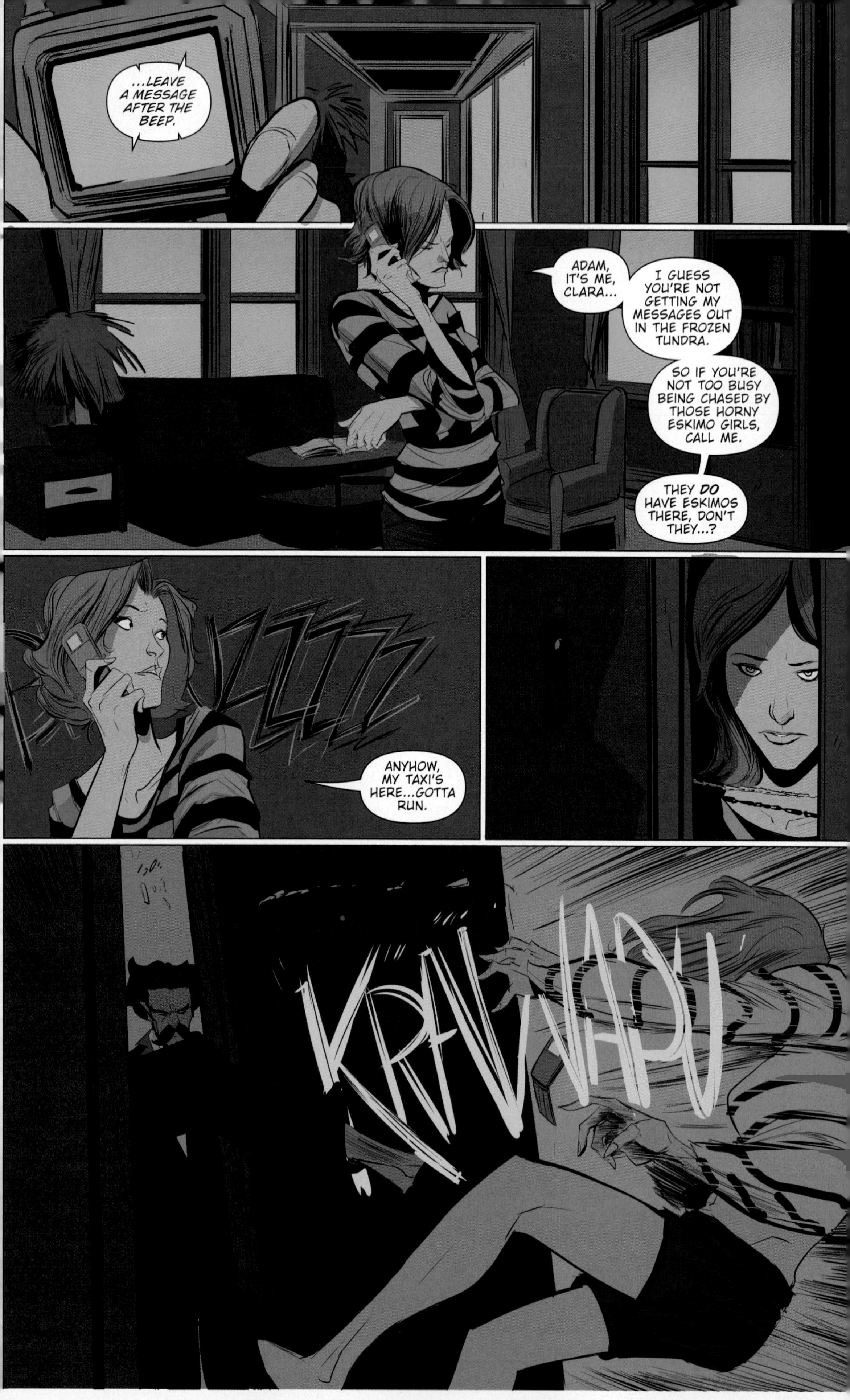
...LEAVE A MESSAGE AFTER THE BEEP.
ADAM, IT'S ME, CLARA...
I GUESS YOU'RE NOT GETTING MY MESSAGES OUT IN THE FROZEN TUNDRA.
SO IF YOU'RE NOT TOO BUSY BEING CHASED BY THOSE HORNY ESKIMO GIRLS, CALL ME.
THEY DO HAVE ESKIMOS THERE, DON'T THEY...?
ANYHOW, MY TAXI'S HERE...GOTTA RUN.

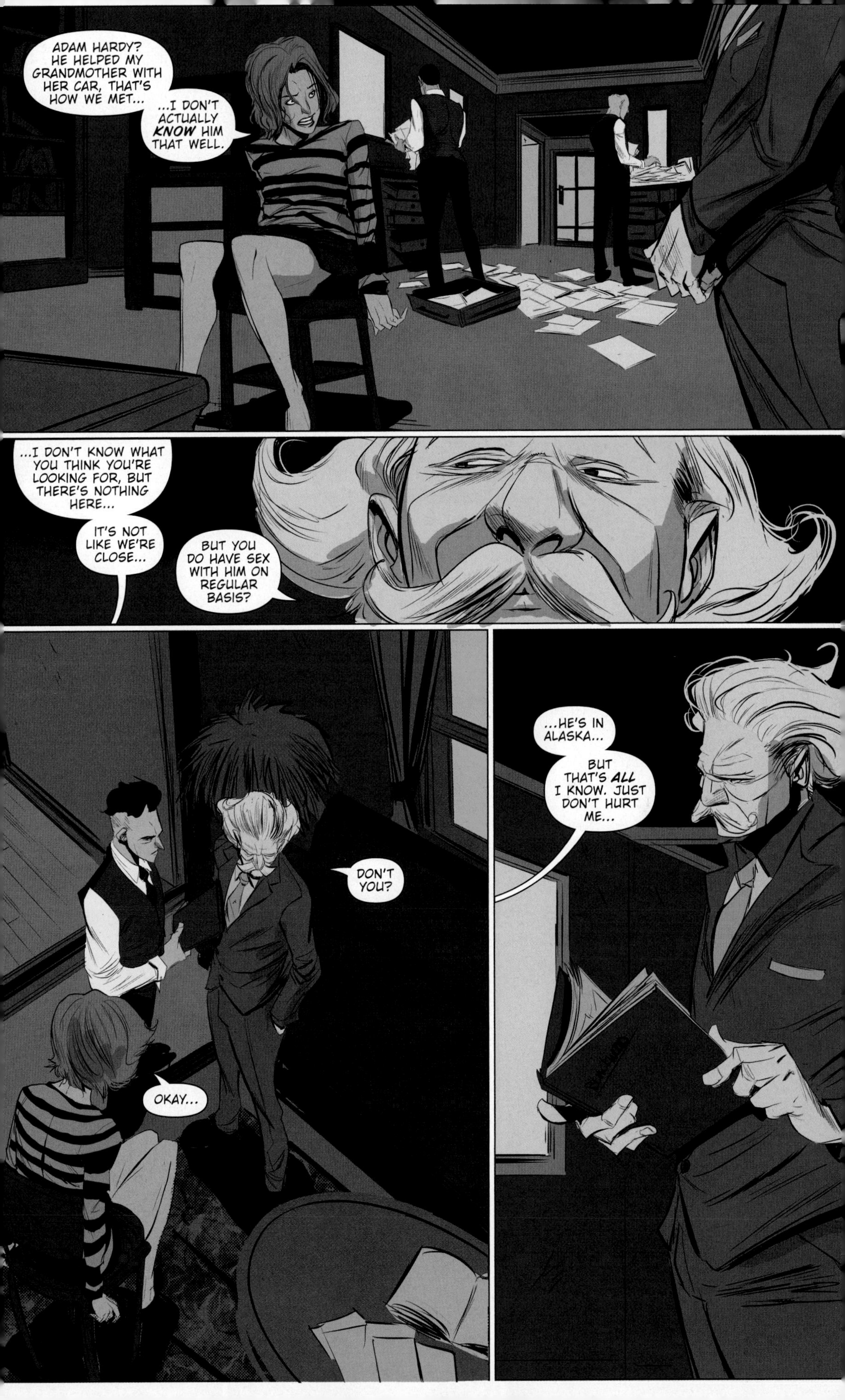
ADAM HARDY? HE HELPED MY GRANDMOTHER WITH HER CAR, THAT'S HOW WE MET...
...I DON'T ACTUALLY **KNOW** HIM THAT WELL.
...I DON'T KNOW WHAT YOU THINK YOU'RE LOOKING FOR, BUT THERE'S NOTHING HERE...
IT'S NOT LIKE WE'RE CLOSE...
BUT YOU DO HAVE SEX WITH HIM ON REGULAR BASIS?
DON'T YOU?
OKAY...
...HE'S IN ALASKA...
BUT THAT'S ***ALL*** I KNOW. JUST DON'T HURT ME...

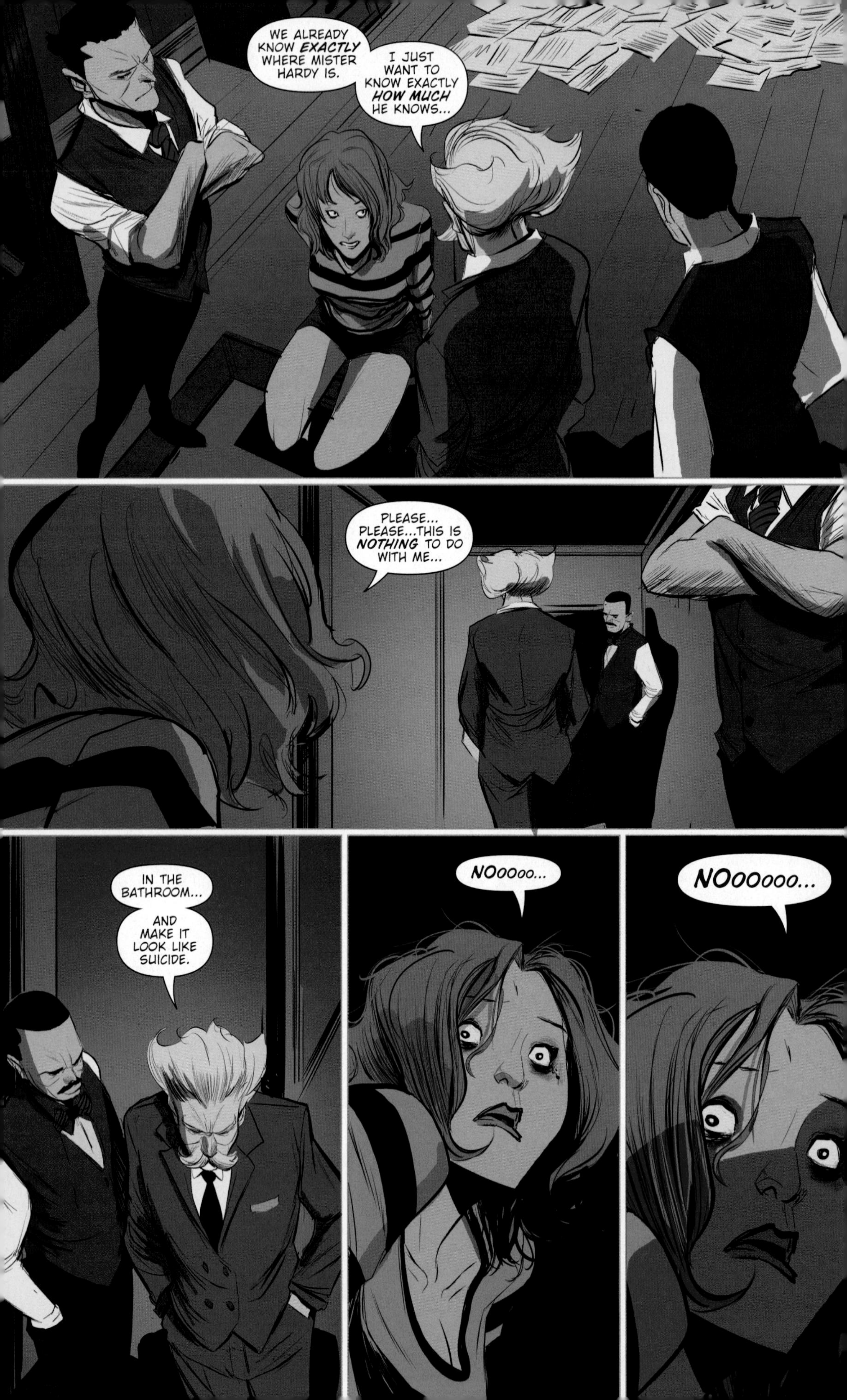
WE ALREADY KNOW EXACTLY WHERE MISTER HARDY IS.
I JUST WANT TO KNOW EXACTLY HOW MUCH HE KNOWS...
PLEASE... PLEASE...THIS IS NOTHING TO DO WITH ME...
IN THE BATHROOM...
AND MAKE IT LOOK LIKE SUICIDE.
NOooooo...
NOoooooo...

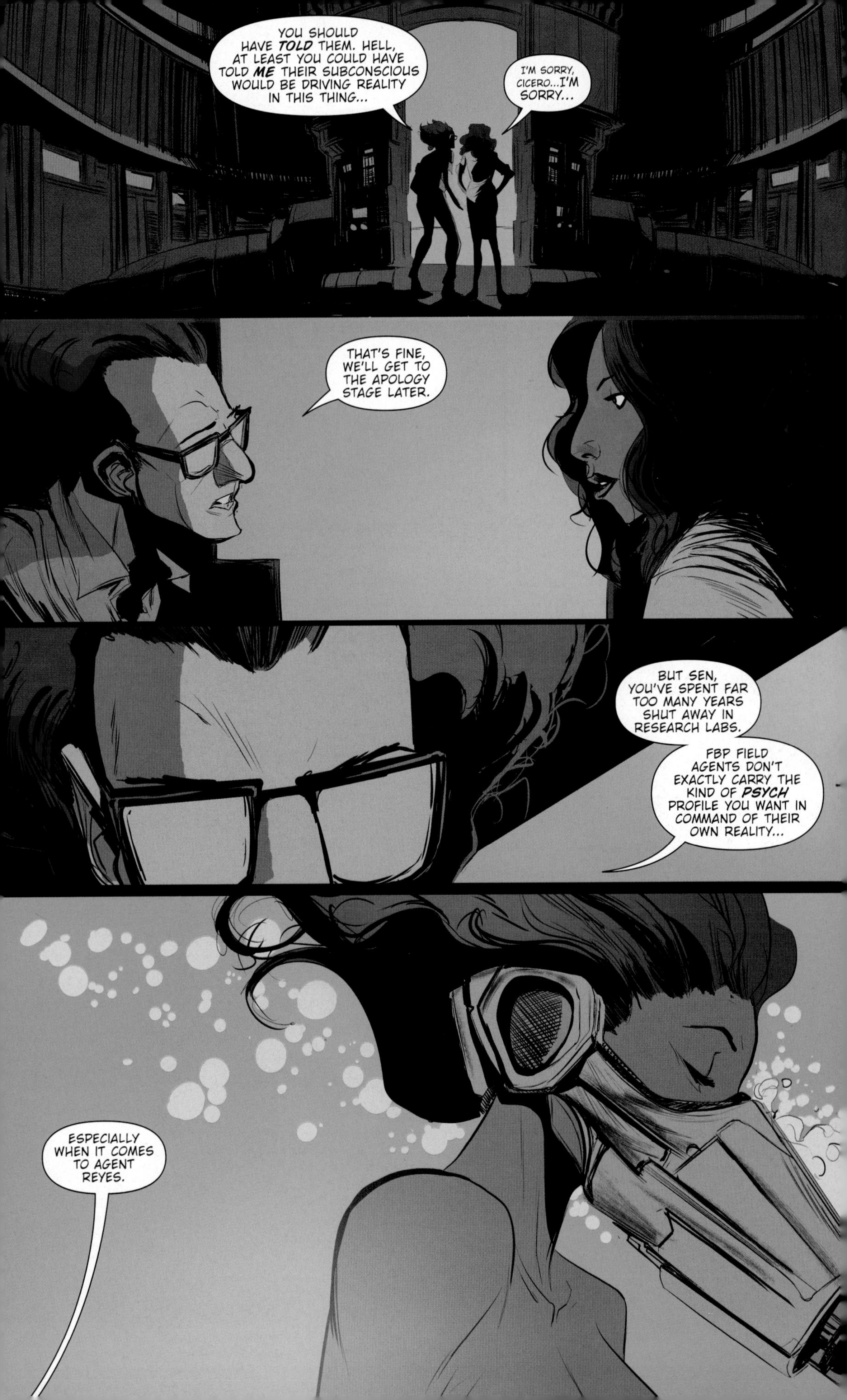
YOU SHOULD HAVE TOLD THEM. HELL, AT LEAST YOU COULD HAVE TOLD ME THEIR SUBCONSCIOUS WOULD BE DRIVING REALITY IN THIS THING...
I'M SORRY, CICERO...I'M SORRY...
THAT'S FINE, WE'LL GET TO THE APOLOGY STAGE LATER.
BUT SEN, YOU'VE SPENT FAR TOO MANY YEARS SHUT AWAY IN RESEARCH LABS.
FBP FIELD AGENTS DON'T EXACTLY CARRY THE KIND OF PSYCH PROFILE YOU WANT IN COMMAND OF THEIR OWN REALITY...
ESPECIALLY WHEN IT COMES TO AGENT REYES.

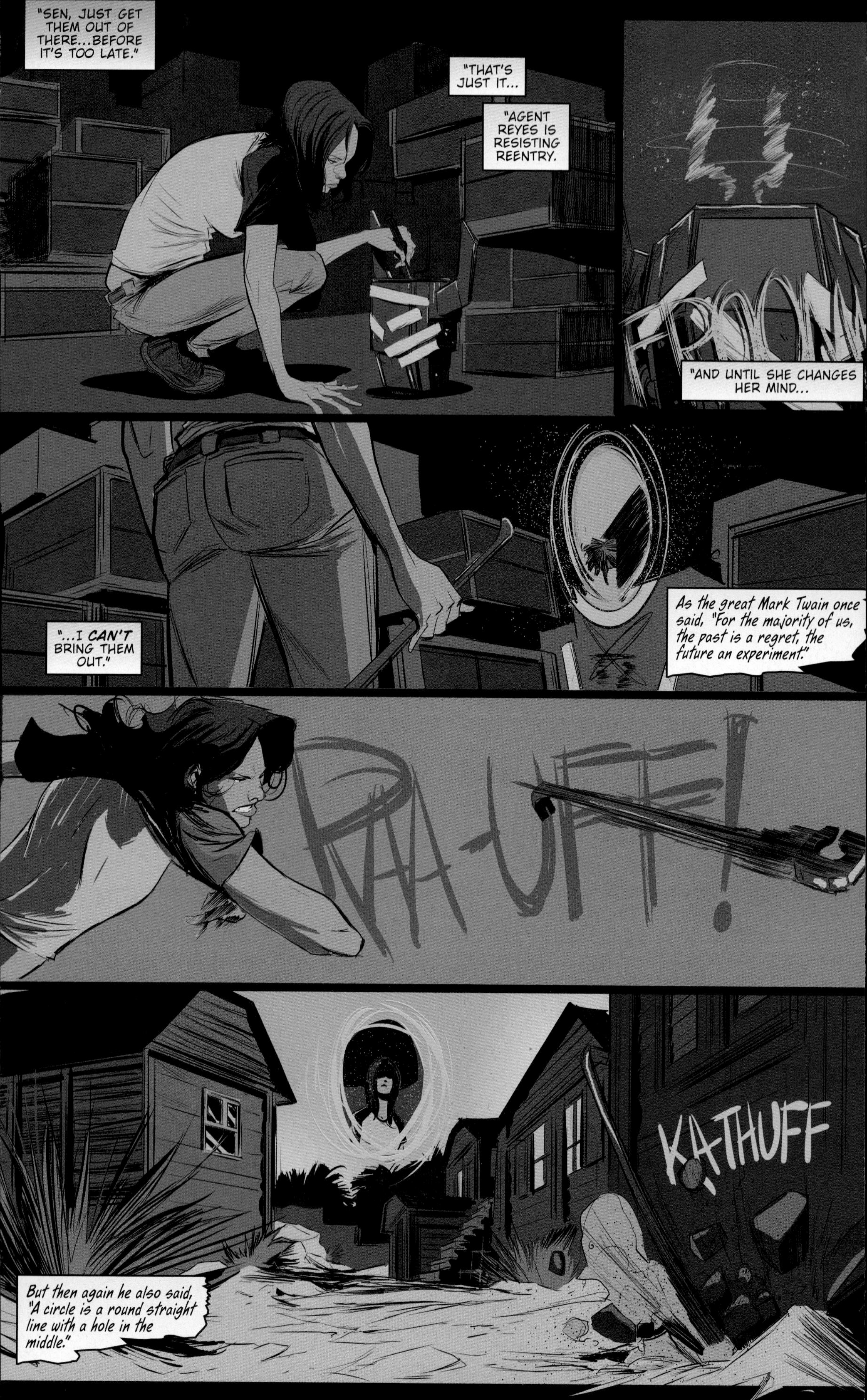
"SEN, JUST GET THEM OUT OF THERE...BEFORE IT'S TOO LATE."
"THAT'S JUST IT...
"AGENT REYES IS RESISTING REENTRY.
FPOOM
"AND UNTIL SHE CHANGES HER MIND...
"...I CAN'T BRING THEM OUT."
As the great Mark Twain once said, "For the majority of us, the past is a regret, the future an experiment."
KRA-UFF!
KATHUFF
But then again he also said, "A circle is a round straight line with a hole in the middle."

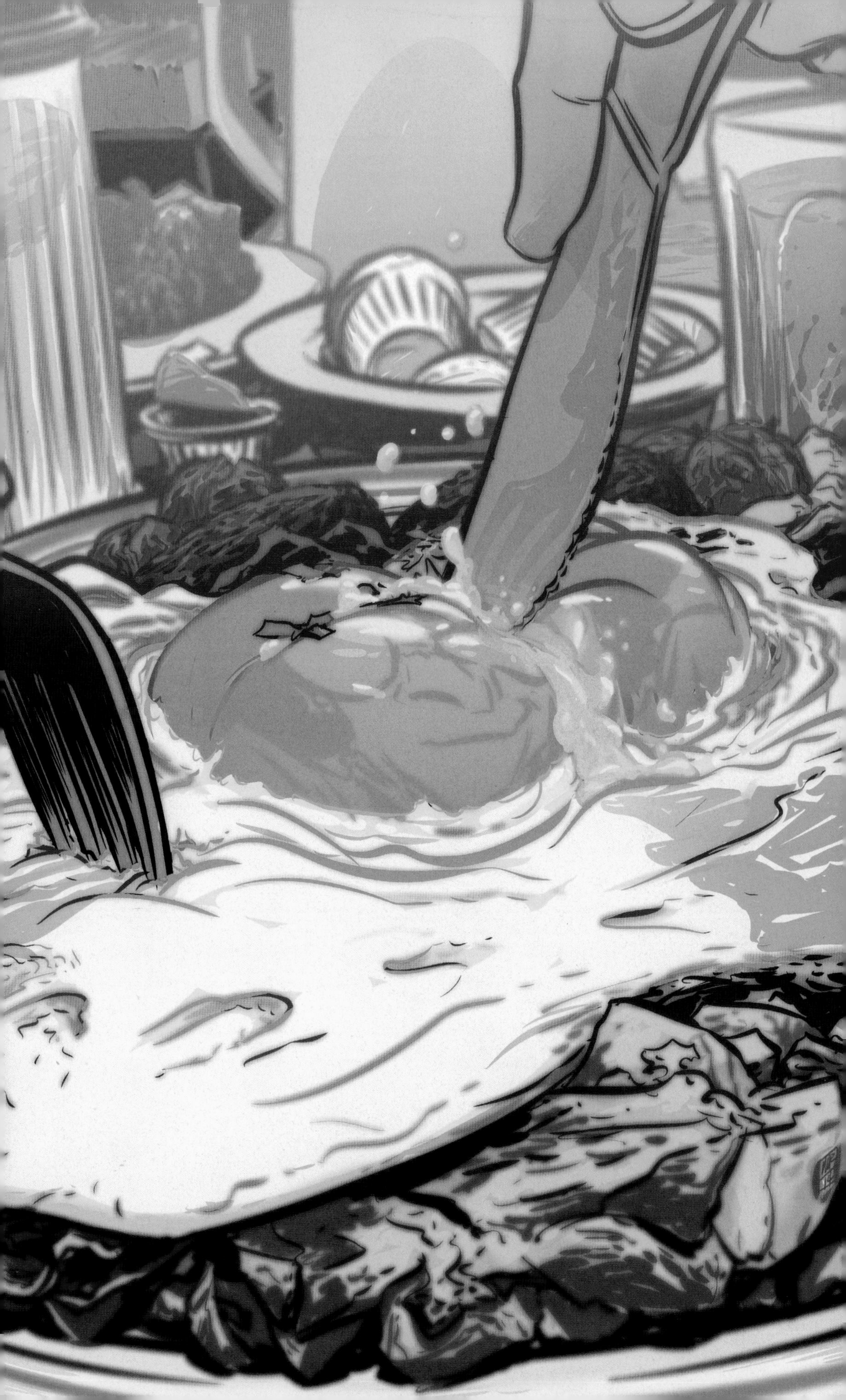

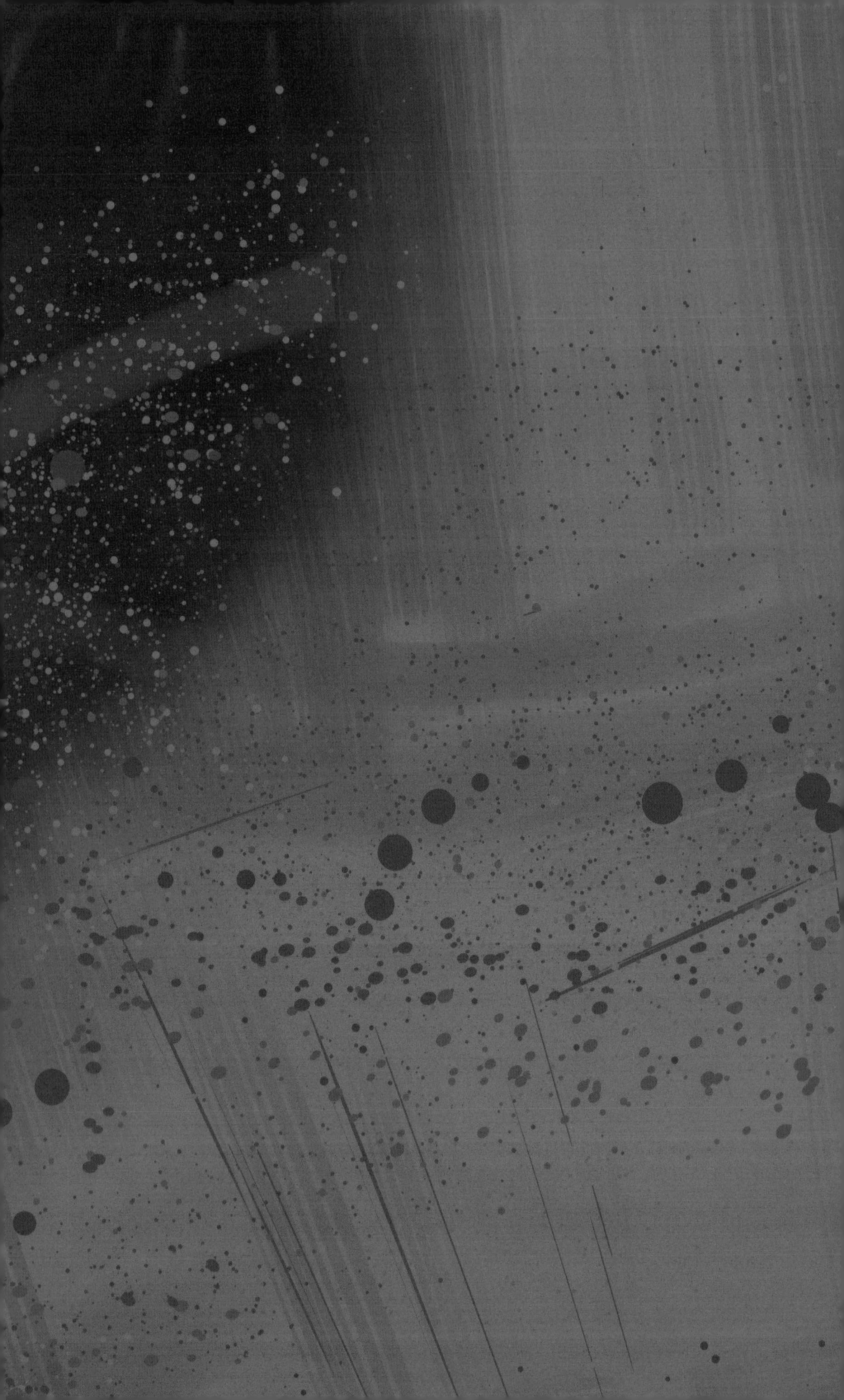

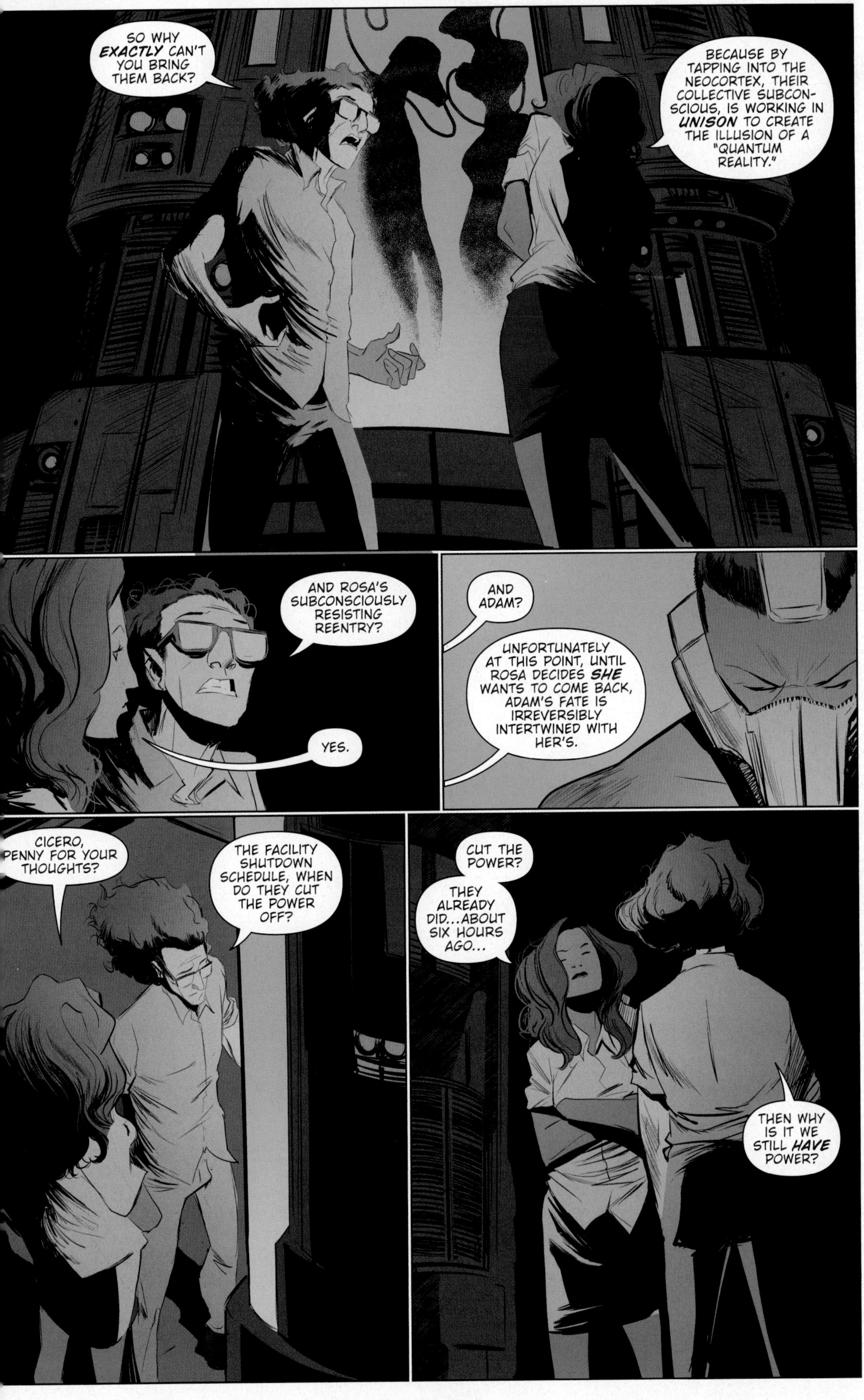

SO WHY EXACTLY CAN'T YOU BRING THEM BACK?
BECAUSE BY TAPPING INTO THE NEOCORTEX, THEIR COLLECTIVE SUBCONSCIOUS, IS WORKING IN UNISON TO CREATE THE ILLUSION OF A "QUANTUM REALITY."
AND ROSA'S SUBCONSCIOUSLY RESISTING REENTRY?
YES.
AND ADAM?
UNFORTUNATELY AT THIS POINT, UNTIL ROSA DECIDES SHE WANTS TO COME BACK, ADAM'S FATE IS IRREVERSIBLY INTERTWINED WITH HER'S.
CICERO, PENNY FOR YOUR THOUGHTS?
THE FACILITY SHUTDOWN SCHEDULE, WHEN DO THEY CUT THE POWER OFF?
CUT THE POWER?
THEY ALREADY DID...ABOUT SIX HOURS AGO...
THEN WHY IS IT WE STILL HAVE POWER?

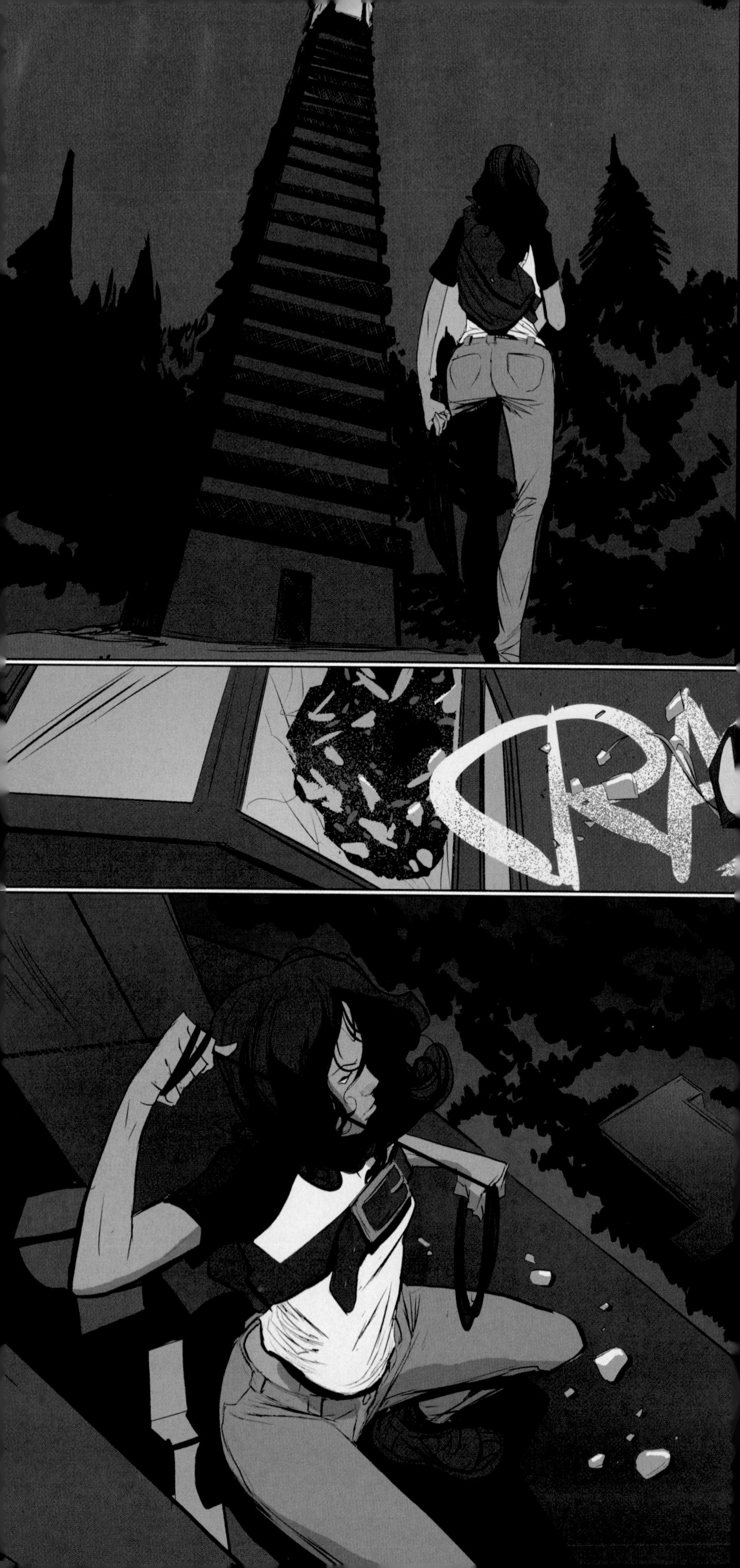
CRA

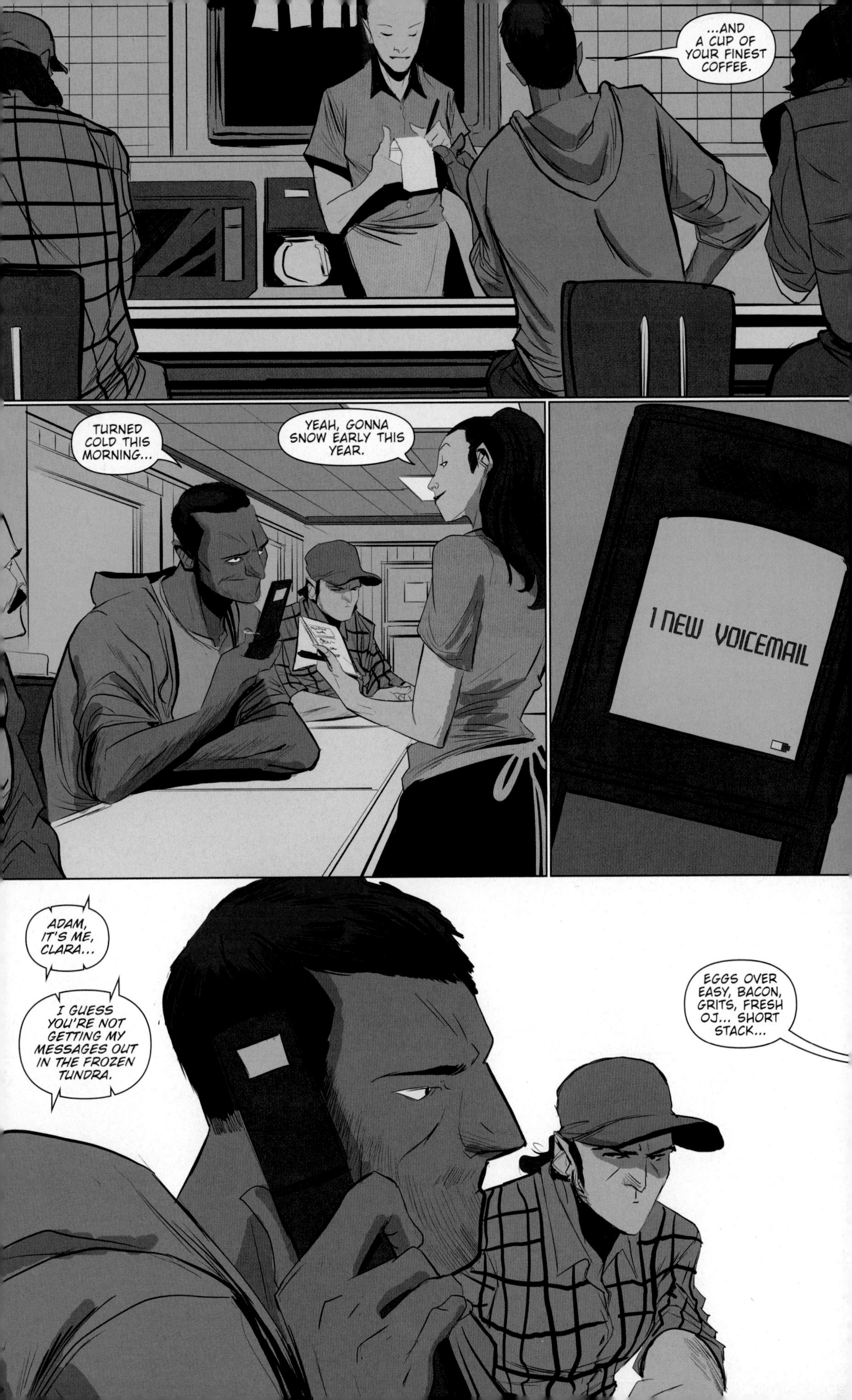
...AND A CUP OF YOUR FINEST COFFEE.
TURNED COLD THIS MORNING...
YEAH, GONNA SNOW EARLY THIS YEAR.
1 NEW VOICEMAIL
ADAM, IT'S ME, CLARA...
I GUESS YOU'RE NOT GETTING MY MESSAGES OUT IN THE FROZEN TUNDRA.
EGGS OVER EASY, BACON, GRITS, FRESH OJ... SHORT STACK...

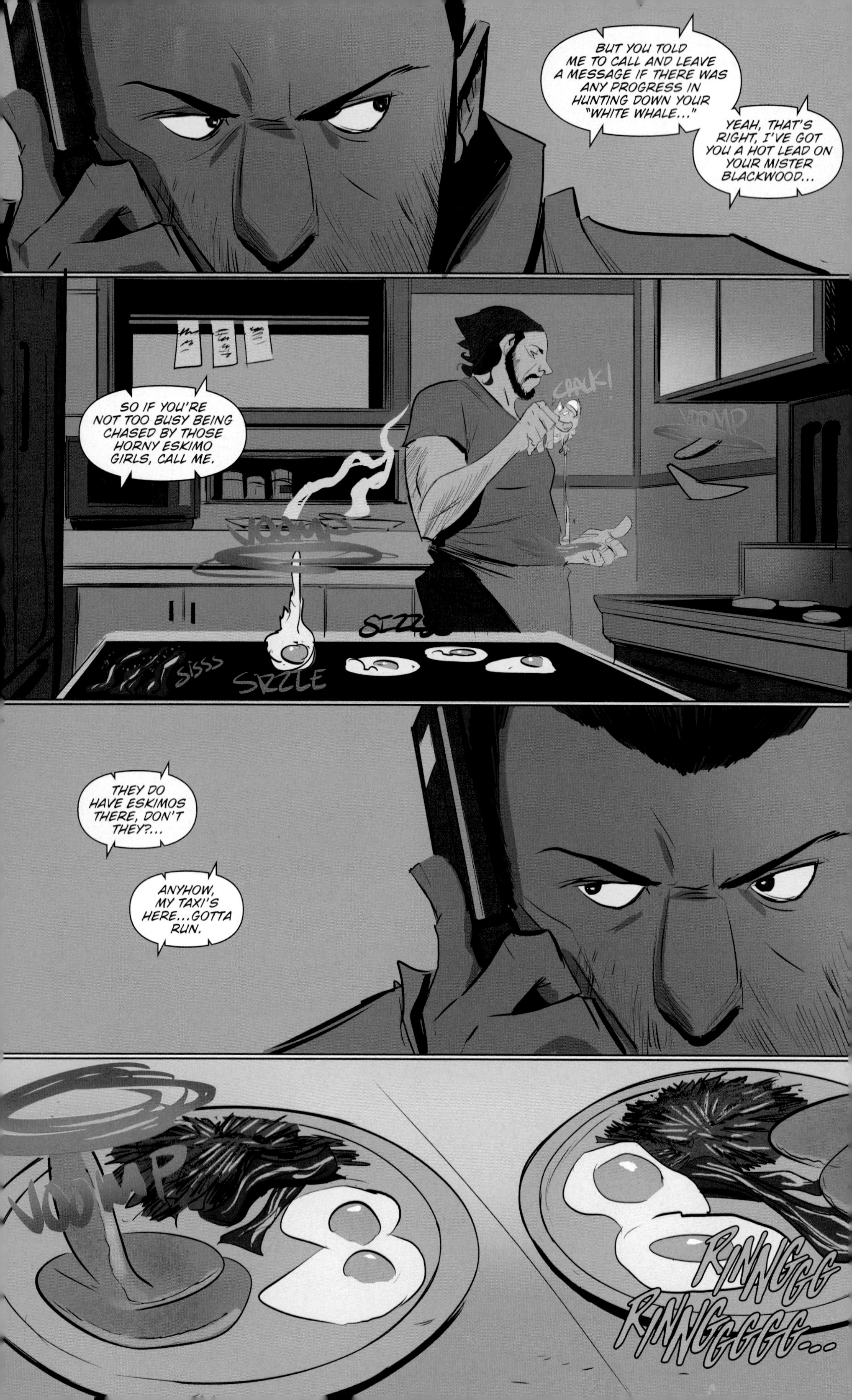
BUT YOU TOLD ME TO CALL AND LEAVE A MESSAGE IF THERE WAS ANY PROGRESS IN HUNTING DOWN YOUR "WHITE WHALE..."
YEAH, THAT'S RIGHT, I'VE GOT YOU A HOT LEAD ON YOUR MISTER BLACKWOOD...
SO IF YOU'RE NOT TOO BUSY BEING CHASED BY THOSE HORNY ESKIMO GIRLS, CALL ME.
CRACK!
VOOMP
VOOMP
SIZZ
SISSS
SIZZLE
THEY DO HAVE ESKIMOS THERE, DON'T THEY?...
ANYHOW, MY TAXI'S HERE...GOTTA RUN.
VOOMP
RINNGGG
RINNGGGGG...

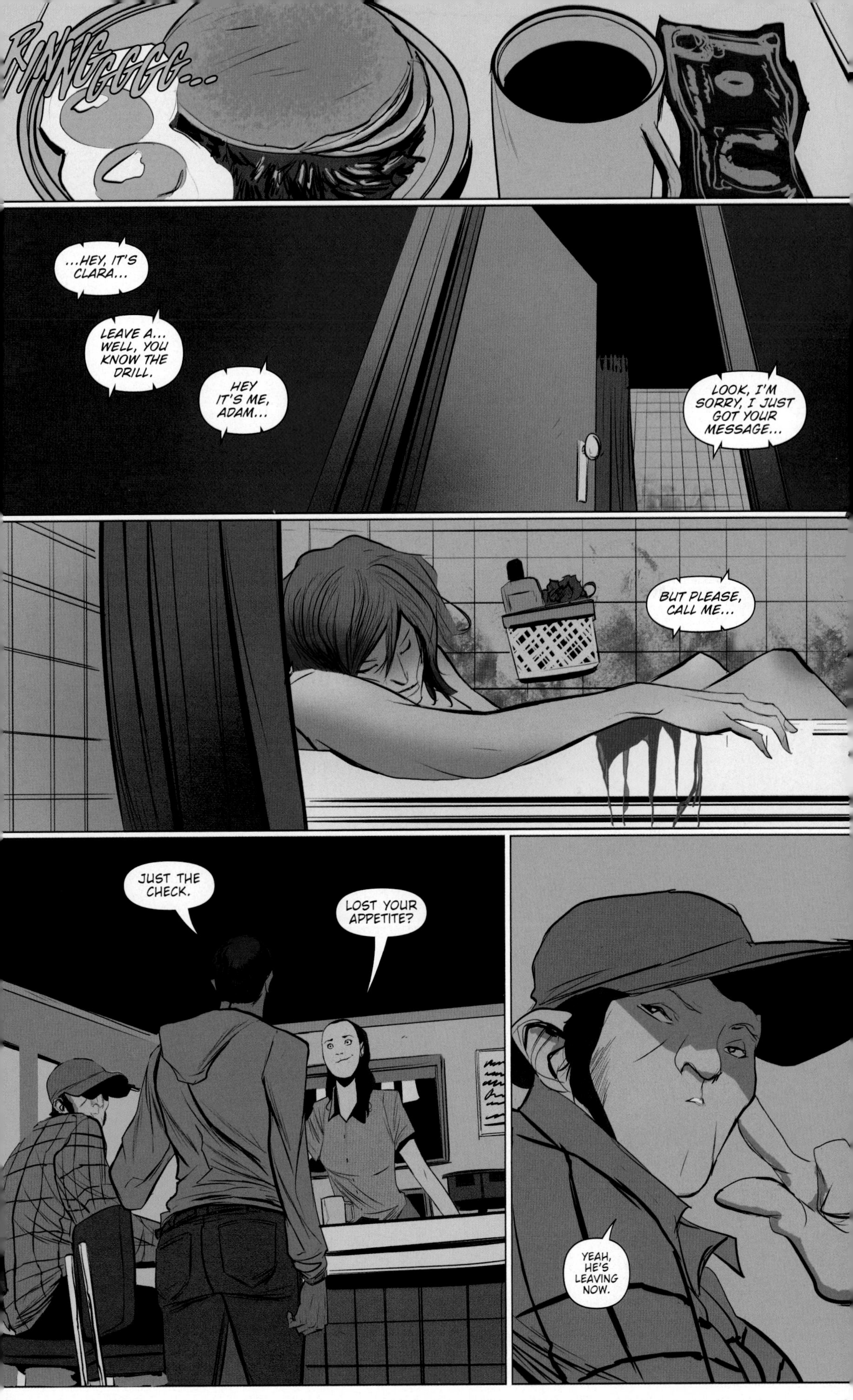
RINGGGG...
...HEY, IT'S CLARA...
LEAVE A... WELL, YOU KNOW THE DRILL.
HEY IT'S ME, ADAM...
LOOK, I'M SORRY, I JUST GOT YOUR MESSAGE...
BUT PLEASE, CALL ME...
JUST THE CHECK.
LOST YOUR APPETITE?
YEAH, HE'S LEAVING NOW.

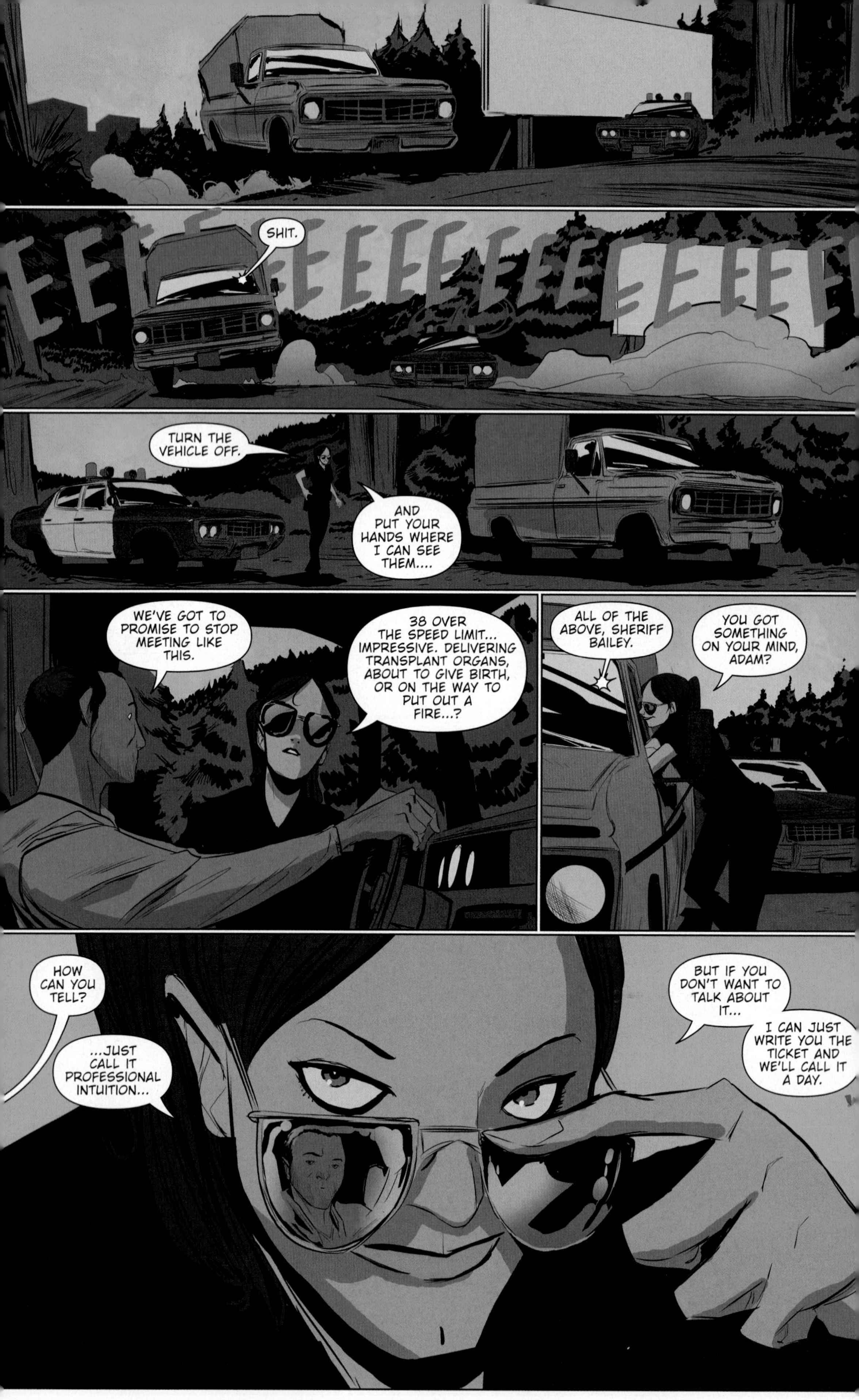
EEEEEEEEEEEEEEEEE
SHIT.
TURN THE VEHICLE OFF.
AND PUT YOUR HANDS WHERE I CAN SEE THEM....
WE'VE GOT TO PROMISE TO STOP MEETING LIKE THIS.
38 OVER THE SPEED LIMIT... IMPRESSIVE. DELIVERING TRANSPLANT ORGANS, ABOUT TO GIVE BIRTH, OR ON THE WAY TO PUT OUT A FIRE...?
ALL OF THE ABOVE, SHERIFF BAILEY.
YOU GOT SOMETHING ON YOUR MIND, ADAM?
HOW CAN YOU TELL?
...JUST CALL IT PROFESSIONAL INTUITION...
BUT IF YOU DON'T WANT TO TALK ABOUT IT...
I CAN JUST WRITE YOU THE TICKET AND WE'LL CALL IT A DAY.

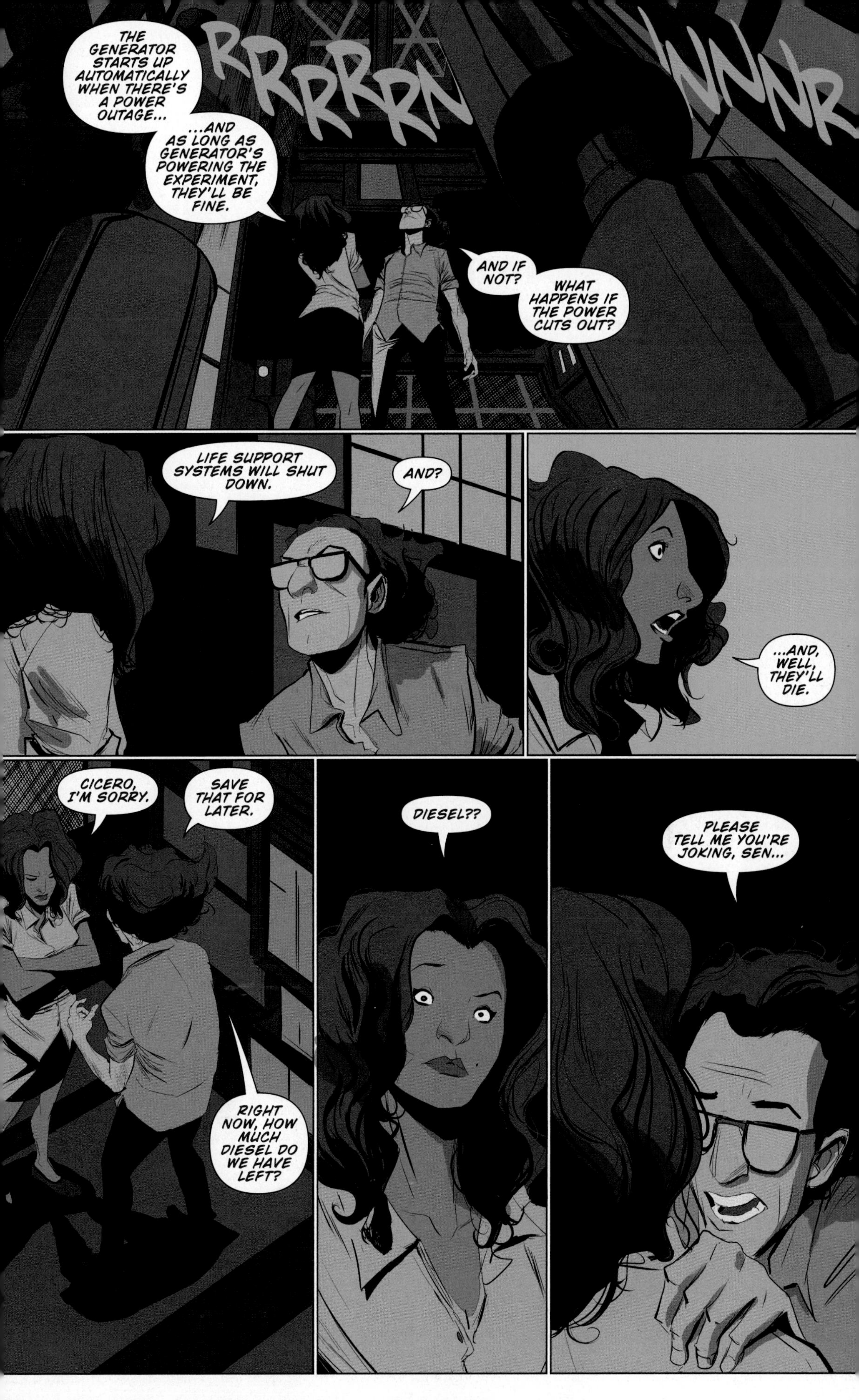
THE GENERATOR STARTS UP AUTOMATICALLY WHEN THERE'S A POWER OUTAGE...
RRRRRN
NNNNR
...AND AS LONG AS GENERATOR'S POWERING THE EXPERIMENT, THEY'LL BE FINE.
AND IF NOT?
WHAT HAPPENS IF THE POWER CUTS OUT?
LIFE SUPPORT SYSTEMS WILL SHUT DOWN.
AND?
...AND, WELL, THEY'LL DIE.
CICERO, I'M SORRY.
SAVE THAT FOR LATER.
RIGHT NOW, HOW MUCH DIESEL DO WE HAVE LEFT?
DIESEL??
PLEASE TELL ME YOU'RE JOKING, SEN...

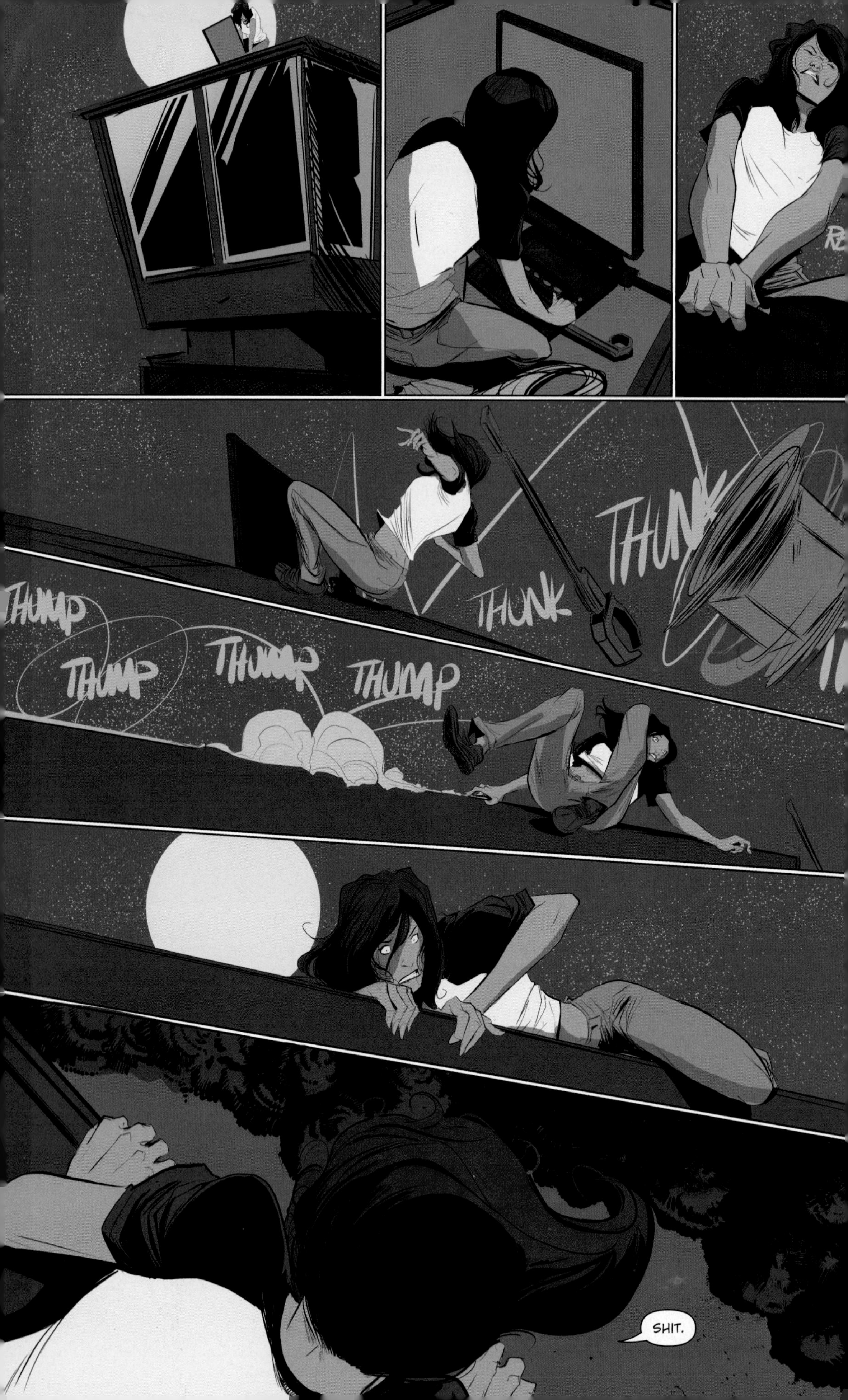
THUNK
THUNK
THUMP
THUMP
THUMP
THUMP
SHIT.

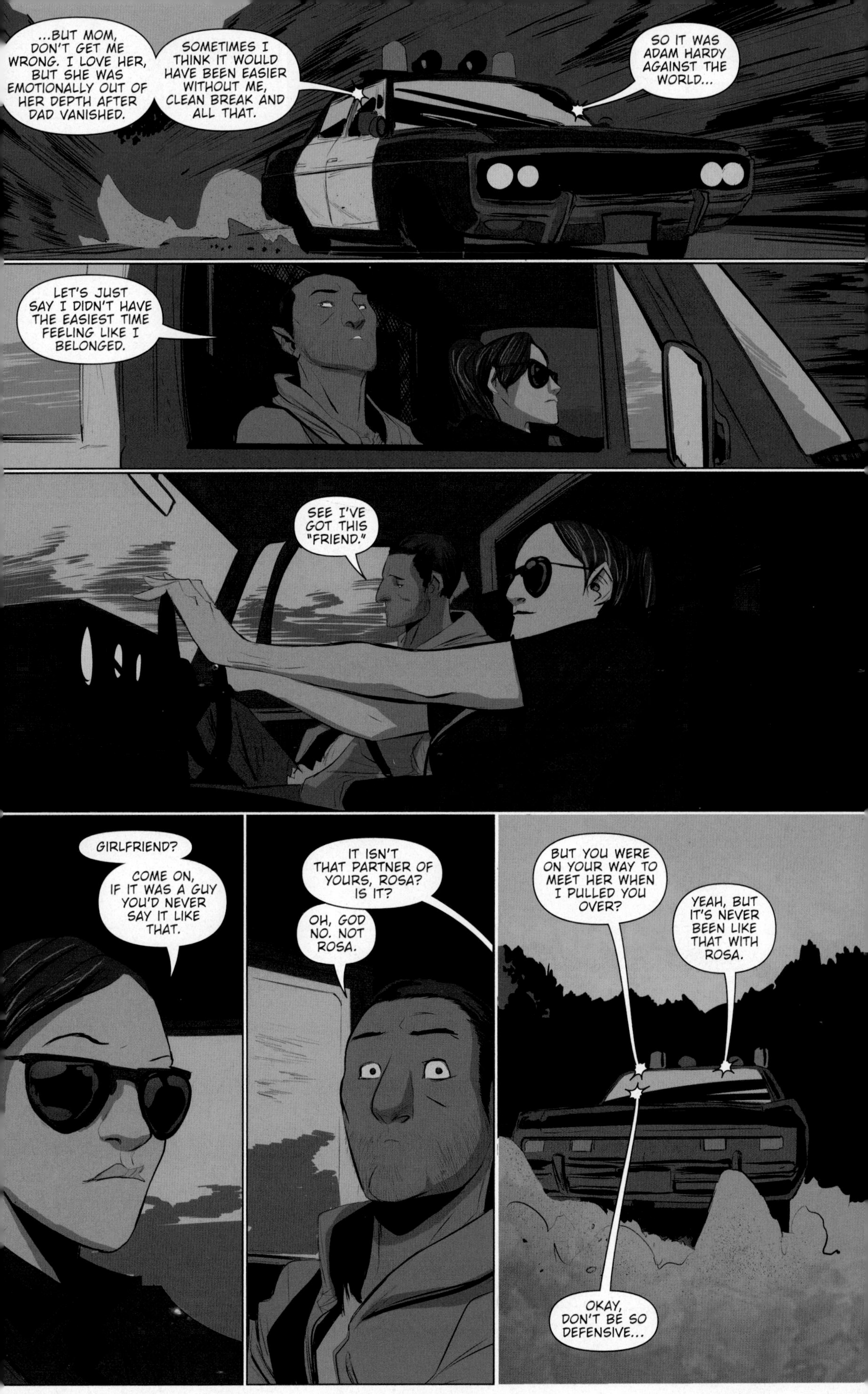
...BUT MOM, DON'T GET ME WRONG. I LOVE HER, BUT SHE WAS EMOTIONALLY OUT OF HER DEPTH AFTER DAD VANISHED.
SOMETIMES I THINK IT WOULD HAVE BEEN EASIER WITHOUT ME, CLEAN BREAK AND ALL THAT.
SO IT WAS ADAM HARDY AGAINST THE WORLD...
LET'S JUST SAY I DIDN'T HAVE THE EASIEST TIME FEELING LIKE I BELONGED.
SEE I'VE GOT THIS "FRIEND."
GIRLFRIEND?
COME ON, IF IT WAS A GUY YOU'D NEVER SAY IT LIKE THAT.
IT ISN'T THAT PARTNER OF YOURS, ROSA? IS IT?
OH, GOD NO. NOT ROSA.
BUT YOU WERE ON YOUR WAY TO MEET HER WHEN I PULLED YOU OVER?
YEAH, BUT IT'S NEVER BEEN LIKE THAT WITH ROSA.
OKAY, DON'T BE SO DEFENSIVE...

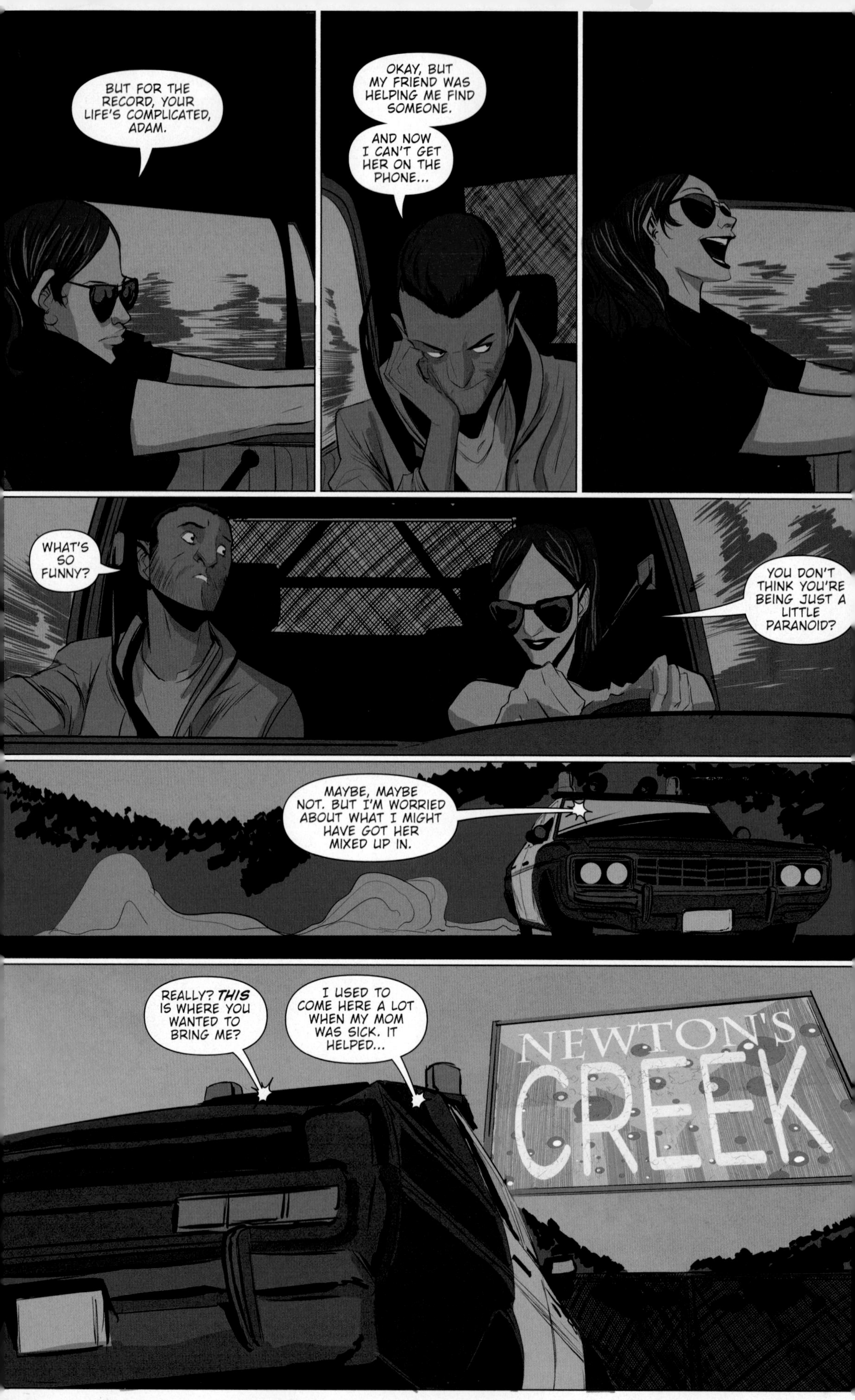
BUT FOR THE RECORD, YOUR LIFE'S COMPLICATED, ADAM.
OKAY, BUT MY FRIEND WAS HELPING ME FIND SOMEONE.
AND NOW I CAN'T GET HER ON THE PHONE...
WHAT'S SO FUNNY?
YOU DON'T THINK YOU'RE BEING JUST A LITTLE PARANOID?
MAYBE, MAYBE NOT. BUT I'M WORRIED ABOUT WHAT I MIGHT HAVE GOT HER MIXED UP IN.
REALLY? *THIS* IS WHERE YOU WANTED TO BRING ME?
I USED TO COME HERE A LOT WHEN MY MOM WAS SICK. IT HELPED...
NEWTON'S
CREEK

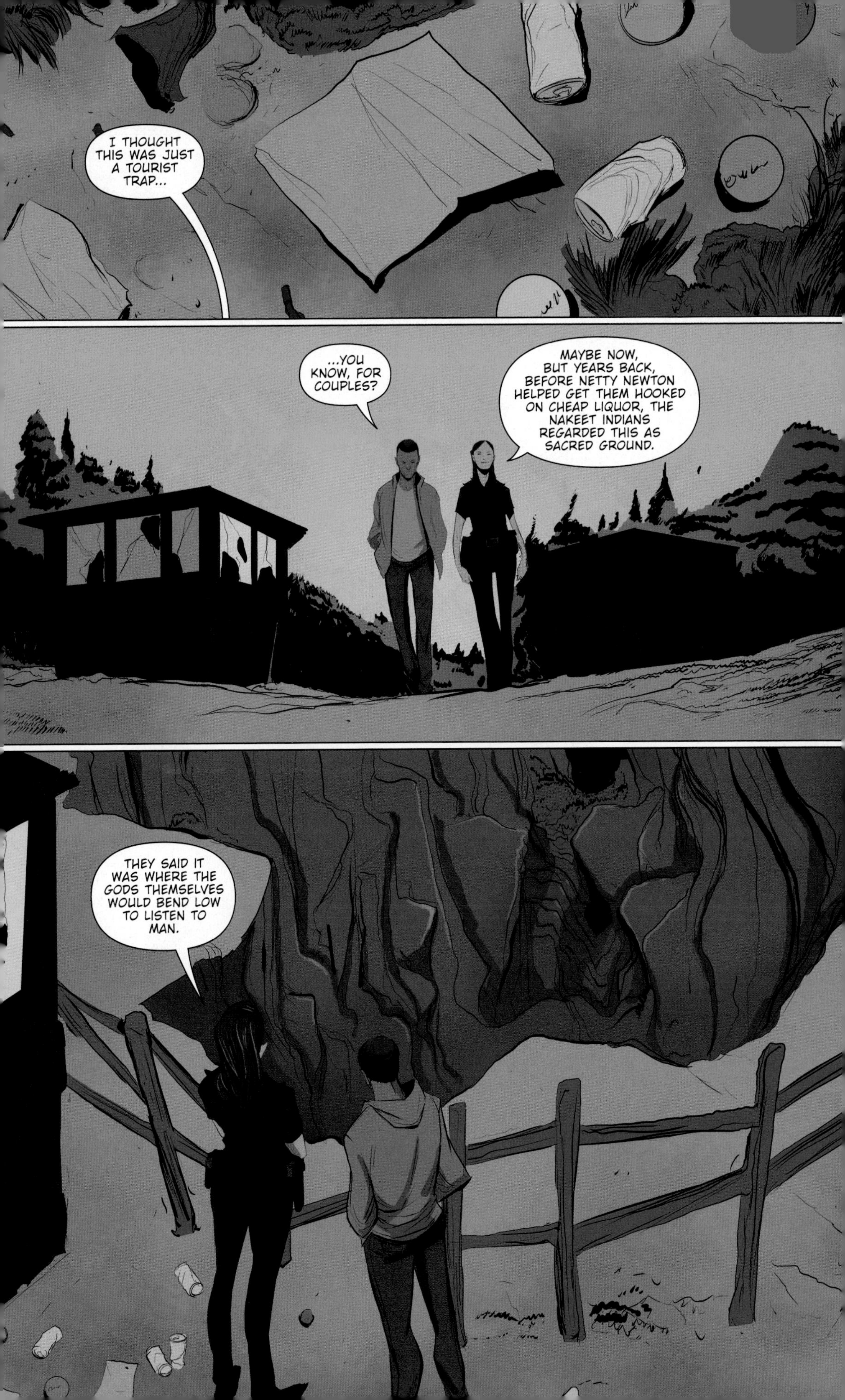
I THOUGHT THIS WAS JUST A TOURIST TRAP...
...YOU KNOW, FOR COUPLES?
MAYBE NOW, BUT YEARS BACK, BEFORE NETTY NEWTON HELPED GET THEM HOOKED ON CHEAP LIQUOR, THE NAKEET INDIANS REGARDED THIS AS SACRED GROUND.
THEY SAID IT WAS WHERE THE GODS THEMSELVES WOULD BEND LOW TO LISTEN TO MAN.

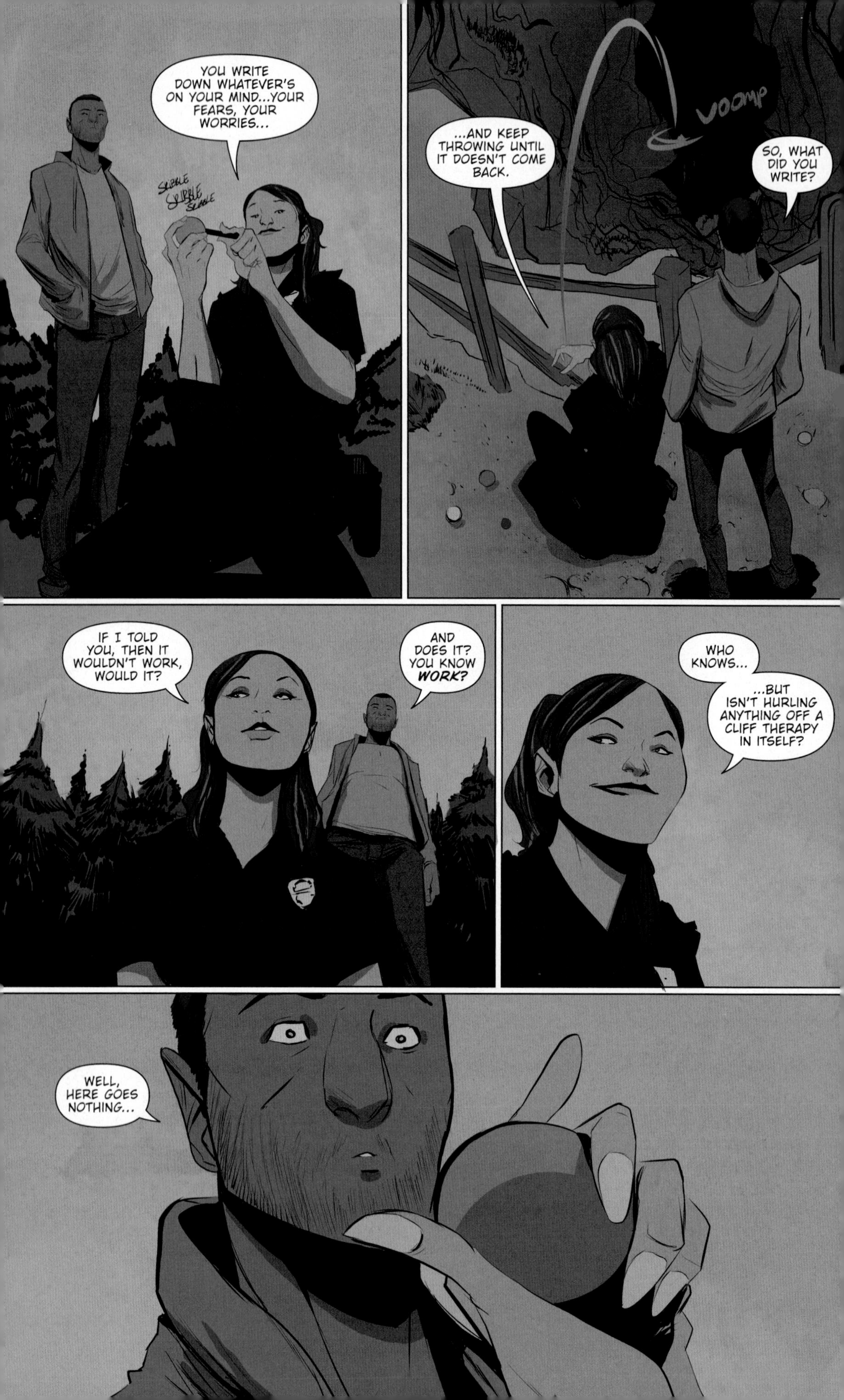
YOU WRITE DOWN WHATEVER'S ON YOUR MIND...YOUR FEARS, YOUR WORRIES...
SKIBBLE SKIBBLE SKIBBLE
...AND KEEP THROWING UNTIL IT DOESN'T COME BACK.
VOOMP
SO, WHAT DID YOU WRITE?
IF I TOLD YOU, THEN IT WOULDN'T WORK, WOULD IT?
AND DOES IT? YOU KNOW **WORK?**
WHO KNOWS...
...BUT ISN'T HURLING ANYTHING OFF A CLIFF THERAPY IN ITSELF?
WELL, HERE GOES NOTHING...

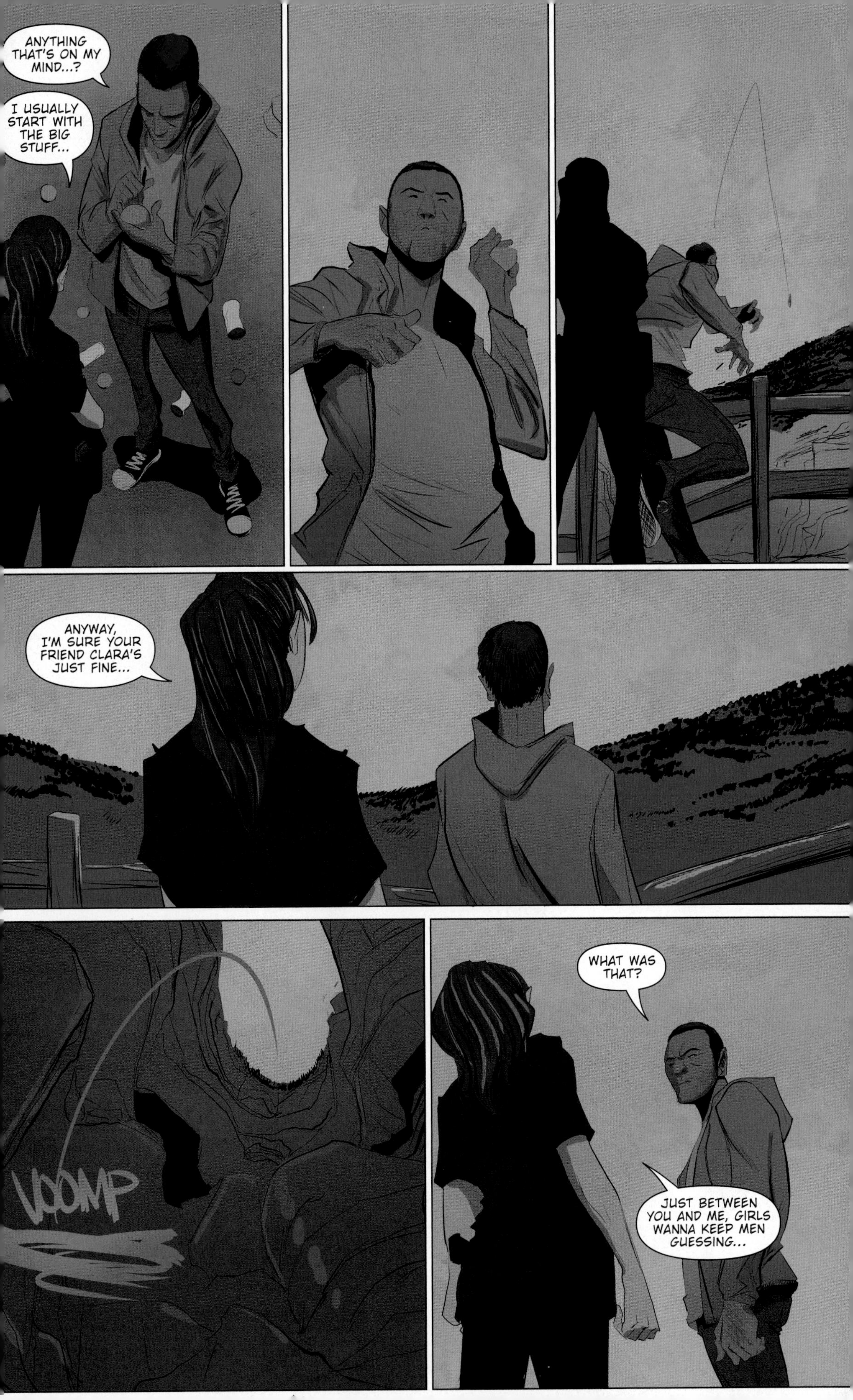
ANYTHING THAT'S ON MY MIND...?
I USUALLY START WITH THE BIG STUFF...
ANYWAY, I'M SURE YOUR FRIEND CLARA'S JUST FINE...
VOOMP
WHAT WAS THAT?
JUST BETWEEN YOU AND ME, GIRLS WANNA KEEP MEN GUESSING...

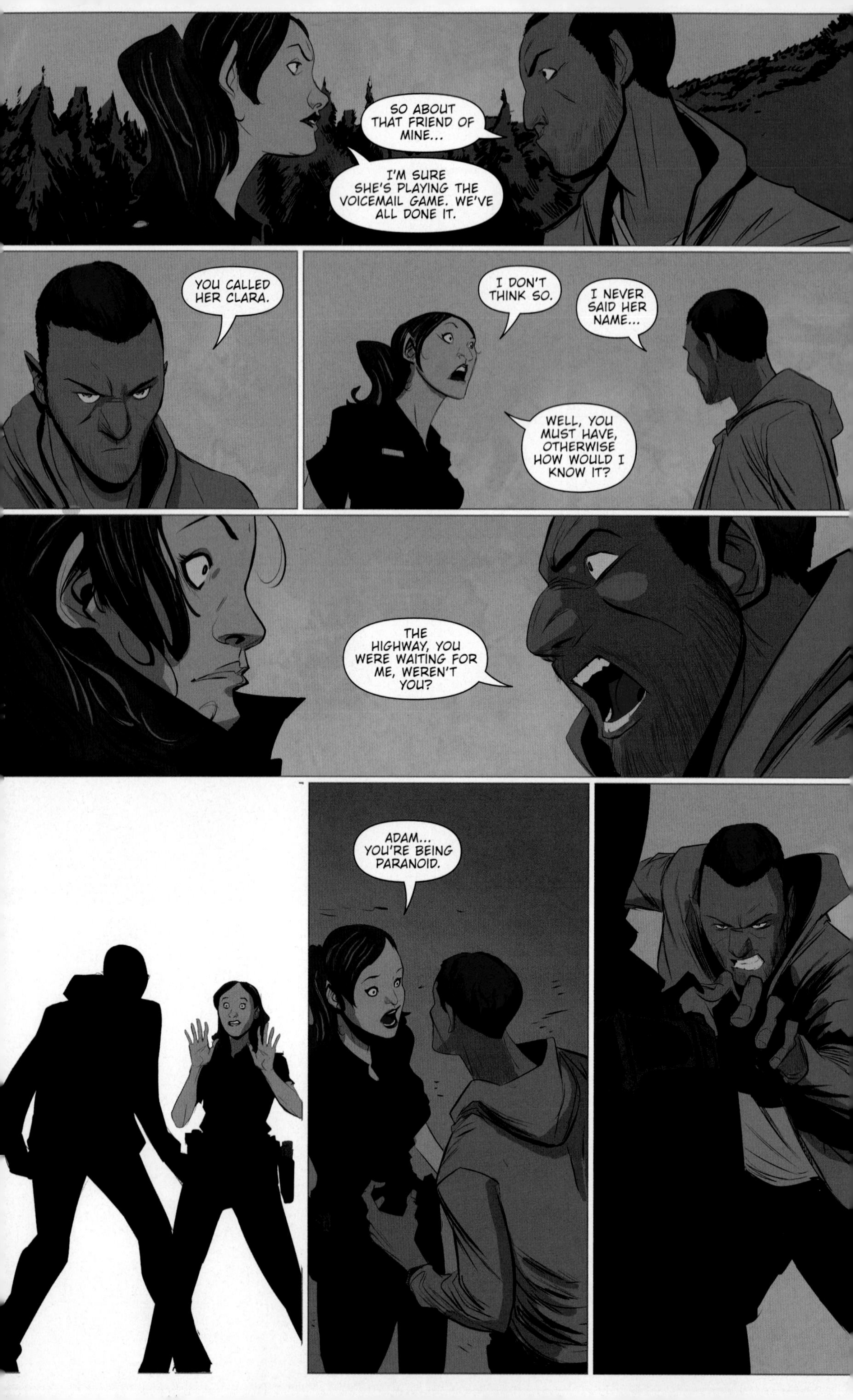
SO ABOUT THAT FRIEND OF MINE...
I'M SURE SHE'S PLAYING THE VOICEMAIL GAME. WE'VE ALL DONE IT.
YOU CALLED HER CLARA.
I DON'T THINK SO.
I NEVER SAID HER NAME...
WELL, YOU MUST HAVE, OTHERWISE HOW WOULD I KNOW IT?
THE HIGHWAY, YOU WERE WAITING FOR ME, WEREN'T YOU?
ADAM... YOU'RE BEING PARANOID.

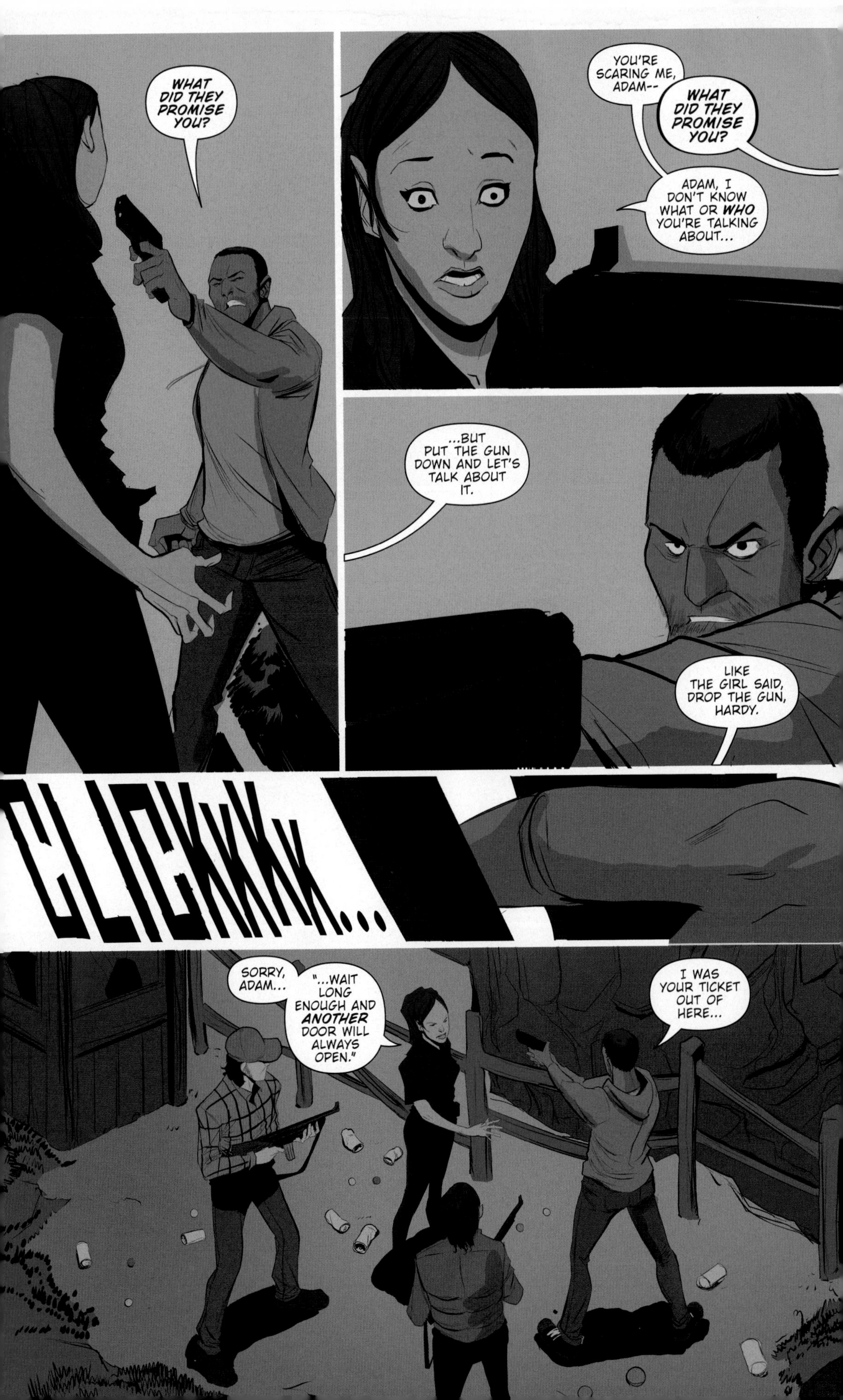
WHAT DID THEY PROMISE YOU?
YOU'RE SCARING ME, ADAM--
WHAT DID THEY PROMISE YOU?
ADAM, I DON'T KNOW WHAT OR WHO YOU'RE TALKING ABOUT...
...BUT PUT THE GUN DOWN AND LET'S TALK ABOUT IT.
LIKE THE GIRL SAID, DROP THE GUN, HARDY.
CLICKKKK...
SORRY, ADAM...
"...WAIT LONG ENOUGH AND ANOTHER DOOR WILL ALWAYS OPEN."
I WAS YOUR TICKET OUT OF HERE...

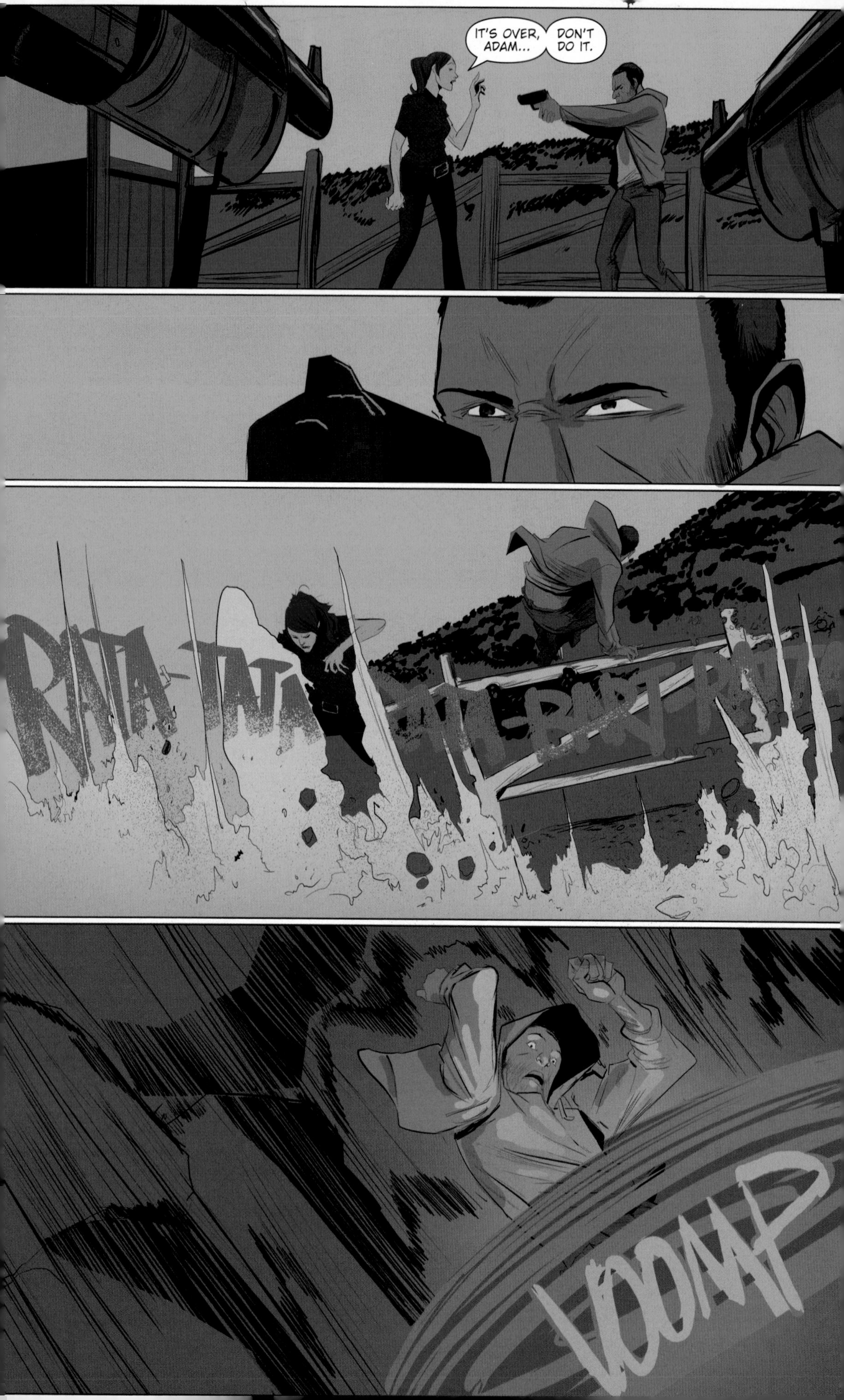
IT'S OVER, ADAM...
DON'T DO IT.
RATA-TATA
VOOMP

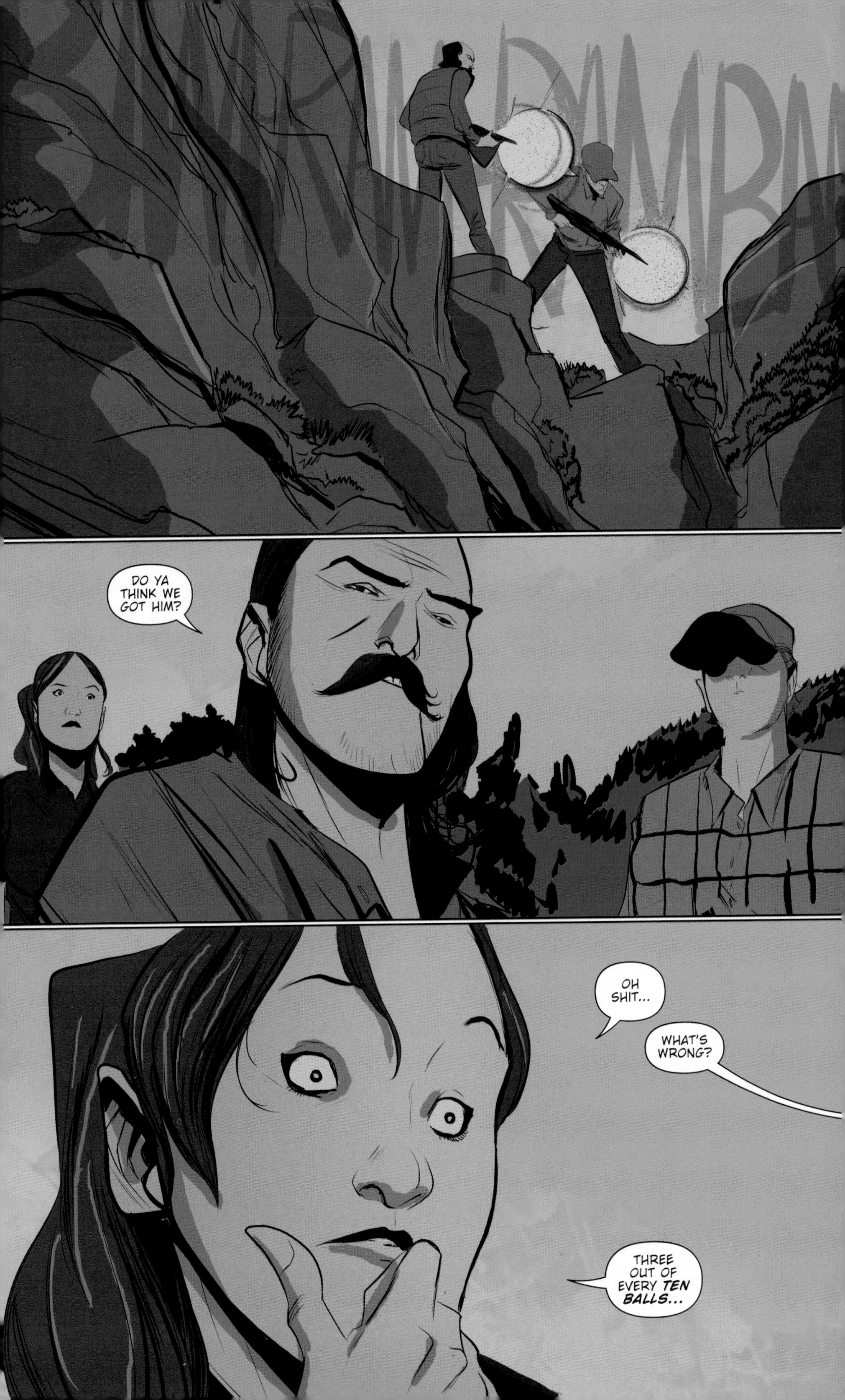
DO YA THINK WE GOT HIM?
OH SHIT...
WHAT'S WRONG?
THREE OUT OF EVERY *TEN BALLS...*

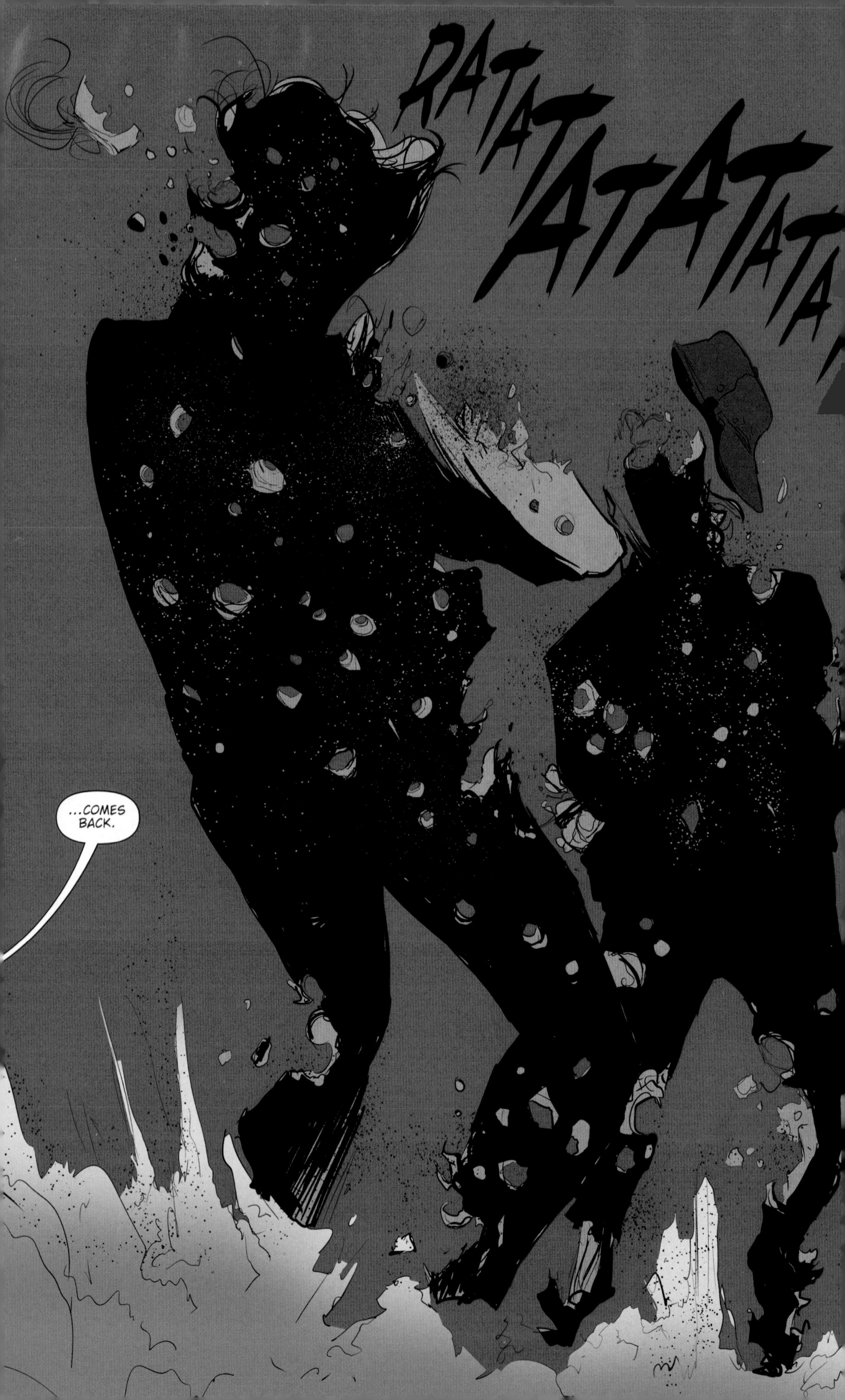
RATATATATATATAT
...COMES BACK.

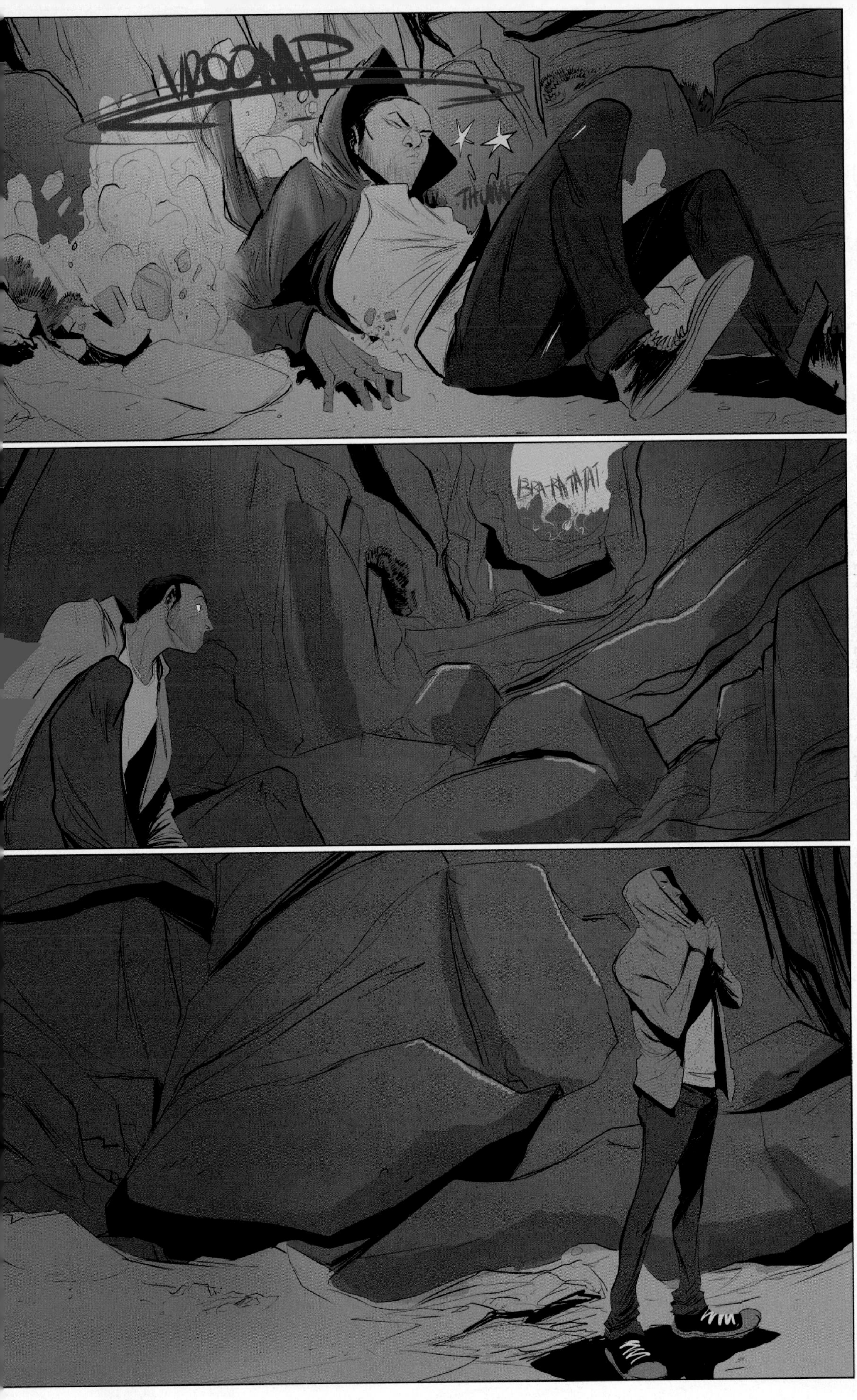
VROOMP
BRA-RA-TA-TAT

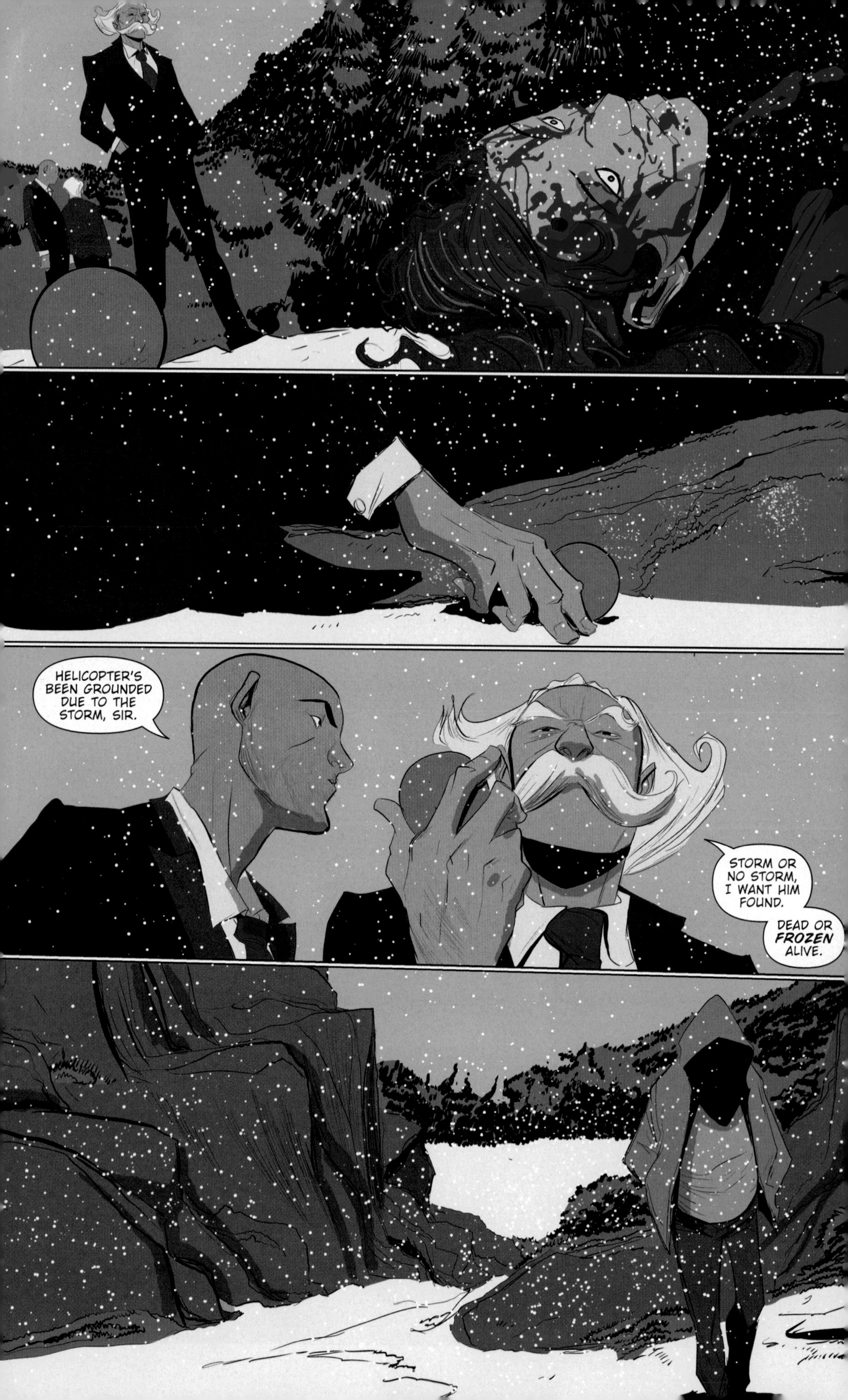
HELICOPTER'S BEEN GROUNDED DUE TO THE STORM, SIR.
STORM OR NO STORM, I WANT HIM FOUND.
DEAD OR *FROZEN* ALIVE.

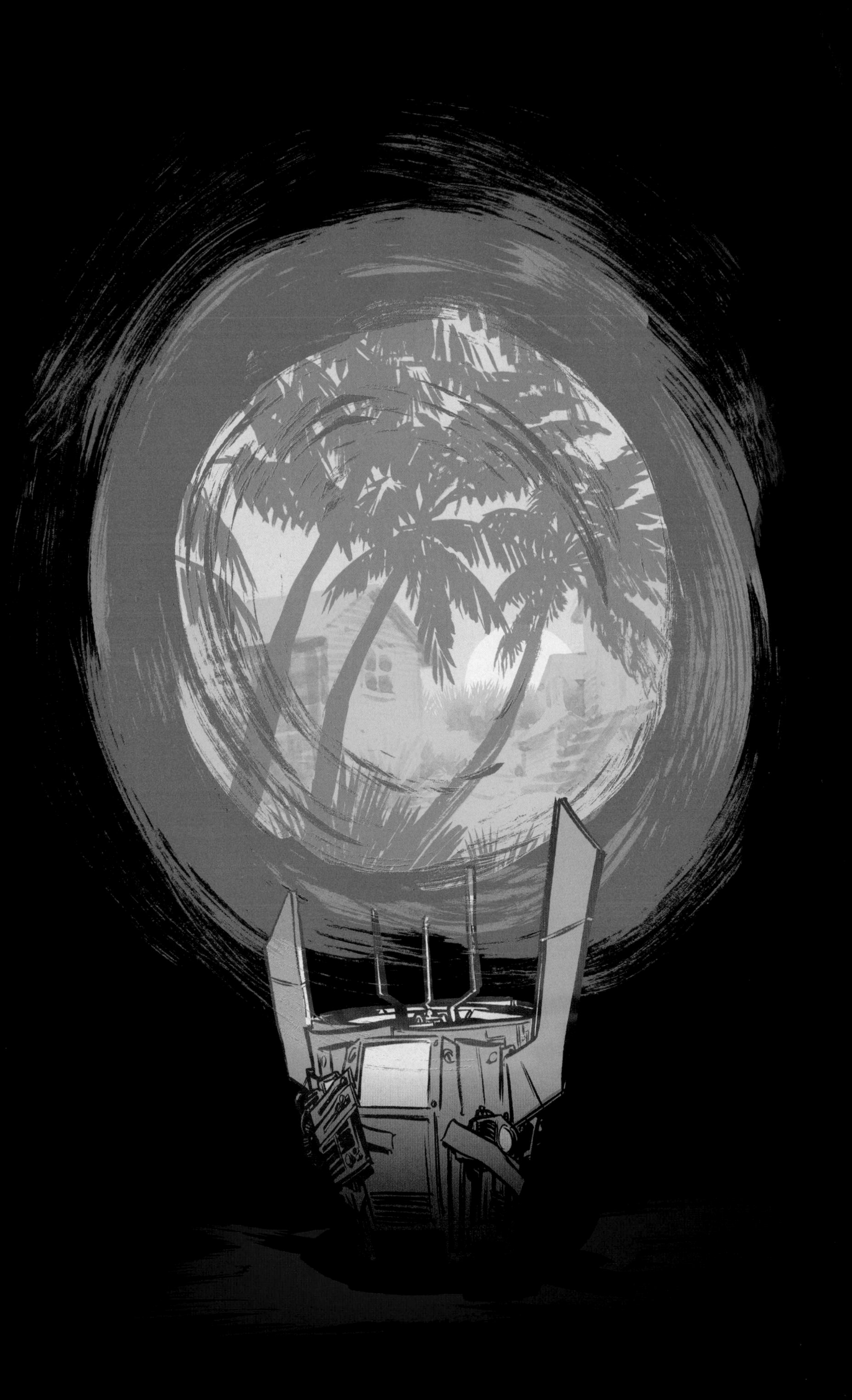

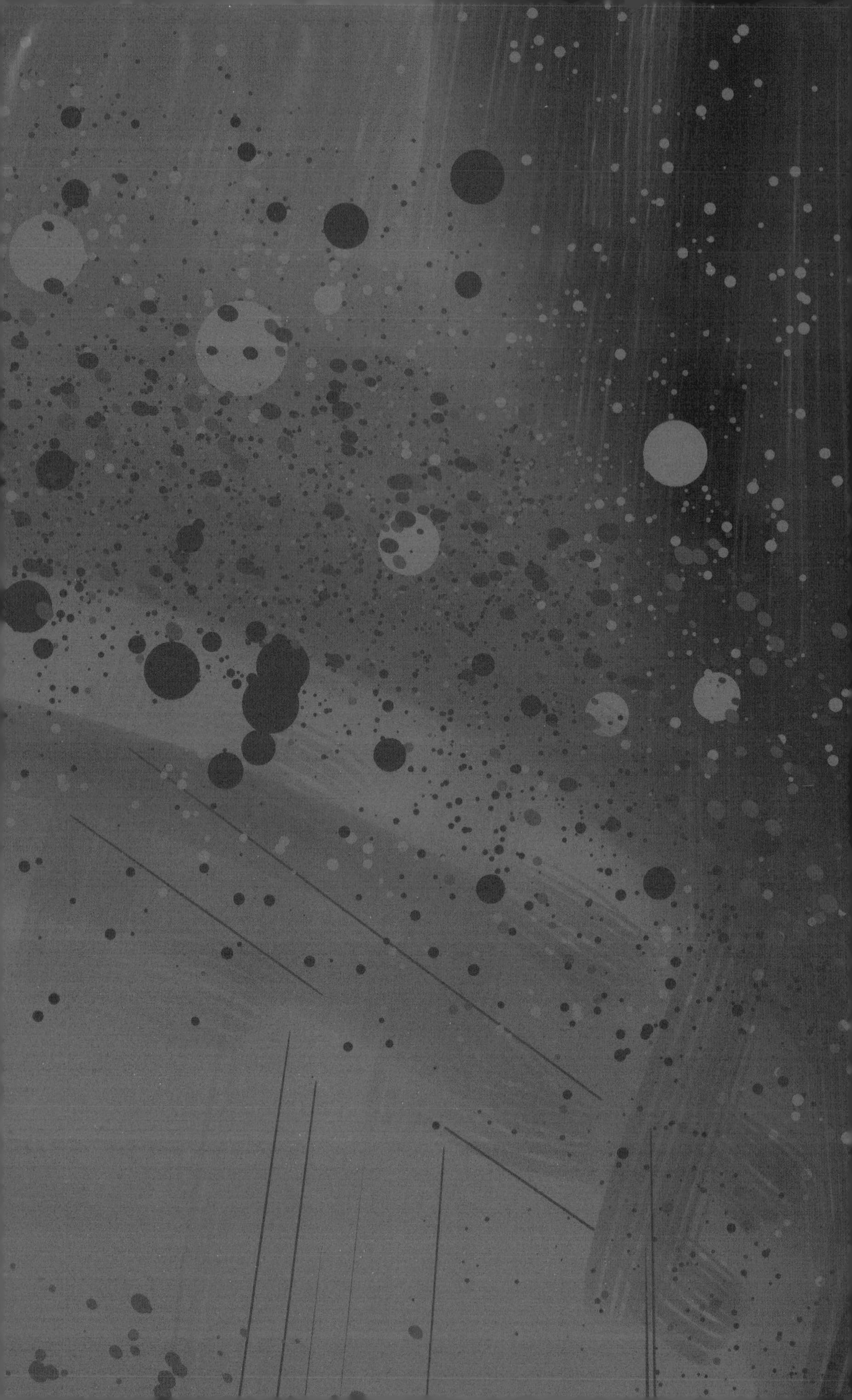

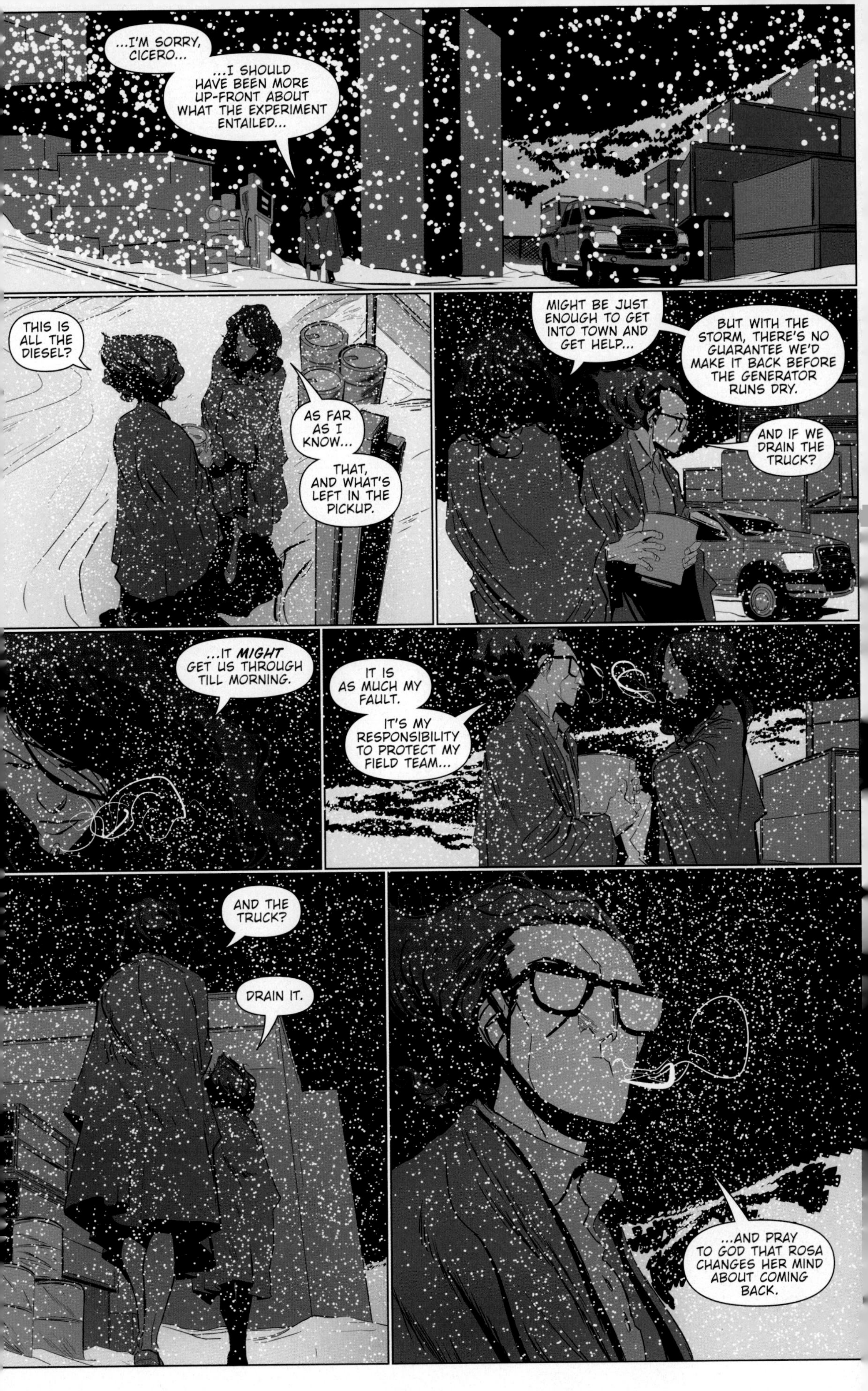
...I'M SORRY, CICERO...
...I SHOULD HAVE BEEN MORE UP-FRONT ABOUT WHAT THE EXPERIMENT ENTAILED...
THIS IS ALL THE DIESEL?
AS FAR AS I KNOW...
THAT, AND WHAT'S LEFT IN THE PICKUP.
MIGHT BE JUST ENOUGH TO GET INTO TOWN AND GET HELP...
BUT WITH THE STORM, THERE'S NO GUARANTEE WE'D MAKE IT BACK BEFORE THE GENERATOR RUNS DRY.
AND IF WE DRAIN THE TRUCK?
...IT *MIGHT* GET US THROUGH TILL MORNING.
IT IS AS MUCH MY FAULT.
IT'S MY RESPONSIBILITY TO PROTECT MY FIELD TEAM...
AND THE TRUCK?
DRAIN IT.
...AND PRAY TO GOD THAT ROSA CHANGES HER MIND ABOUT COMING BACK.

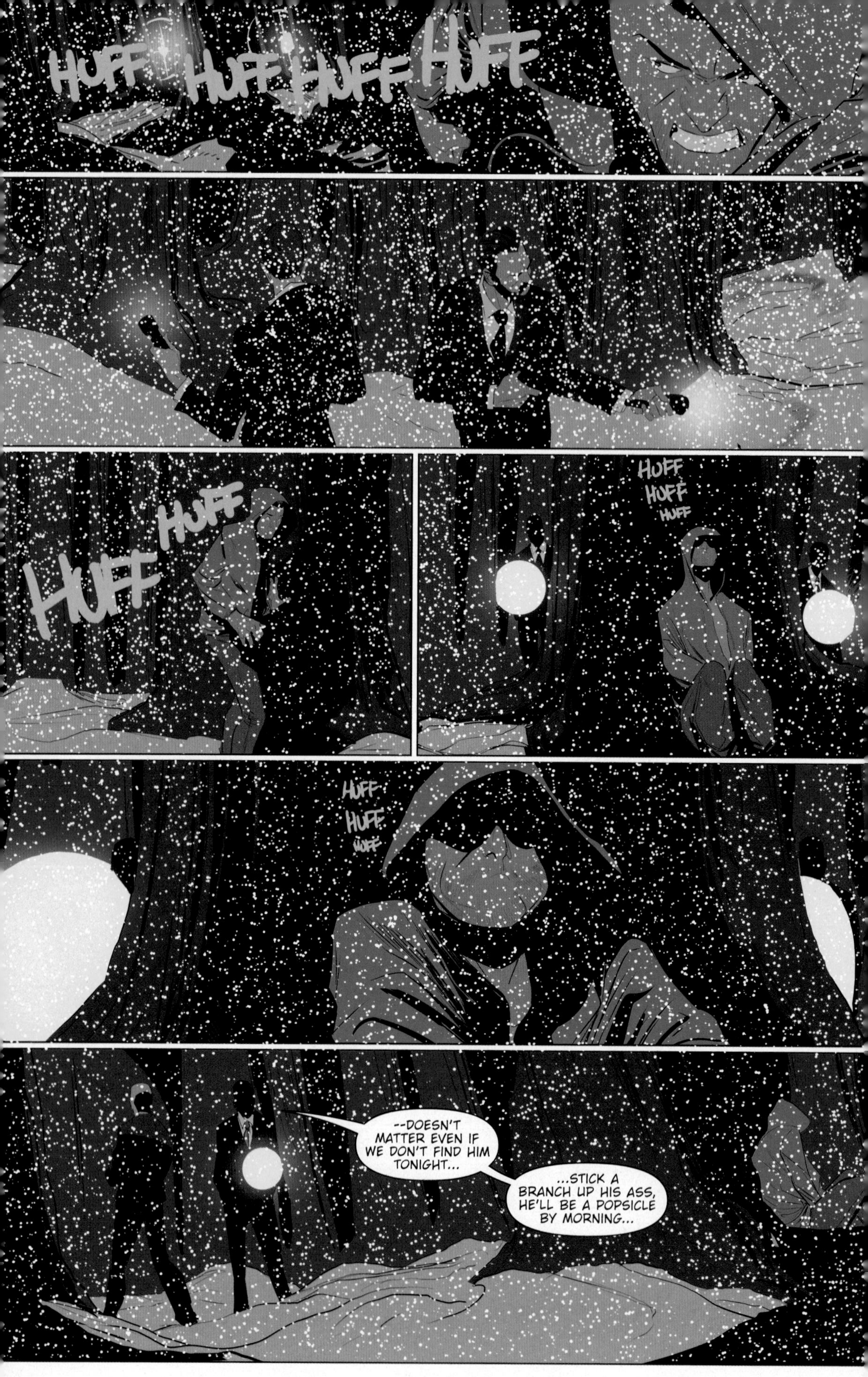
HUFF HUFF HUFF HUFF
HUFF HUFF
HUFF HUFF HUFF
HUFF HUFF HUFF
--DOESN'T MATTER EVEN IF WE DON'T FIND HIM TONIGHT...
...STICK A BRANCH UP HIS ASS, HE'LL BE A POPSICLE BY MORNING...

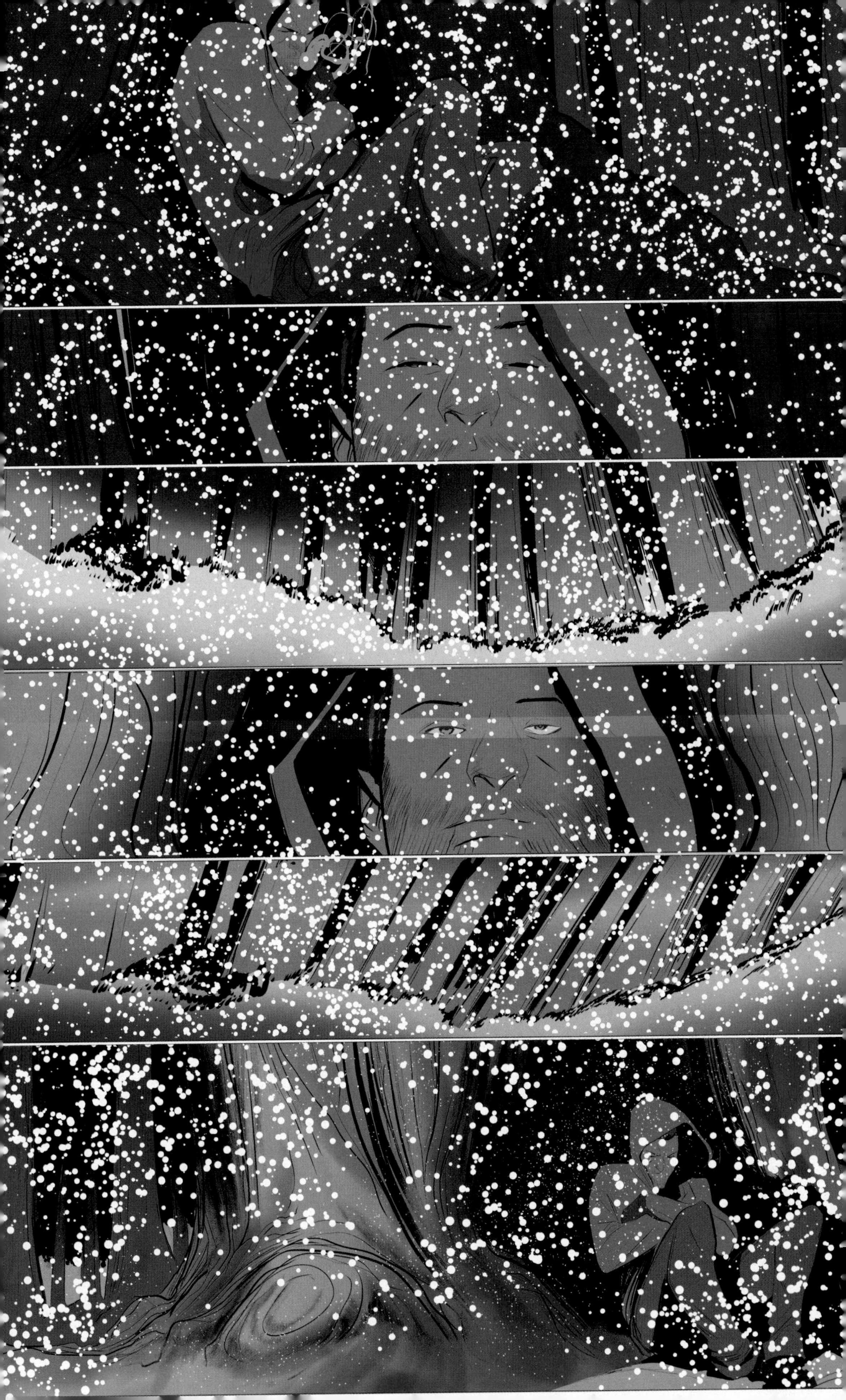

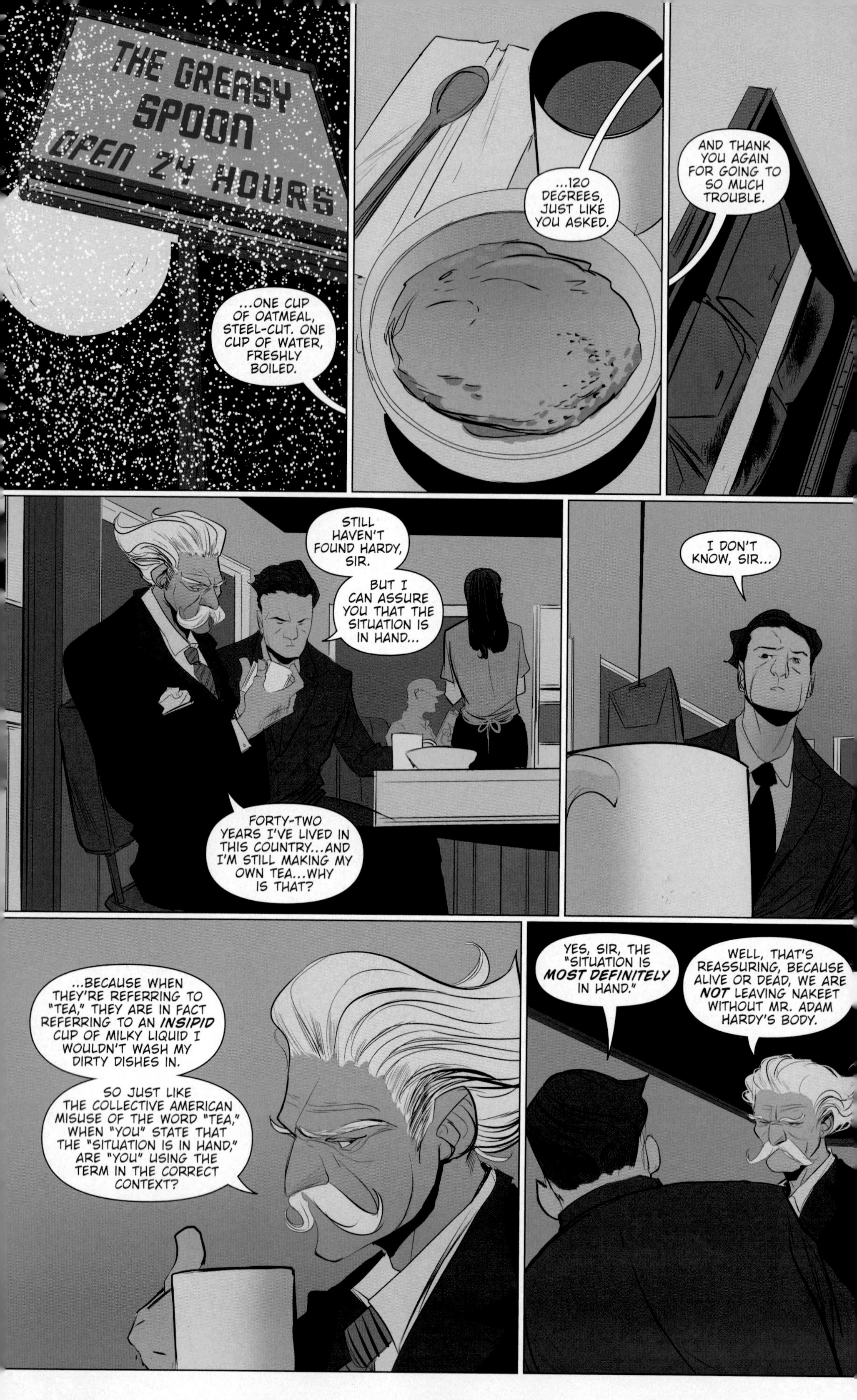
THE GREASY SPOON
OPEN 24 HOURS
...ONE CUP OF OATMEAL, STEEL-CUT. ONE CUP OF WATER, FRESHLY BOILED.
...120 DEGREES, JUST LIKE YOU ASKED.
AND THANK YOU AGAIN FOR GOING TO SO MUCH TROUBLE.
STILL HAVEN'T FOUND HARDY, SIR.
BUT I CAN ASSURE YOU THAT THE SITUATION IS IN HAND...
FORTY-TWO YEARS I'VE LIVED IN THIS COUNTRY...AND I'M STILL MAKING MY OWN TEA...WHY IS THAT?
I DON'T KNOW, SIR...
...BECAUSE WHEN THEY'RE REFERRING TO "TEA," THEY ARE IN FACT REFERRING TO AN *INSIPID* CUP OF MILKY LIQUID I WOULDN'T WASH MY DIRTY DISHES IN.
SO JUST LIKE THE COLLECTIVE AMERICAN MISUSE OF THE WORD "TEA," WHEN "YOU" STATE THAT THE "SITUATION IS IN HAND," ARE "YOU" USING THE TERM IN THE CORRECT CONTEXT?
YES, SIR, THE "SITUATION IS *MOST DEFINITELY* IN HAND."
WELL, THAT'S REASSURING, BECAUSE ALIVE OR DEAD, WE ARE *NOT* LEAVING NAKEET WITHOUT MR. ADAM HARDY'S BODY.

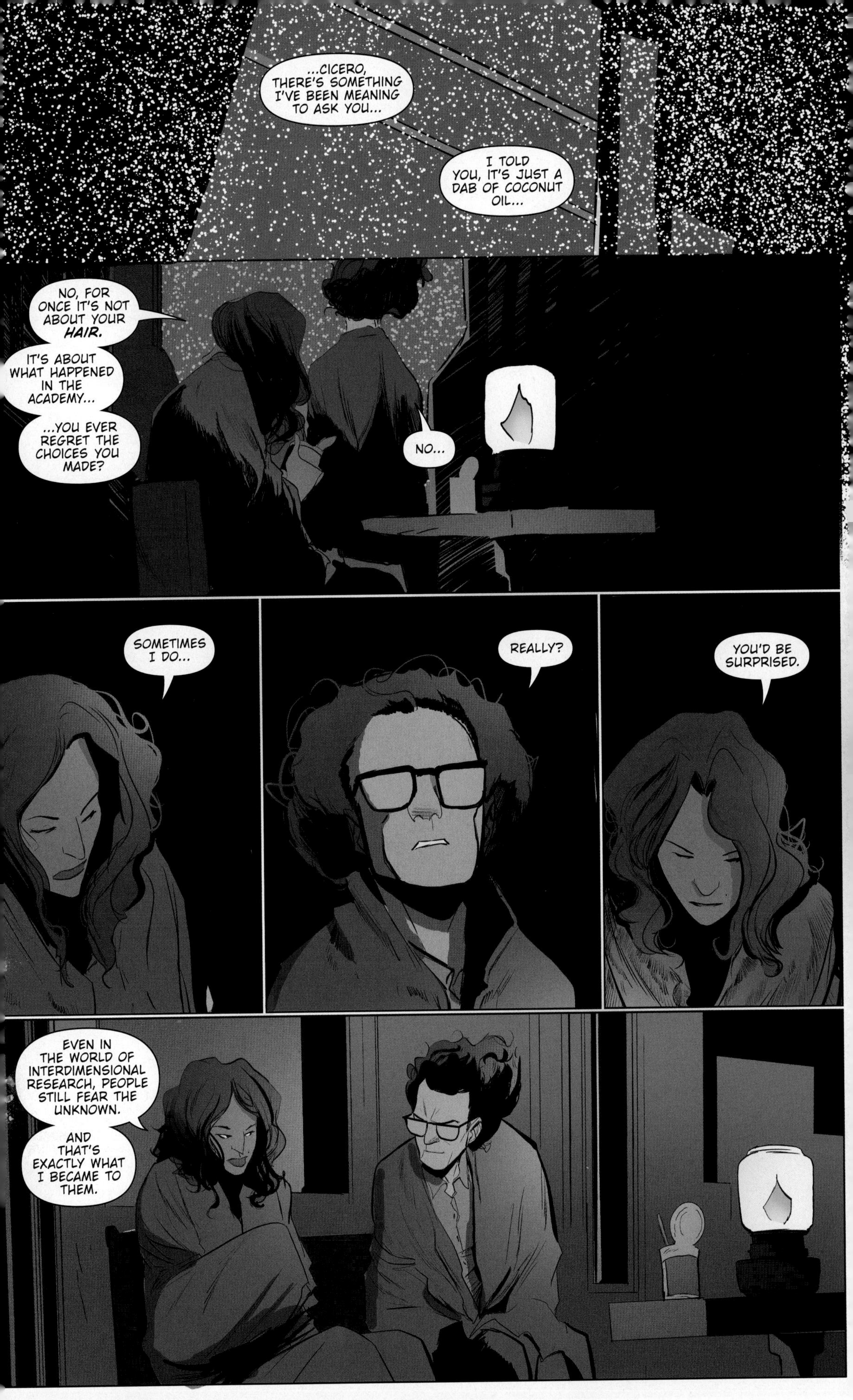
...CICERO, THERE'S SOMETHING I'VE BEEN MEANING TO ASK YOU...
I TOLD YOU, IT'S JUST A DAB OF COCONUT OIL...
NO, FOR ONCE IT'S NOT ABOUT YOUR *HAIR.*
IT'S ABOUT WHAT HAPPENED IN THE ACADEMY...
...YOU EVER REGRET THE CHOICES YOU MADE?
NO...
SOMETIMES I DO...
REALLY?
YOU'D BE SURPRISED.
EVEN IN THE WORLD OF INTERDIMENSIONAL RESEARCH, PEOPLE STILL FEAR THE UNKNOWN.
AND THAT'S EXACTLY WHAT I BECAME TO THEM.

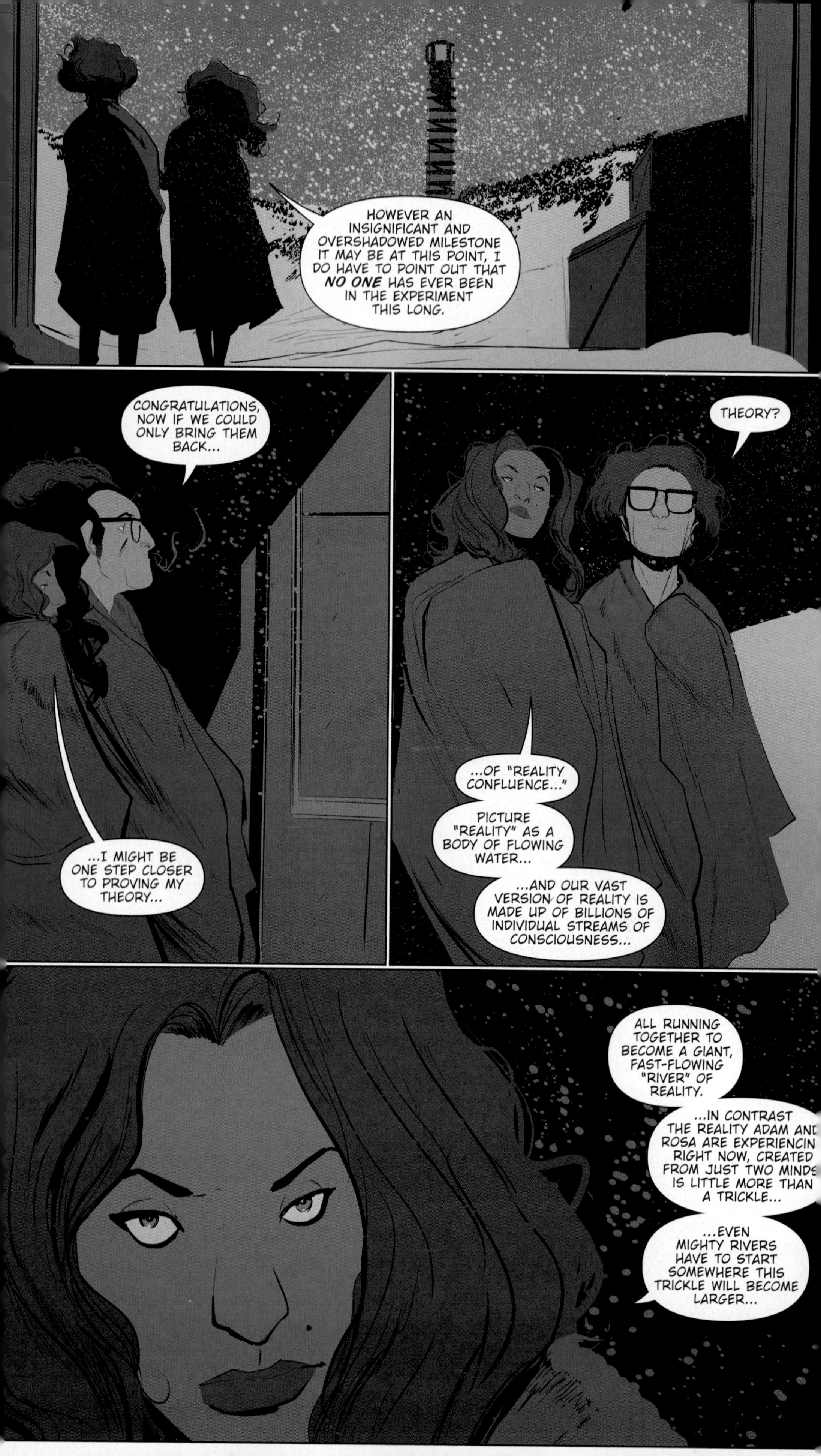
HOWEVER AN INSIGNIFICANT AND OVERSHADOWED MILESTONE IT MAY BE AT THIS POINT, I DO HAVE TO POINT OUT THAT NO ONE HAS EVER BEEN IN THE EXPERIMENT THIS LONG.
CONGRATULATIONS, NOW IF WE COULD ONLY BRING THEM BACK...
...I MIGHT BE ONE STEP CLOSER TO PROVING MY THEORY...
THEORY?
...OF "REALITY CONFLUENCE..."
PICTURE "REALITY" AS A BODY OF FLOWING WATER...
...AND OUR VAST VERSION OF REALITY IS MADE UP OF BILLIONS OF INDIVIDUAL STREAMS OF CONSCIOUSNESS...
ALL RUNNING TOGETHER TO BECOME A GIANT, FAST-FLOWING "RIVER" OF REALITY.
...IN CONTRAST THE REALITY ADAM AND ROSA ARE EXPERIENCIN RIGHT NOW, CREATED FROM JUST TWO MINDS IS LITTLE MORE THAN A TRICKLE...
...EVEN MIGHTY RIVERS HAVE TO START SOMEWHERE THIS TRICKLE WILL BECOME LARGER...

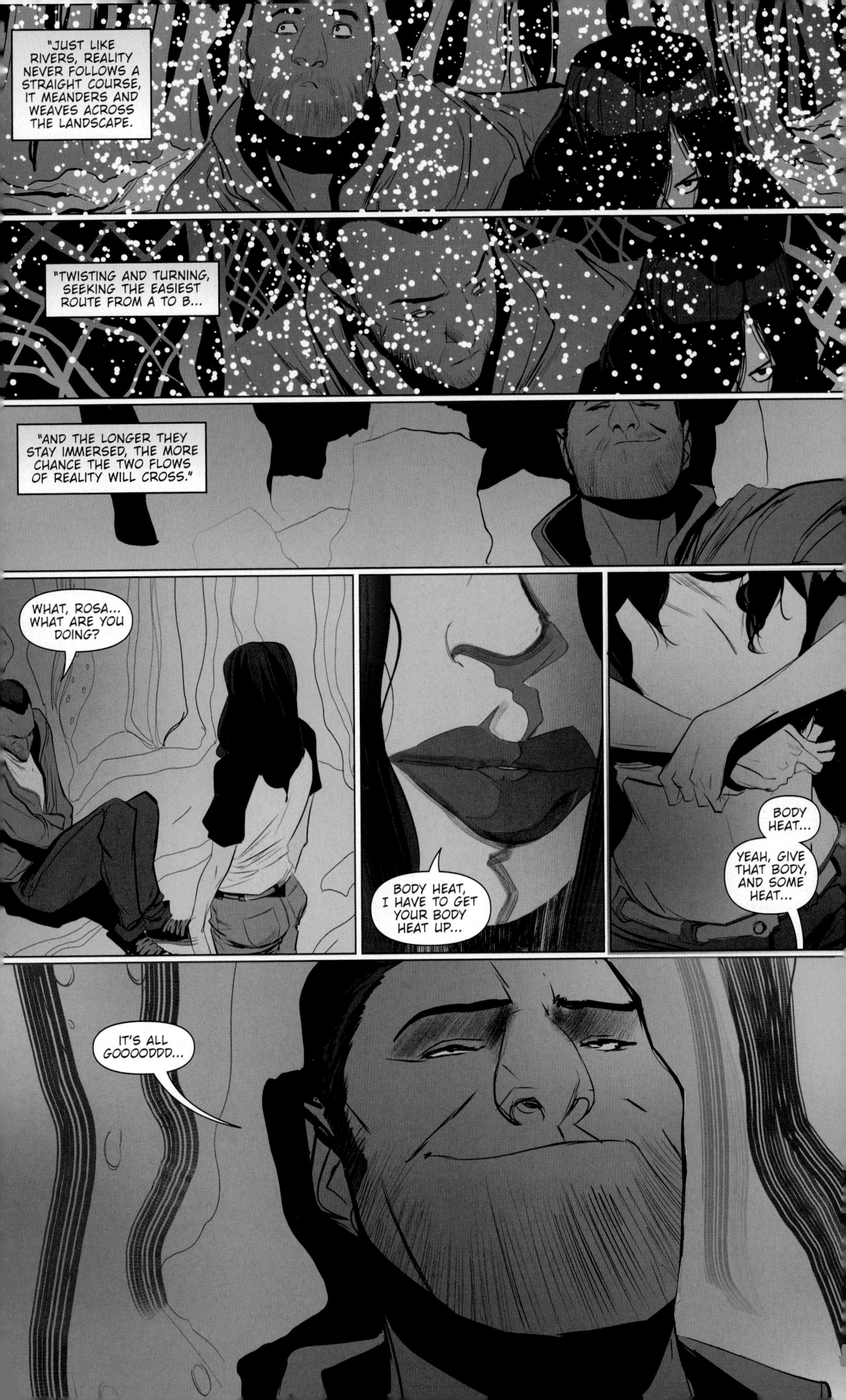
"JUST LIKE RIVERS, REALITY NEVER FOLLOWS A STRAIGHT COURSE, IT MEANDERS AND WEAVES ACROSS THE LANDSCAPE.
"TWISTING AND TURNING, SEEKING THE EASIEST ROUTE FROM A TO B...
"AND THE LONGER THEY STAY IMMERSED, THE MORE CHANCE THE TWO FLOWS OF REALITY WILL CROSS."
WHAT, ROSA... WHAT ARE YOU DOING?
BODY HEAT, I HAVE TO GET YOUR BODY HEAT UP...
BODY HEAT...
YEAH, GIVE THAT BODY, AND SOME HEAT...
IT'S ALL GOOOODDD...

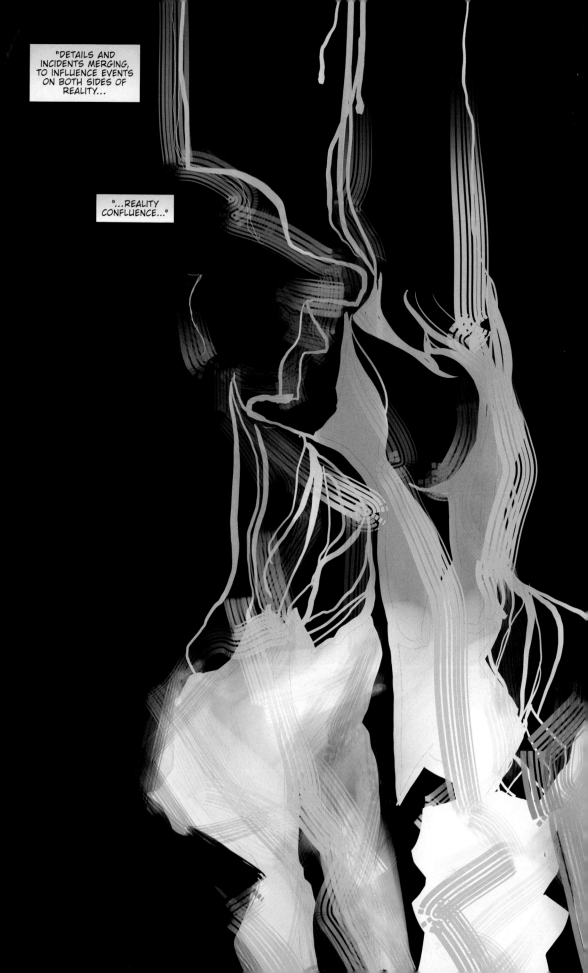

"DETAILS AND INCIDENTS MERGING, TO INFLUENCE EVENTS ON BOTH SIDES OF REALITY..."

"...REALITY CONFLUENCE..."

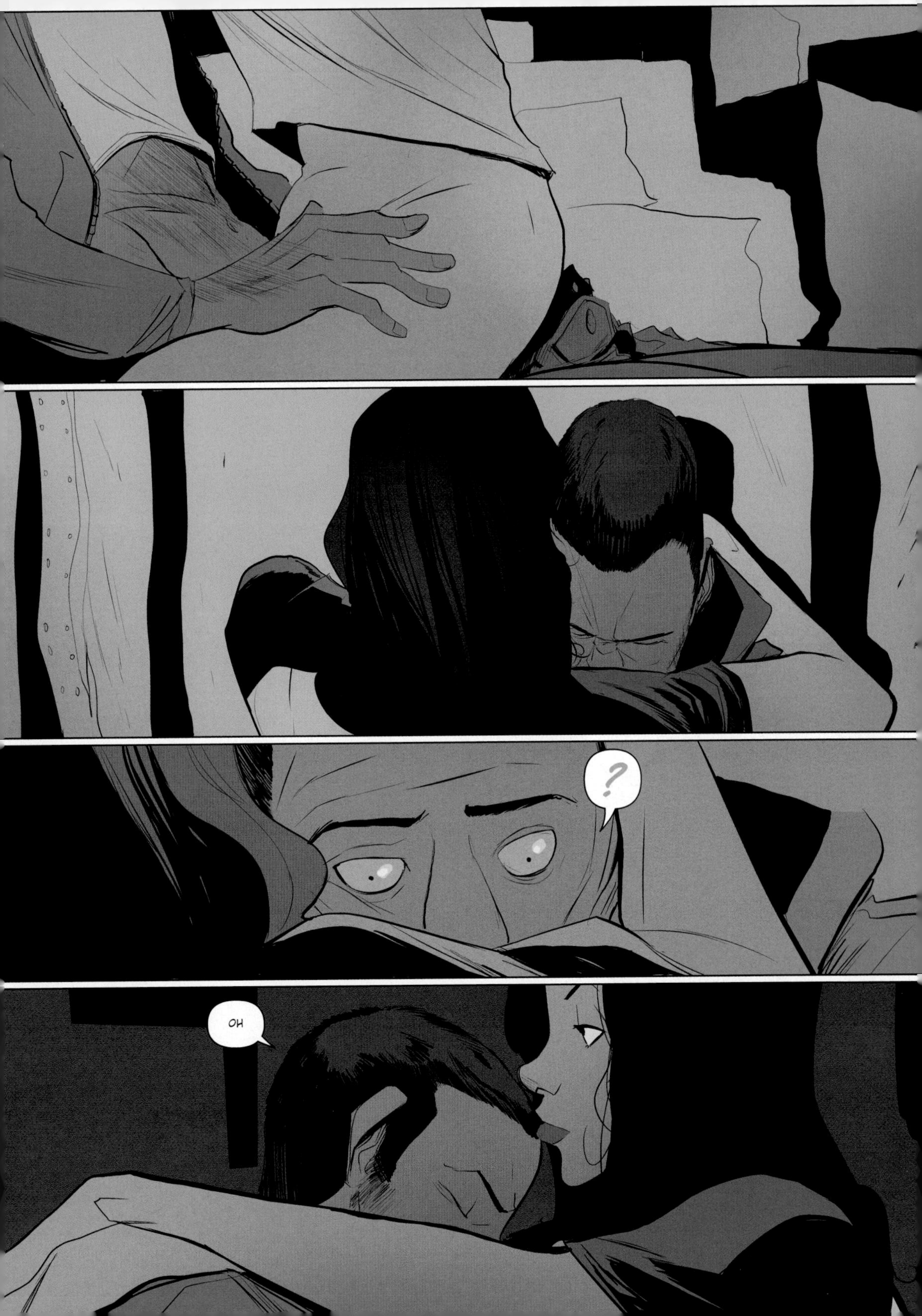
?
OH

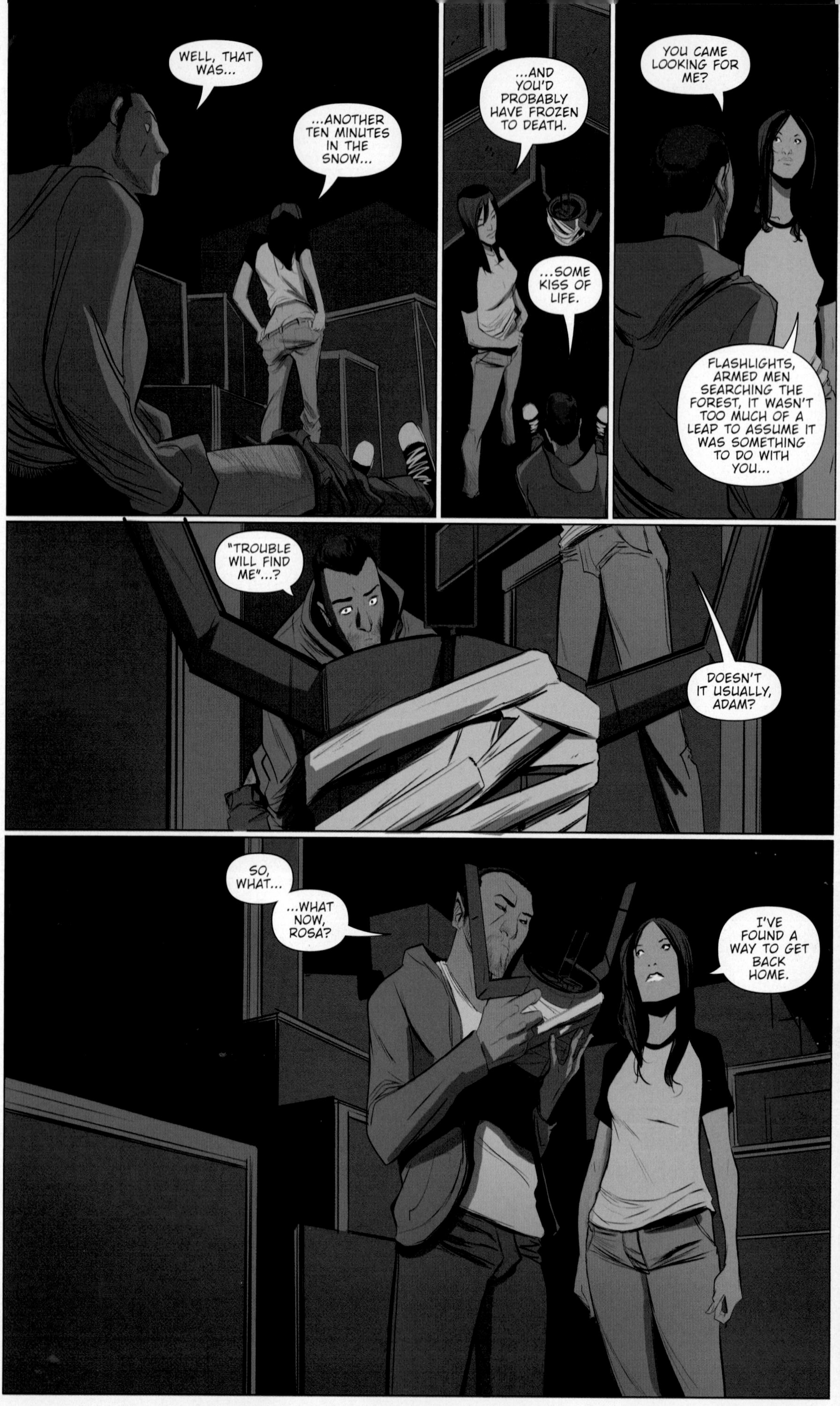
WELL, THAT WAS...
...ANOTHER TEN MINUTES IN THE SNOW...
...AND YOU'D PROBABLY HAVE FROZEN TO DEATH.
...SOME KISS OF LIFE.
YOU CAME LOOKING FOR ME?
FLASHLIGHTS, ARMED MEN SEARCHING THE FOREST, IT WASN'T TOO MUCH OF A LEAP TO ASSUME IT WAS SOMETHING TO DO WITH YOU...
"TROUBLE WILL FIND ME"...?
DOESN'T IT USUALLY, ADAM?
SO, WHAT...
...WHAT NOW, ROSA?
I'VE FOUND A WAY TO GET BACK HOME.

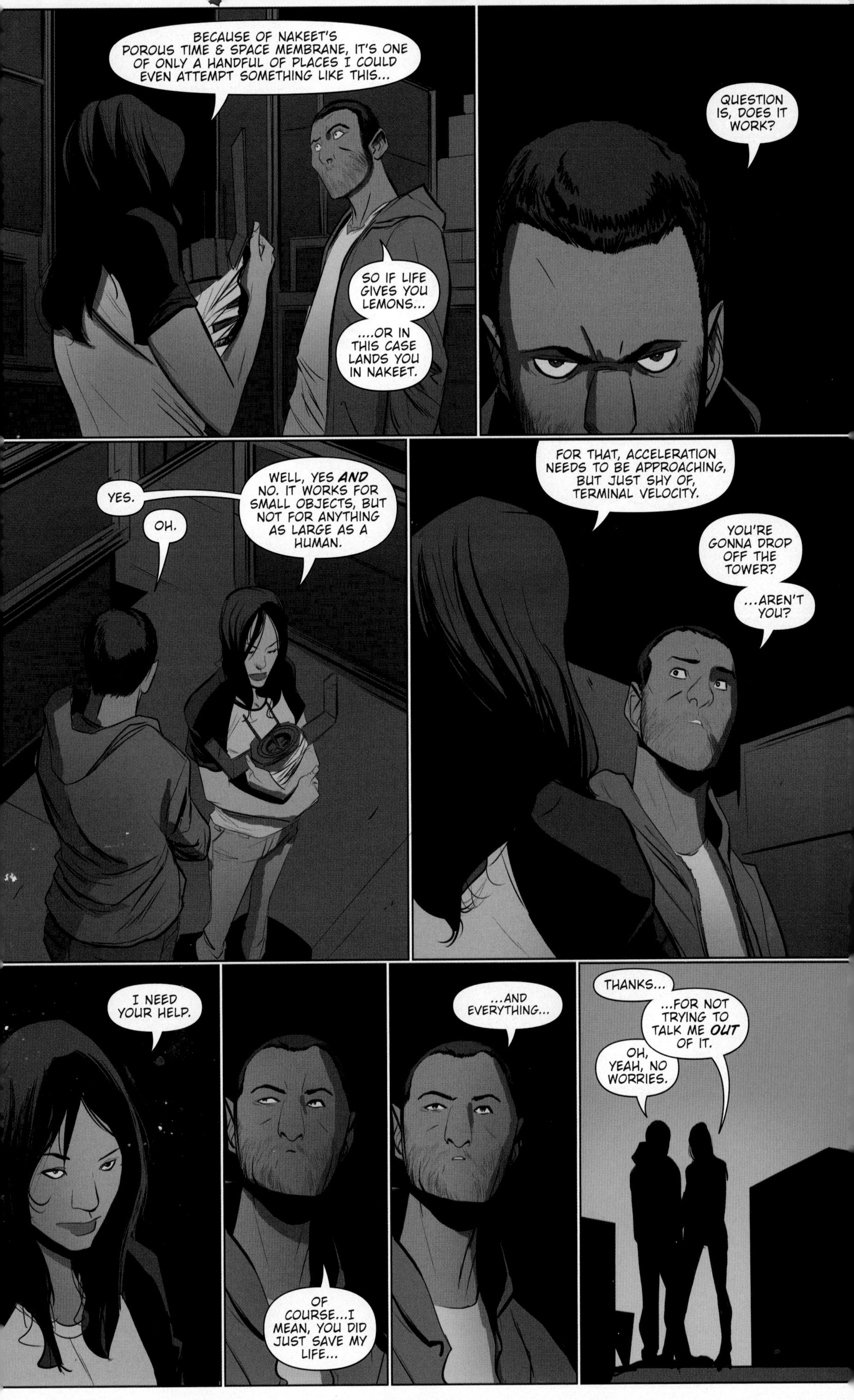
BECAUSE OF NAKEET'S POROUS TIME & SPACE MEMBRANE, IT'S ONE OF ONLY A HANDFUL OF PLACES I COULD EVEN ATTEMPT SOMETHING LIKE THIS...
SO IF LIFE GIVES YOU LEMONS...
....OR IN THIS CASE LANDS YOU IN NAKEET.
QUESTION IS, DOES IT WORK?
YES.
OH.
WELL, YES AND NO. IT WORKS FOR SMALL OBJECTS, BUT NOT FOR ANYTHING AS LARGE AS A HUMAN.
FOR THAT, ACCELERATION NEEDS TO BE APPROACHING, BUT JUST SHY OF, TERMINAL VELOCITY.
YOU'RE GONNA DROP OFF THE TOWER?
...AREN'T YOU?
I NEED YOUR HELP.
OF COURSE...I MEAN, YOU DID JUST SAVE MY LIFE...
...AND EVERYTHING...
THANKS...
...FOR NOT TRYING TO TALK ME OUT OF IT.
OH, YEAH, NO WORRIES.

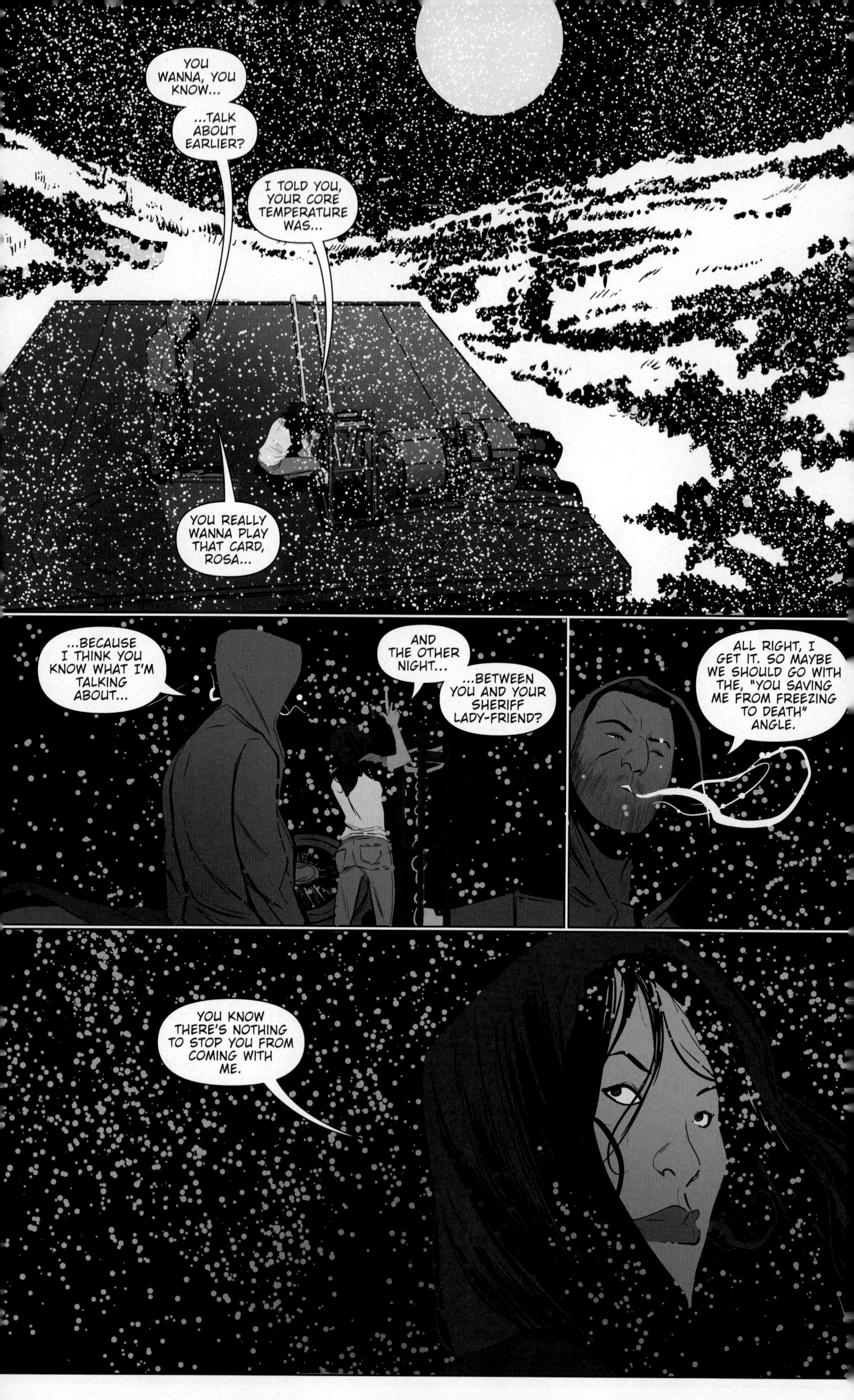
YOU WANNA, YOU KNOW...
...TALK ABOUT EARLIER?
I TOLD YOU, YOUR CORE TEMPERATURE WAS...
YOU REALLY WANNA PLAY THAT CARD, ROSA...
...BECAUSE I THINK YOU KNOW WHAT I'M TALKING ABOUT...
AND THE OTHER NIGHT...
...BETWEEN YOU AND YOUR SHERIFF LADY-FRIEND?
ALL RIGHT, I GET IT. SO MAYBE WE SHOULD GO WITH THE, "YOU SAVING ME FROM FREEZING TO DEATH" ANGLE.
YOU KNOW THERE'S NOTHING TO STOP YOU FROM COMING WITH ME.

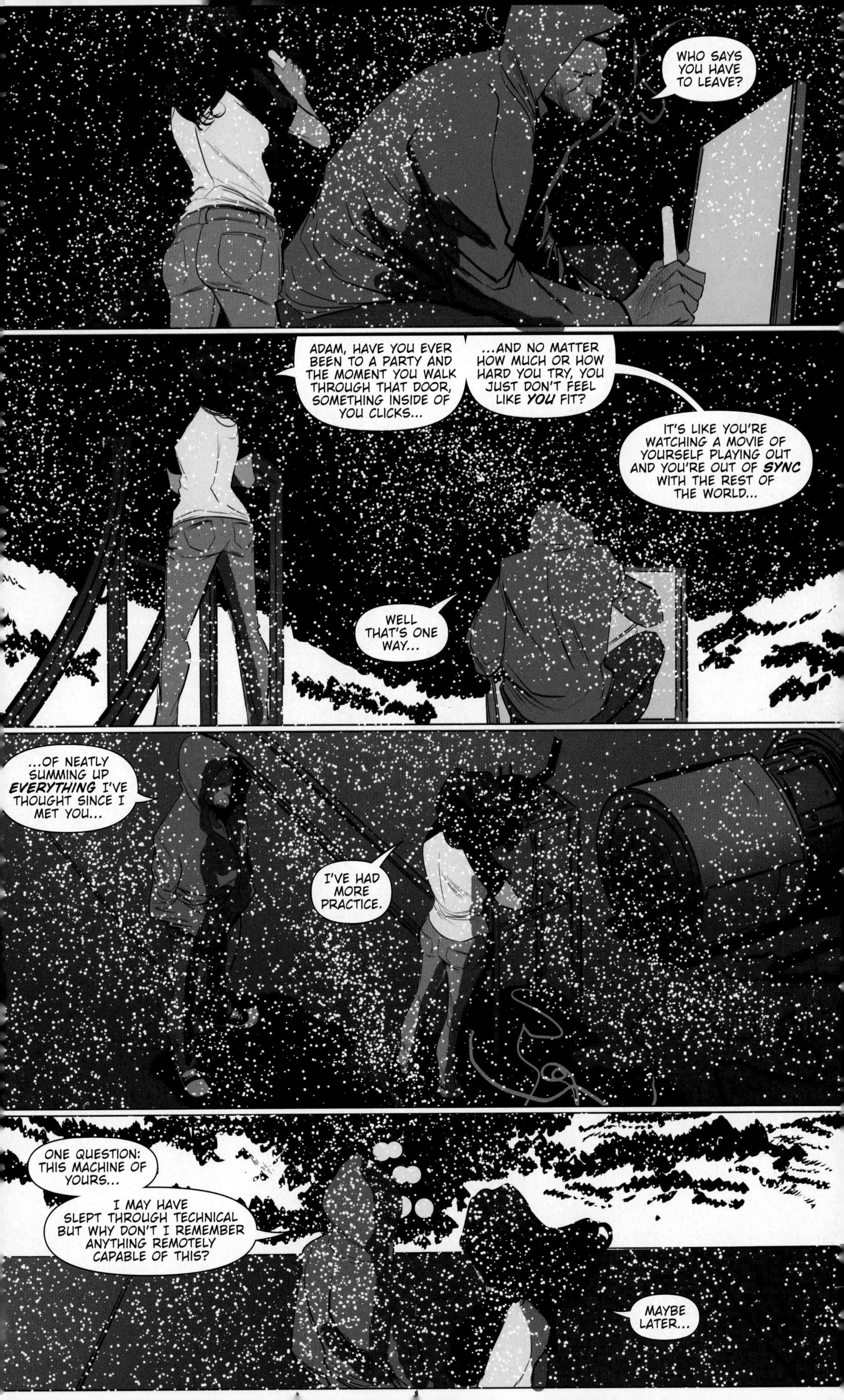
WHO SAYS YOU HAVE TO LEAVE?
ADAM, HAVE YOU EVER BEEN TO A PARTY AND THE MOMENT YOU WALK THROUGH THAT DOOR, SOMETHING INSIDE OF YOU CLICKS...
...AND NO MATTER HOW MUCH OR HOW HARD YOU TRY, YOU JUST DON'T FEEL LIKE ***YOU*** FIT?
IT'S LIKE YOU'RE WATCHING A MOVIE OF YOURSELF PLAYING OUT AND YOU'RE OUT OF ***SYNC*** WITH THE REST OF THE WORLD...
WELL THAT'S ONE WAY...
...OF NEATLY SUMMING UP ***EVERYTHING*** I'VE THOUGHT SINCE I MET YOU...
I'VE HAD MORE PRACTICE.
ONE QUESTION: THIS MACHINE OF YOURS...
I MAY HAVE SLEPT THROUGH TECHNICAL BUT WHY DON'T I REMEMBER ANYTHING REMOTELY CAPABLE OF THIS?
MAYBE LATER...

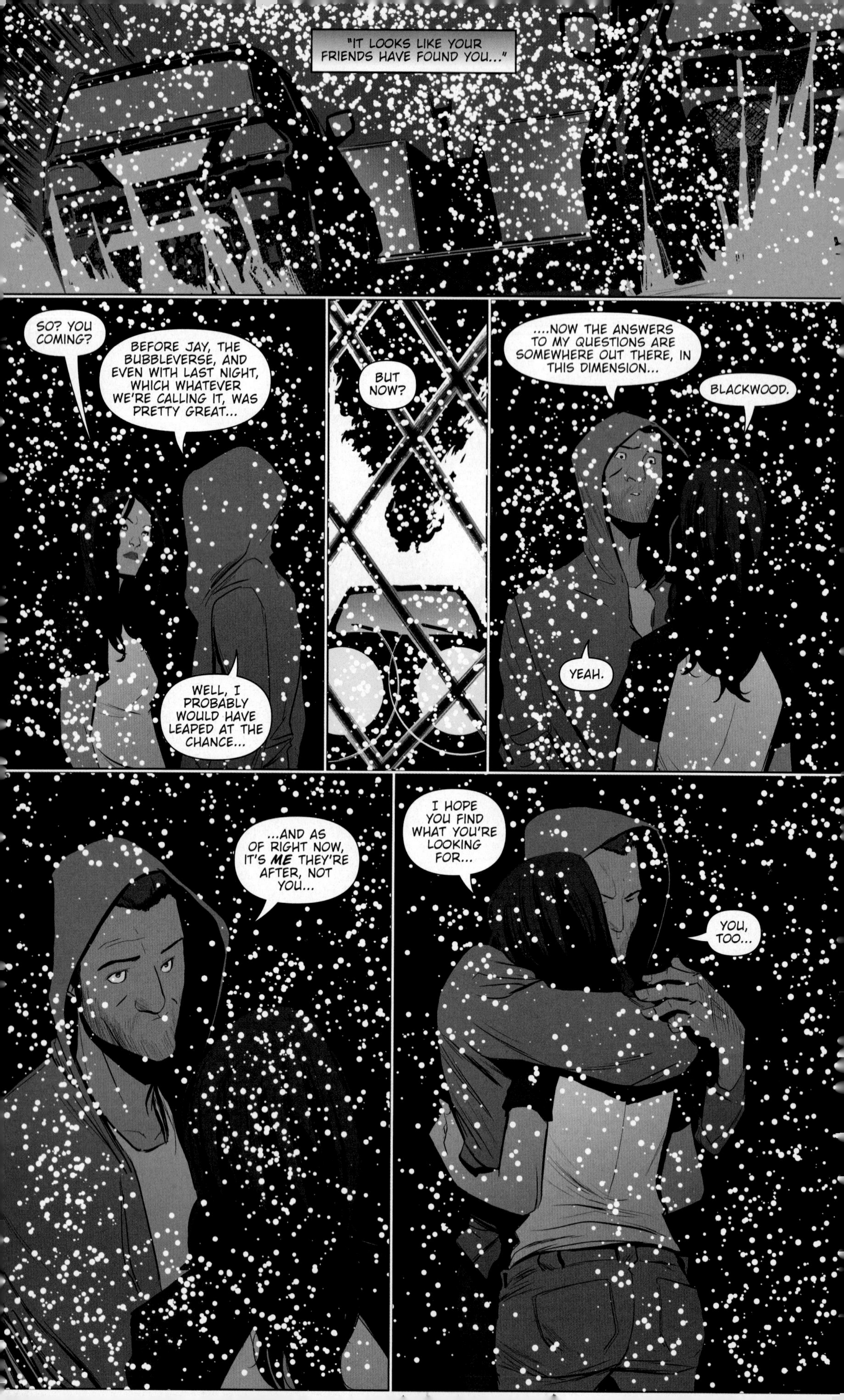
"IT LOOKS LIKE YOUR FRIENDS HAVE FOUND YOU..."
SO? YOU COMING?
BEFORE JAY, THE BUBBLEVERSE, AND EVEN WITH LAST NIGHT, WHICH WHATEVER WE'RE CALLING IT, WAS PRETTY GREAT...
WELL, I PROBABLY WOULD HAVE LEAPED AT THE CHANCE...
BUT NOW?
....NOW THE ANSWERS TO MY QUESTIONS ARE SOMEWHERE OUT THERE, IN THIS DIMENSION...
BLACKWOOD.
YEAH.
...AND AS OF RIGHT NOW, IT'S ME THEY'RE AFTER, NOT YOU...
I HOPE YOU FIND WHAT YOU'RE LOOKING FOR...
YOU, TOO...

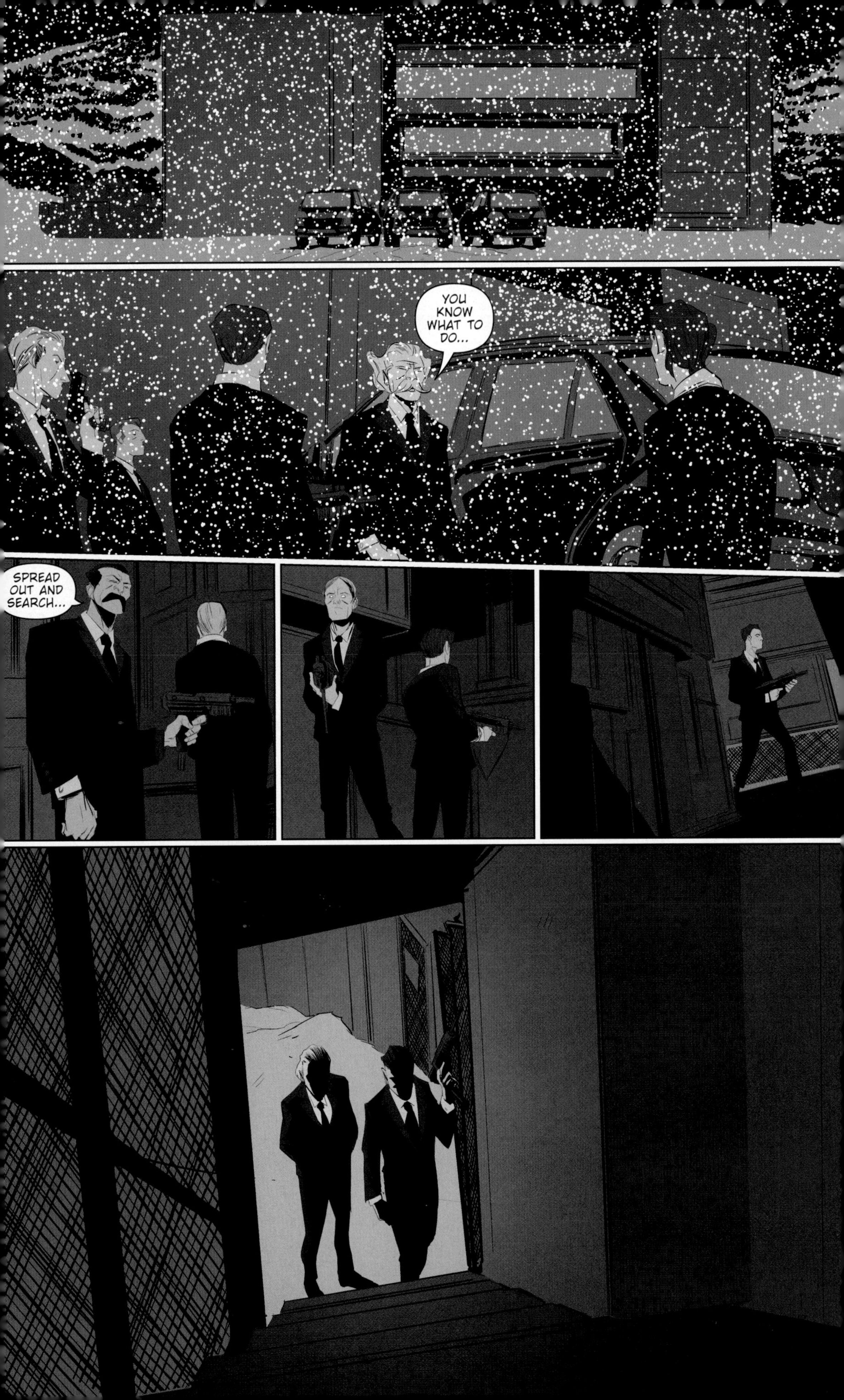
YOU KNOW WHAT TO DO...
SPREAD OUT AND SEARCH...

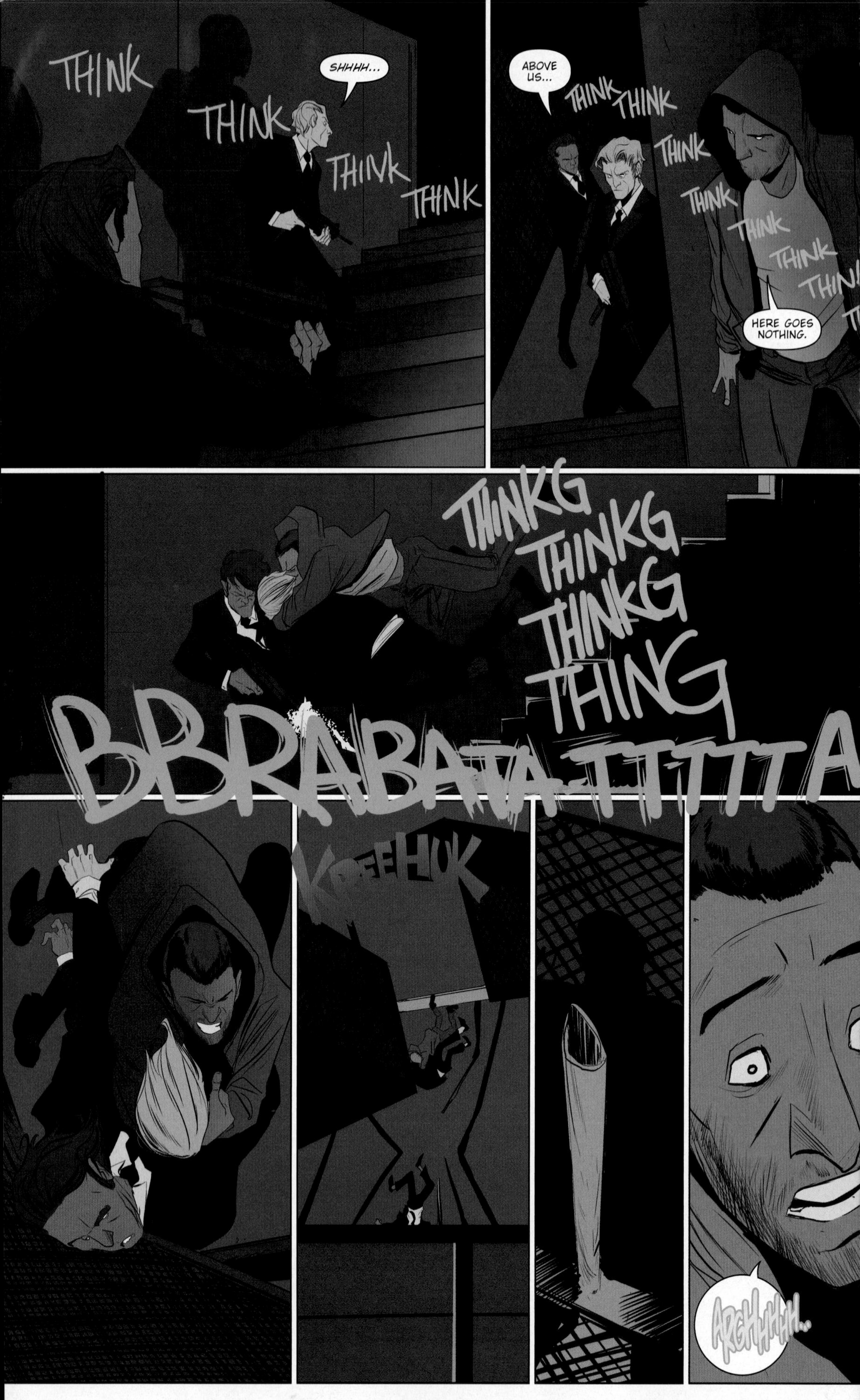
THINK
SHHHH...
THINK
THINK
THINK
ABOVE US...
THINK THINK
THINK
THINK
THINK
THINK
HERE GOES NOTHING.
THINKG
THINKG
THINKG
THING
BBRABATA-TTTTTA
KREEHUK
ARGHHHHH..

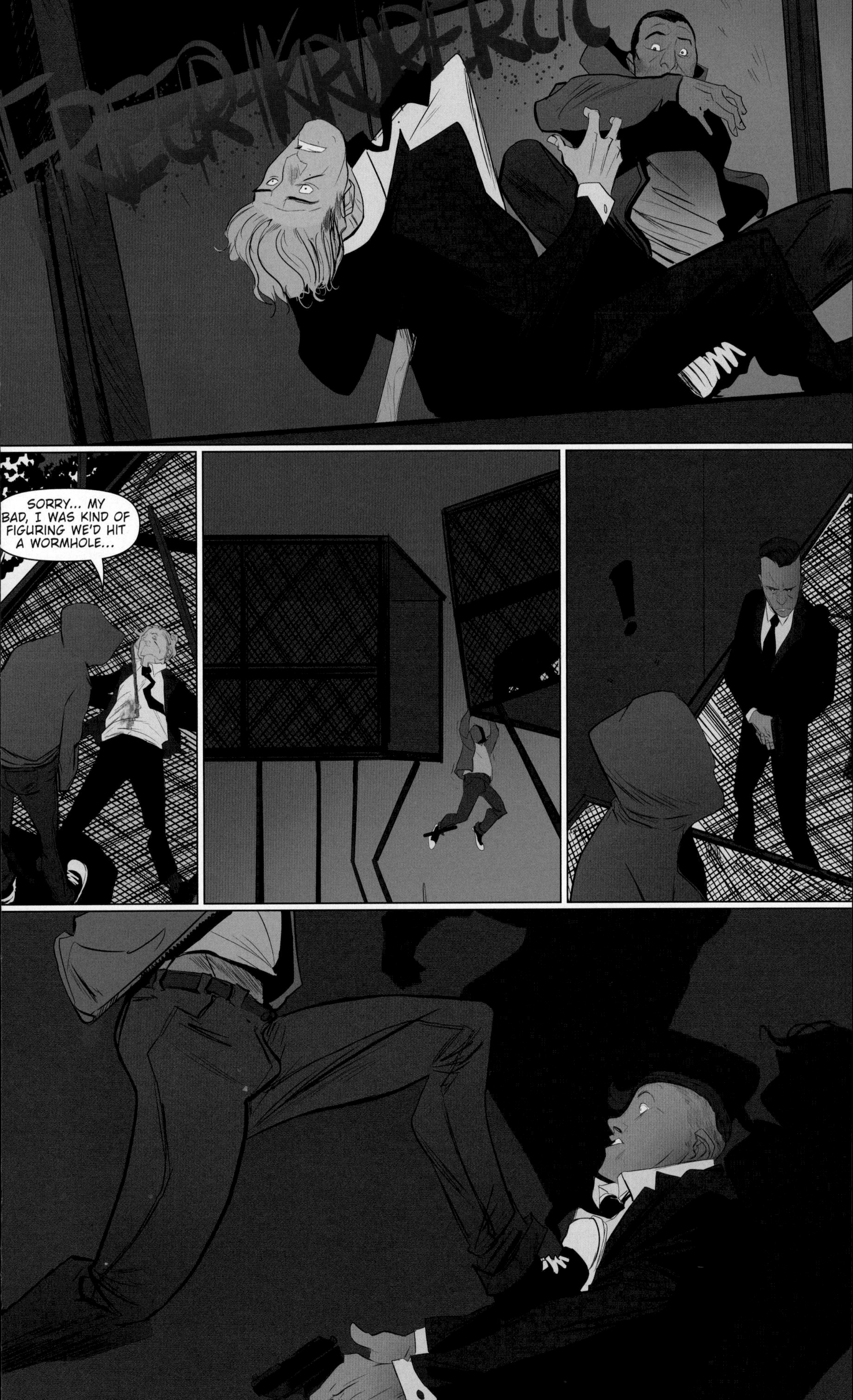
SORRY... MY BAD, I WAS KIND OF FIGURING WE'D HIT A WORMHOLE...
!

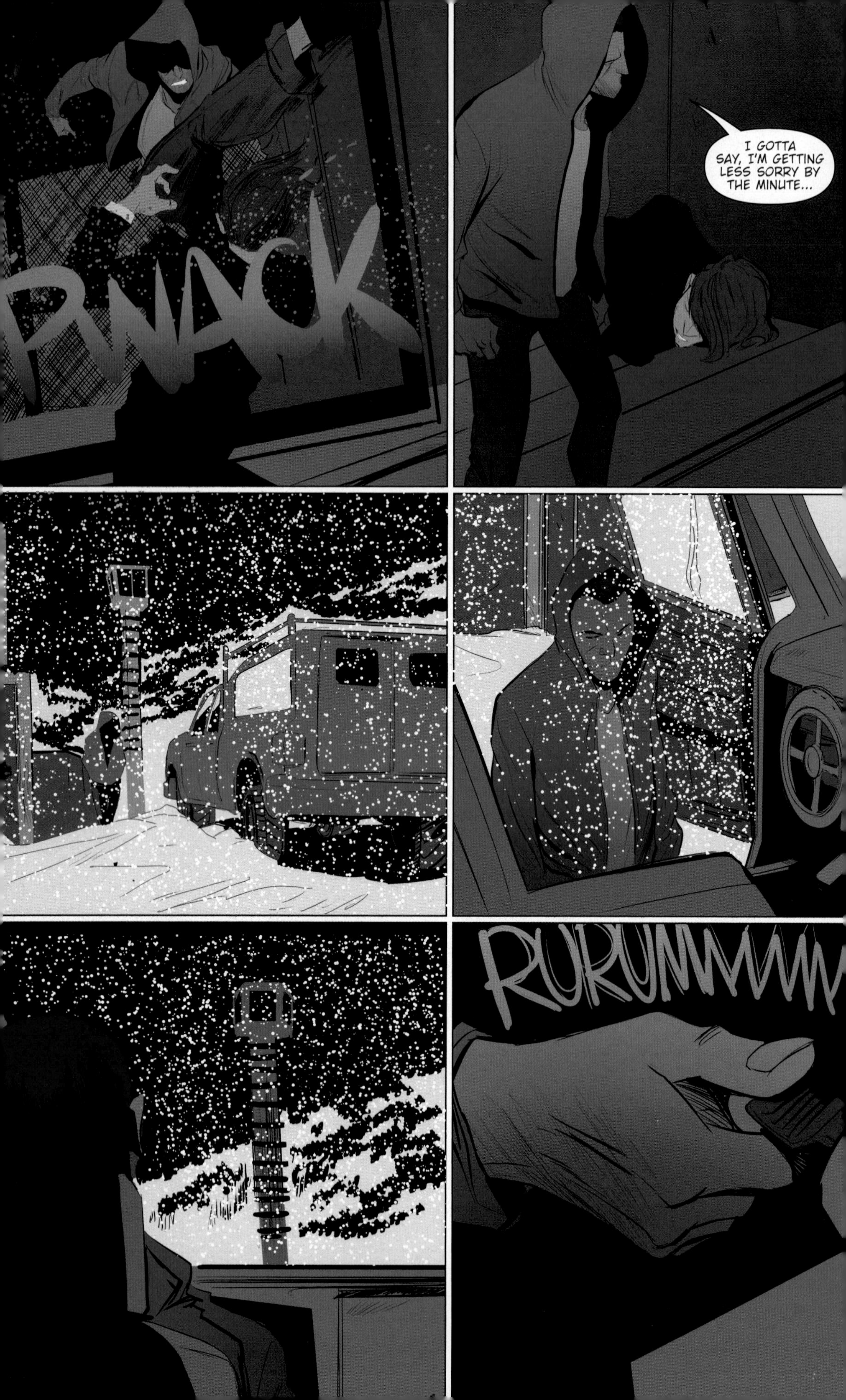
BWACK
I GOTTA SAY, I'M GETTING LESS SORRY BY THE MINUTE...
RURUMMMM

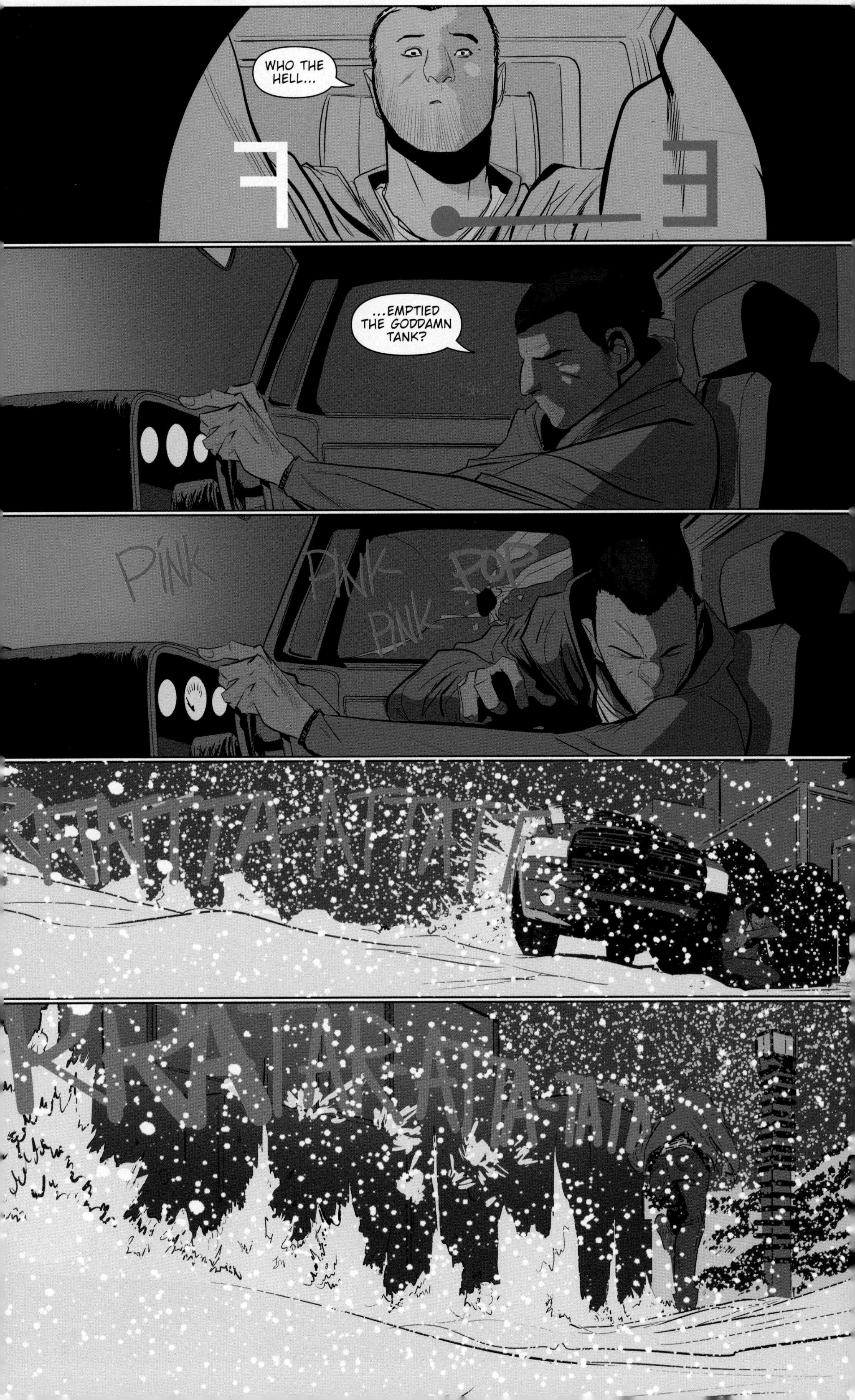
WHO THE HELL...
...EMPTIED THE GODDAMN TANK?
PINK
PINK
POP
PINK

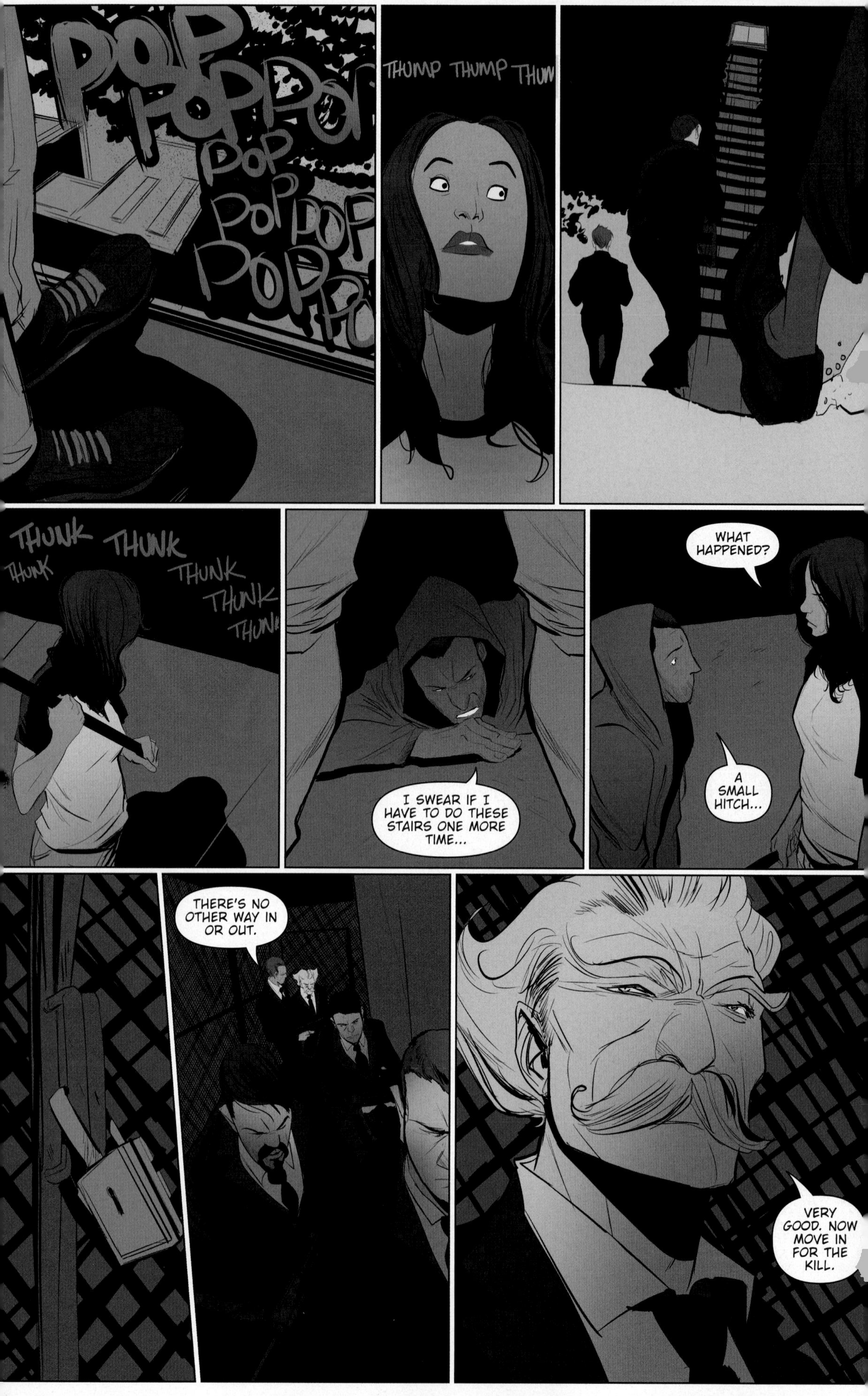
POP POP POP POP
POP
POP POP
POP
THUMP THUMP THUM
THUNK THUNK
THUNK
THUNK
THUNK
THUNK
I SWEAR IF I HAVE TO DO THESE STAIRS ONE MORE TIME...
WHAT HAPPENED?
A SMALL HITCH...
THERE'S NO OTHER WAY IN OR OUT.
VERY GOOD. NOW MOVE IN FOR THE KILL.

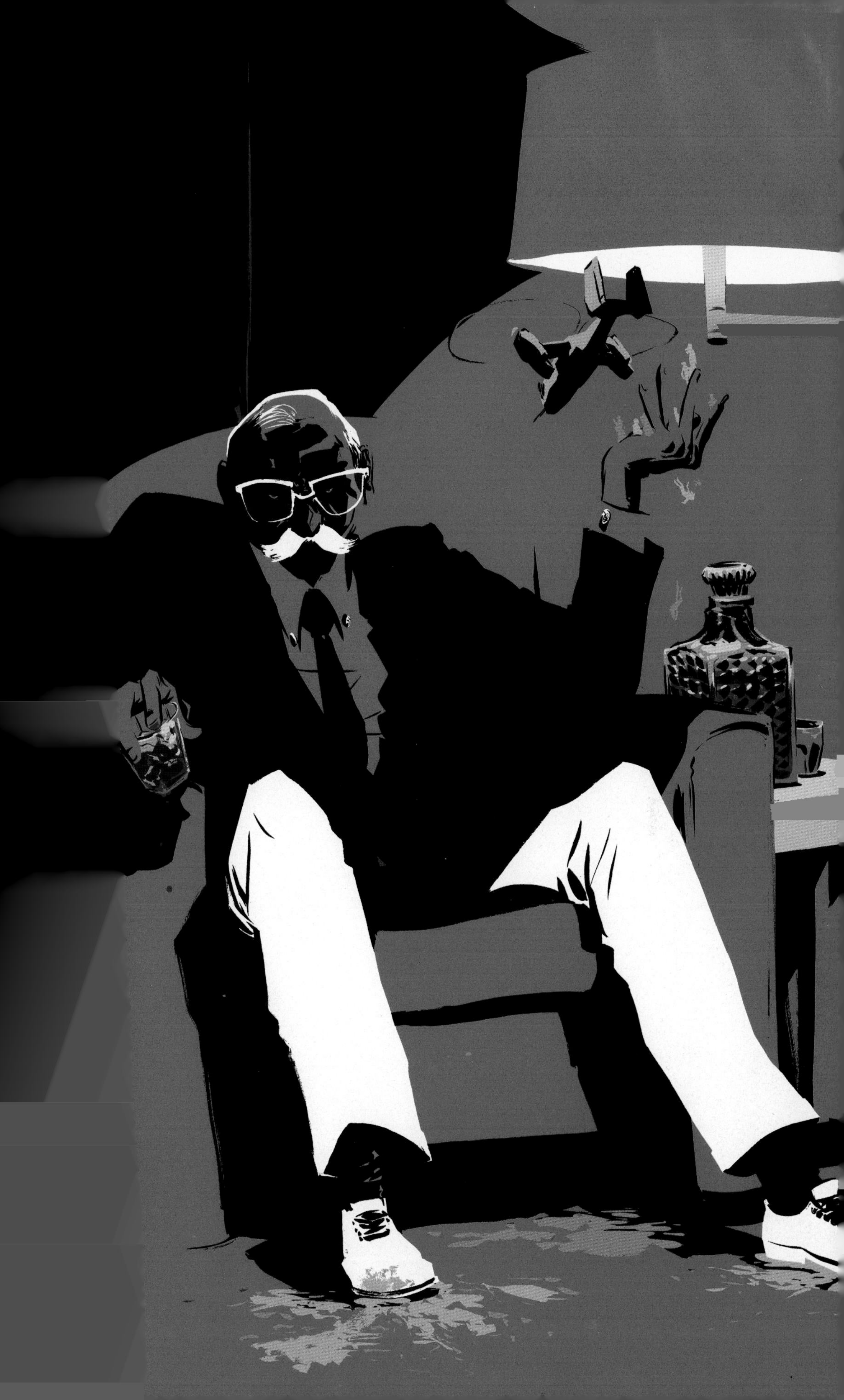

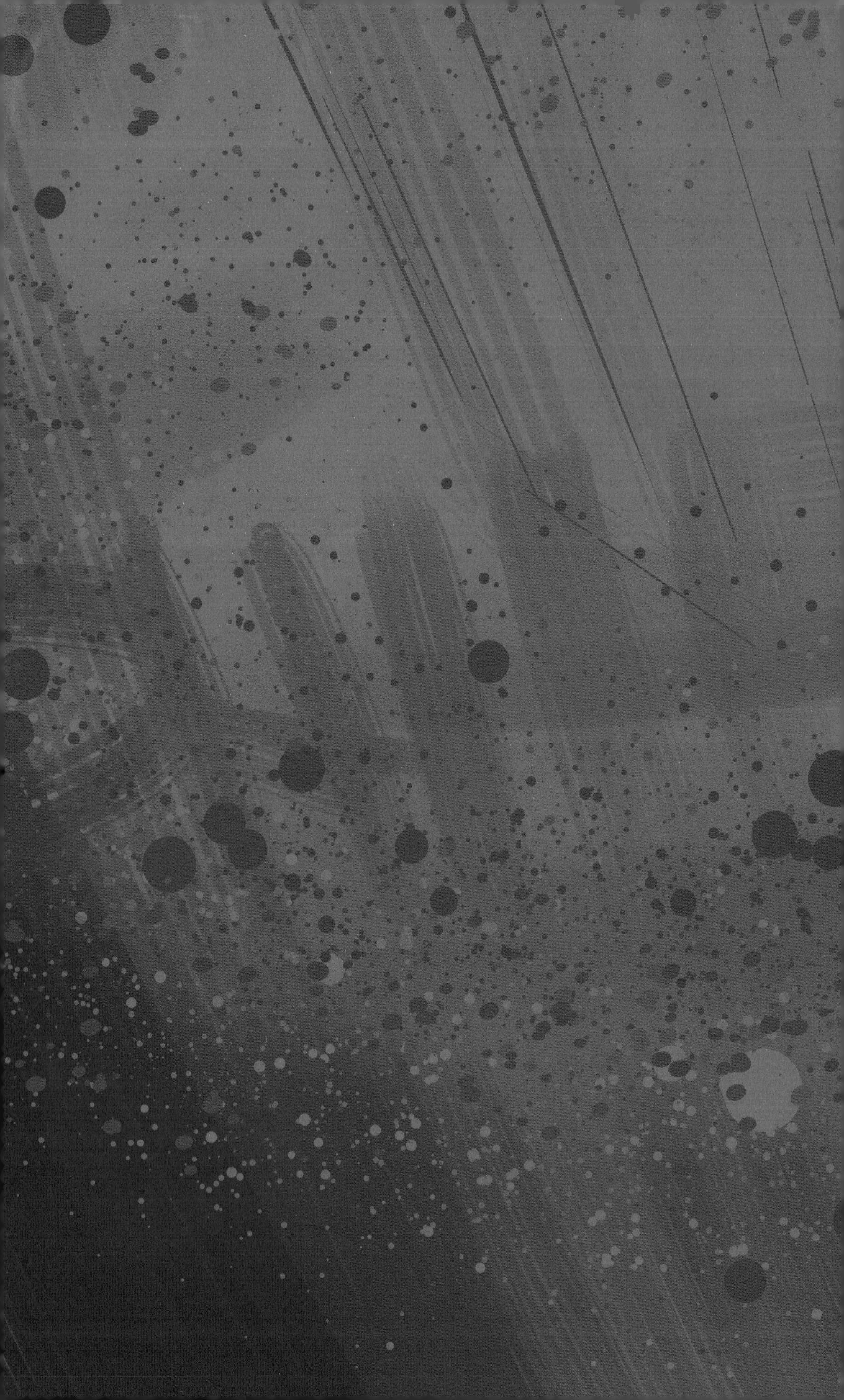

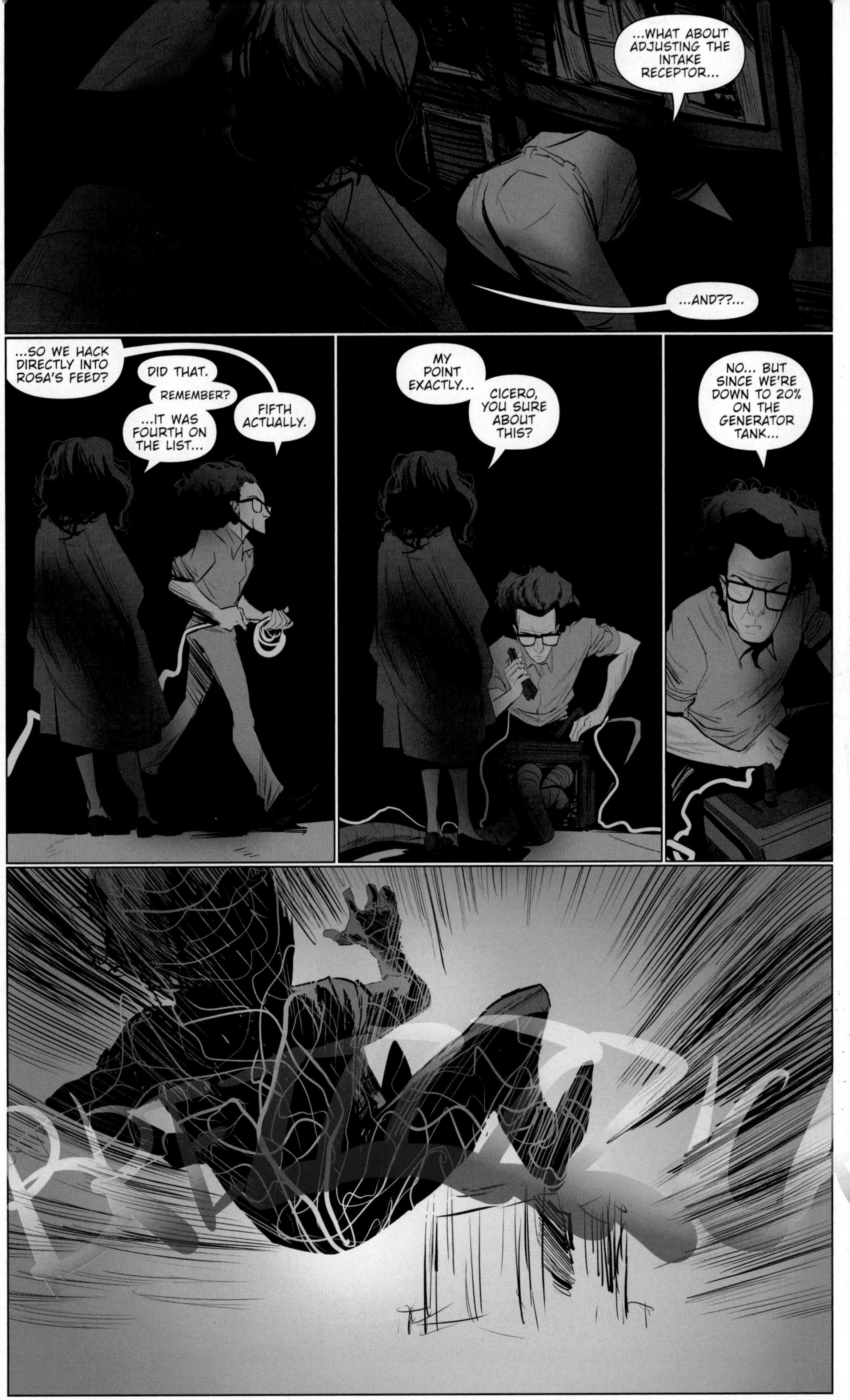
...WHAT ABOUT ADJUSTING THE INTAKE RECEPTOR...
...AND??...
...SO WE HACK DIRECTLY INTO ROSA'S FEED?
DID THAT.
REMEMBER?
...IT WAS FOURTH ON THE LIST...
FIFTH ACTUALLY.
MY POINT EXACTLY...
CICERO, YOU SURE ABOUT THIS?
NO... BUT SINCE WE'RE DOWN TO 20% ON THE GENERATOR TANK...

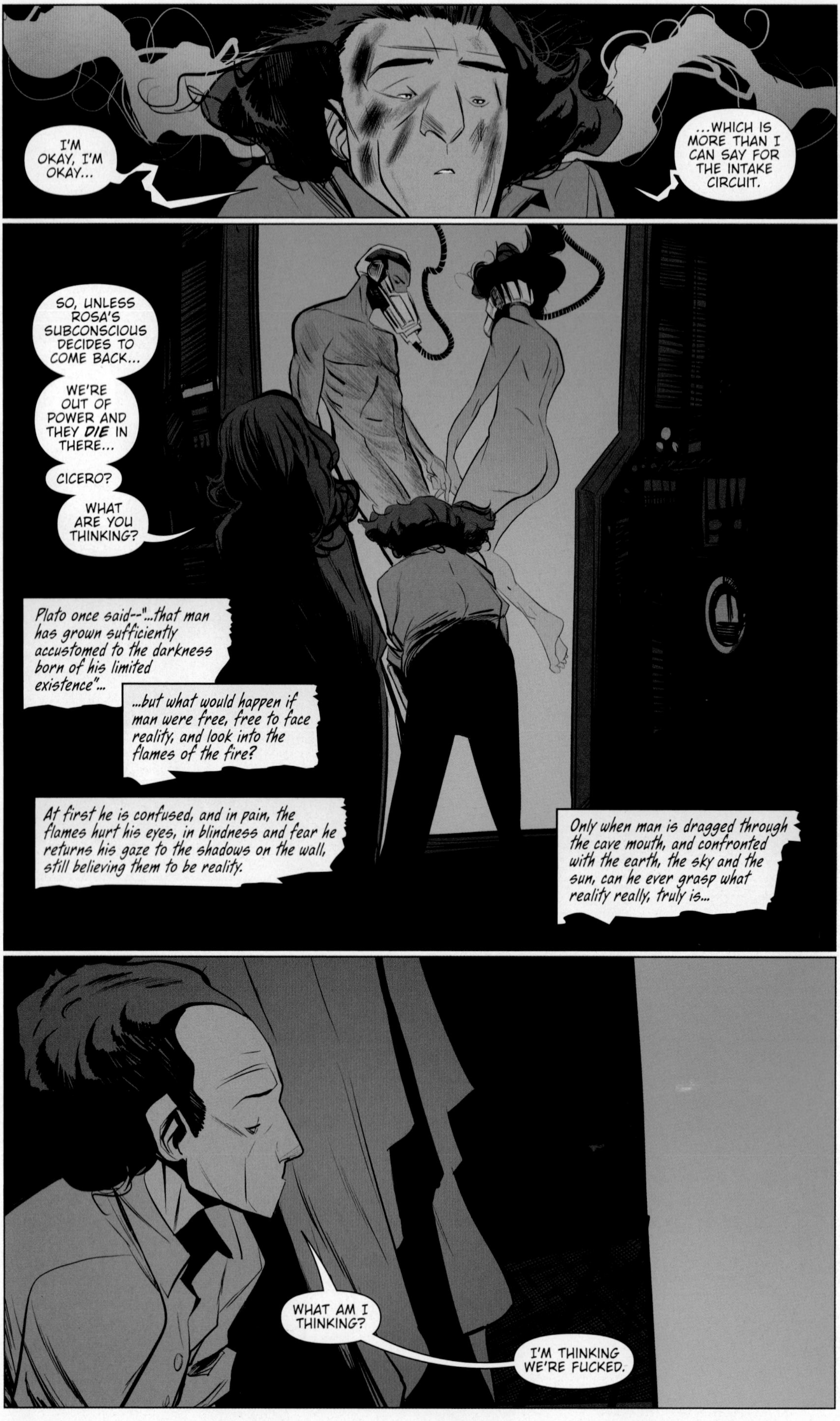

I'M OKAY, I'M OKAY...
...WHICH IS MORE THAN I CAN SAY FOR THE INTAKE CIRCUIT.
SO, UNLESS ROSA'S SUBCONSCIOUS DECIDES TO COME BACK...
WE'RE OUT OF POWER AND THEY DIE IN THERE...
CICERO?
WHAT ARE YOU THINKING?
Plato once said--"...that man has grown sufficiently accustomed to the darkness born of his limited existence"...
...but what would happen if man were free, free to face reality, and look into the flames of the fire?
At first he is confused, and in pain, the flames hurt his eyes, in blindness and fear he returns his gaze to the shadows on the wall, still believing them to be reality.
Only when man is dragged through the cave mouth, and confronted with the earth, the sky and the sun, can he ever grasp what reality really, truly is...
WHAT AM I THINKING?
I'M THINKING WE'RE FUCKED.

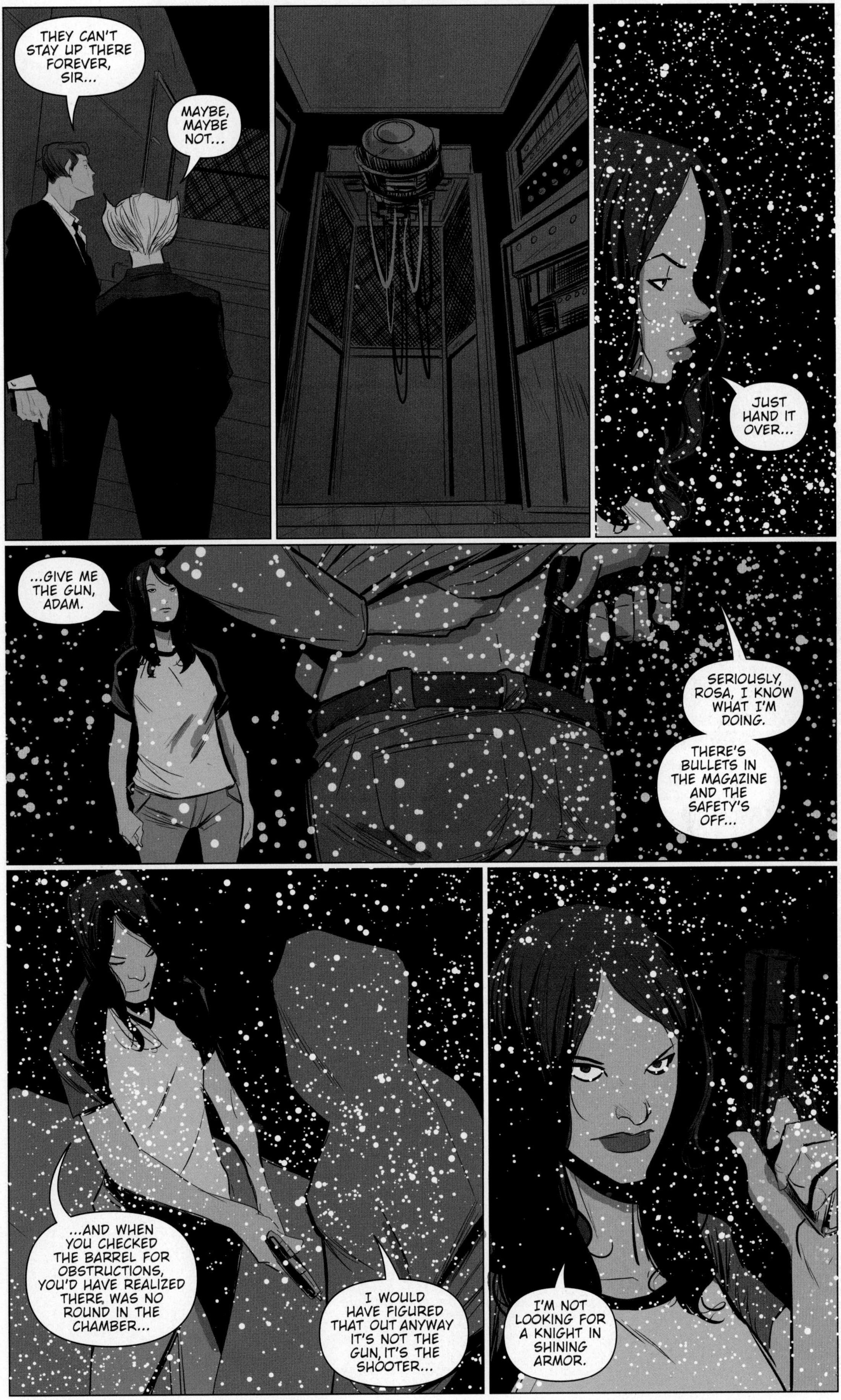
THEY CAN'T STAY UP THERE FOREVER, SIR...
MAYBE, MAYBE NOT...
JUST HAND IT OVER...
...GIVE ME THE GUN, ADAM.
SERIOUSLY, ROSA, I KNOW WHAT I'M DOING.
THERE'S BULLETS IN THE MAGAZINE AND THE SAFETY'S OFF...
...AND WHEN YOU CHECKED THE BARREL FOR OBSTRUCTIONS, YOU'D HAVE REALIZED THERE WAS NO ROUND IN THE CHAMBER...
I WOULD HAVE FIGURED THAT OUT ANYWAY IT'S NOT THE GUN, IT'S THE SHOOTER...
I'M NOT LOOKING FOR A KNIGHT IN SHINING ARMOR.

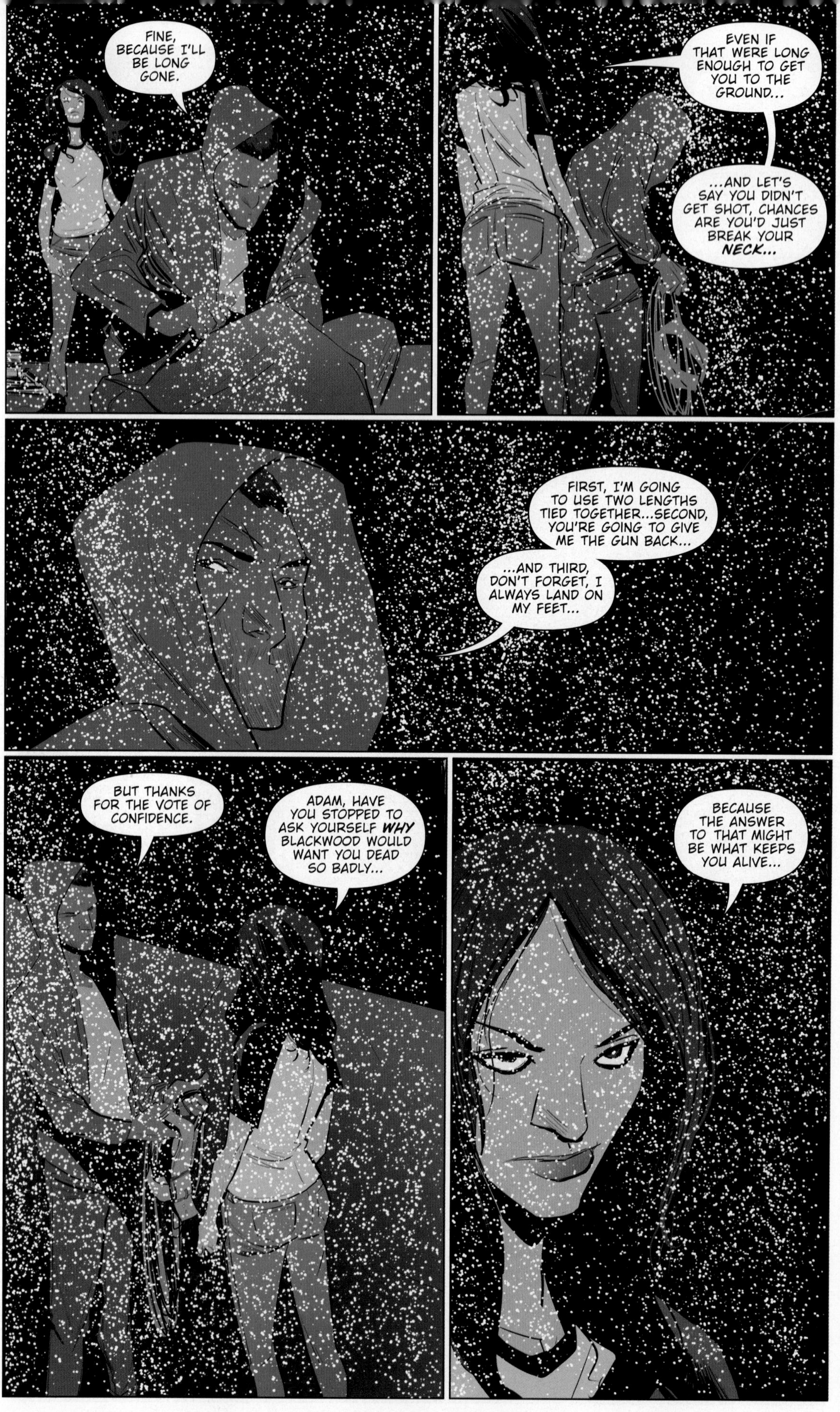
FINE, BECAUSE I'LL BE LONG GONE.
EVEN IF THAT WERE LONG ENOUGH TO GET YOU TO THE GROUND...
...AND LET'S SAY YOU DIDN'T GET SHOT, CHANCES ARE YOU'D JUST BREAK YOUR NECK...
FIRST, I'M GOING TO USE TWO LENGTHS TIED TOGETHER...SECOND, YOU'RE GOING TO GIVE ME THE GUN BACK...
...AND THIRD, DON'T FORGET, I ALWAYS LAND ON MY FEET...
BUT THANKS FOR THE VOTE OF CONFIDENCE.
ADAM, HAVE YOU STOPPED TO ASK YOURSELF WHY BLACKWOOD WOULD WANT YOU DEAD SO BADLY...
BECAUSE THE ANSWER TO THAT MIGHT BE WHAT KEEPS YOU ALIVE...

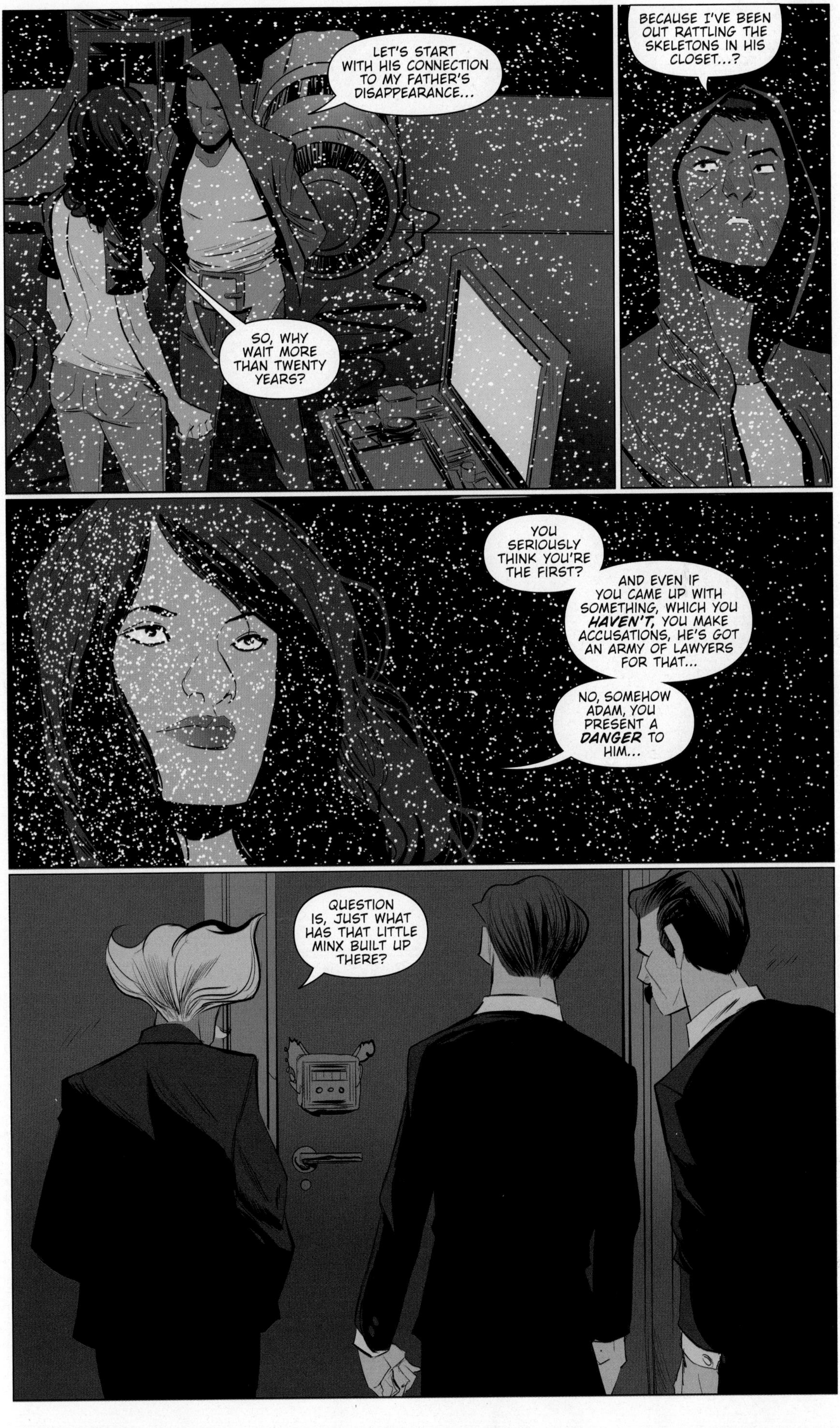
LET'S START WITH HIS CONNECTION TO MY FATHER'S DISAPPEARANCE...
SO, WHY WAIT MORE THAN TWENTY YEARS?
BECAUSE I'VE BEEN OUT RATTLING THE SKELETONS IN HIS CLOSET...?
YOU SERIOUSLY THINK YOU'RE THE FIRST?
AND EVEN IF YOU CAME UP WITH SOMETHING, WHICH YOU HAVEN'T, YOU MAKE ACCUSATIONS, HE'S GOT AN ARMY OF LAWYERS FOR THAT...
NO, SOMEHOW ADAM, YOU PRESENT A DANGER TO HIM...
QUESTION IS, JUST WHAT HAS THAT LITTLE MINX BUILT UP THERE?

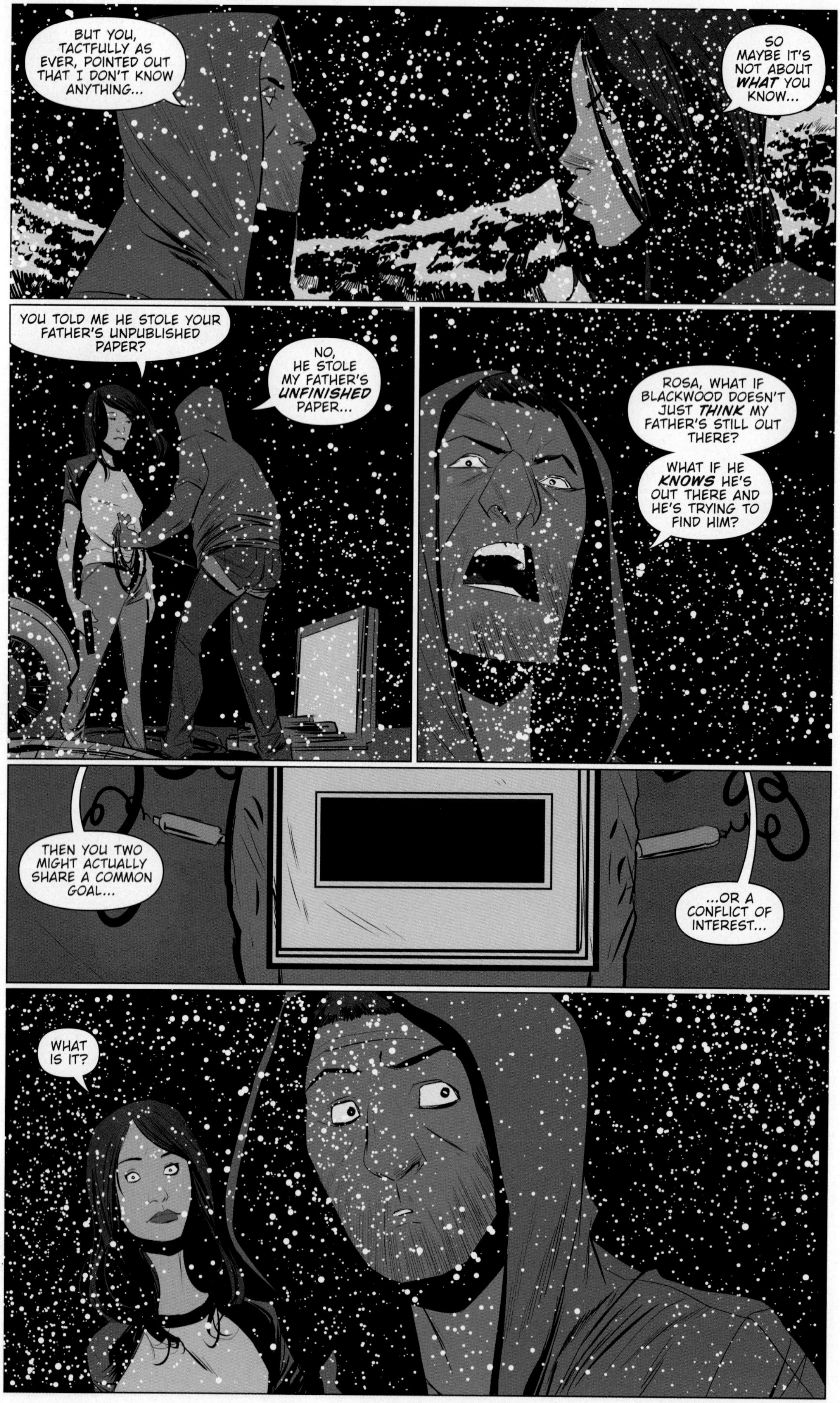
BUT YOU, TACTFULLY AS EVER, POINTED OUT THAT I DON'T KNOW ANYTHING...
SO MAYBE IT'S NOT ABOUT ***WHAT*** YOU KNOW...
YOU TOLD ME HE STOLE YOUR FATHER'S UNPUBLISHED PAPER?
NO, HE STOLE MY FATHER'S ***UNFINISHED*** PAPER...
ROSA, WHAT IF BLACKWOOD DOESN'T JUST ***THINK*** MY FATHER'S STILL OUT THERE?
WHAT IF HE ***KNOWS*** HE'S OUT THERE AND HE'S TRYING TO FIND HIM?
THEN YOU TWO MIGHT ACTUALLY SHARE A COMMON GOAL...
...OR A CONFLICT OF INTEREST...
WHAT IS IT?

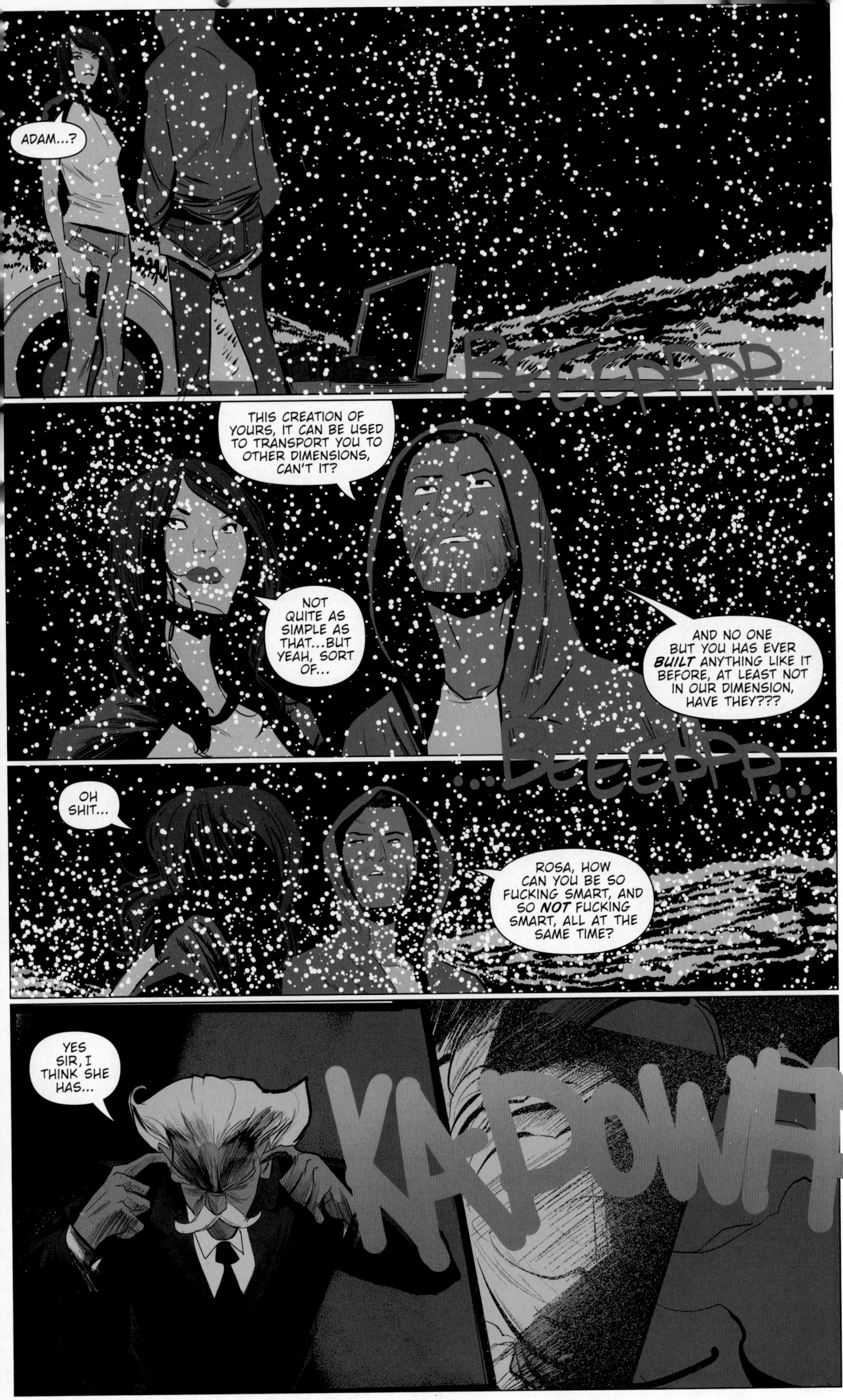
ADAM...?
BEEEPPPP...
THIS CREATION OF YOURS, IT CAN BE USED TO TRANSPORT YOU TO OTHER DIMENSIONS, CAN'T IT?
NOT QUITE AS SIMPLE AS THAT...BUT YEAH, SORT OF...
AND NO ONE BUT YOU HAS EVER *BUILT* ANYTHING LIKE IT BEFORE, AT LEAST NOT IN OUR DIMENSION, HAVE THEY???
...BEEEPPPP...
OH SHIT...
ROSA, HOW CAN YOU BE SO FUCKING SMART, AND SO *NOT* FUCKING SMART, ALL AT THE SAME TIME?
YES SIR, I THINK SHE HAS...
KADOWM

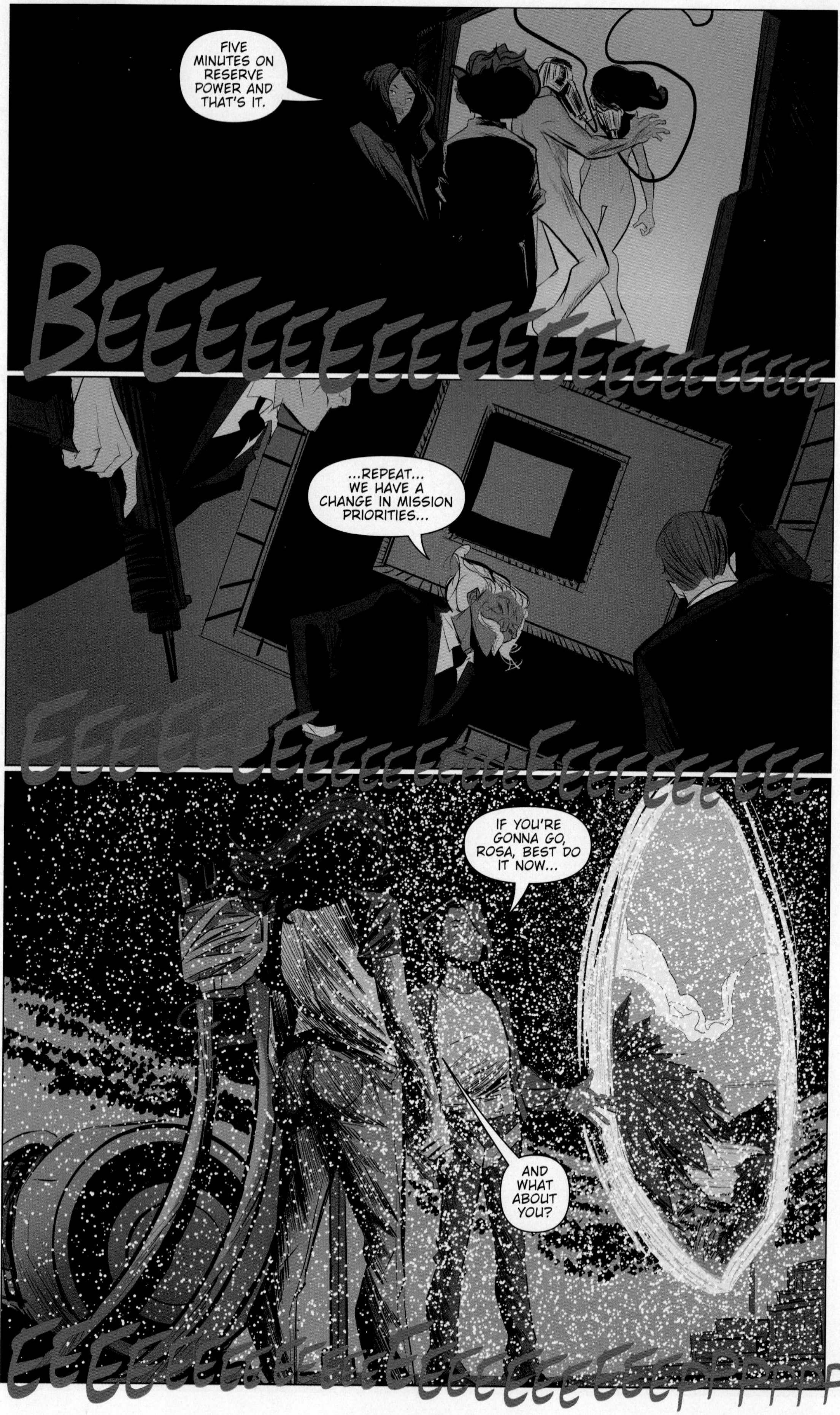
FIVE MINUTES ON RESERVE POWER AND THAT'S IT.
BEEEEEEEEEEEEEEEEEEEEEEEEEE
...REPEAT... WE HAVE A CHANGE IN MISSION PRIORITIES...
EEEEEEEEEEEEEEEEEEEEEEEEEEEEEE
IF YOU'RE GONNA GO, ROSA, BEST DO IT NOW...
AND WHAT ABOUT YOU?
EEEEEEEEEEEEEEEEEEEEEEEEEEEEPPPPP

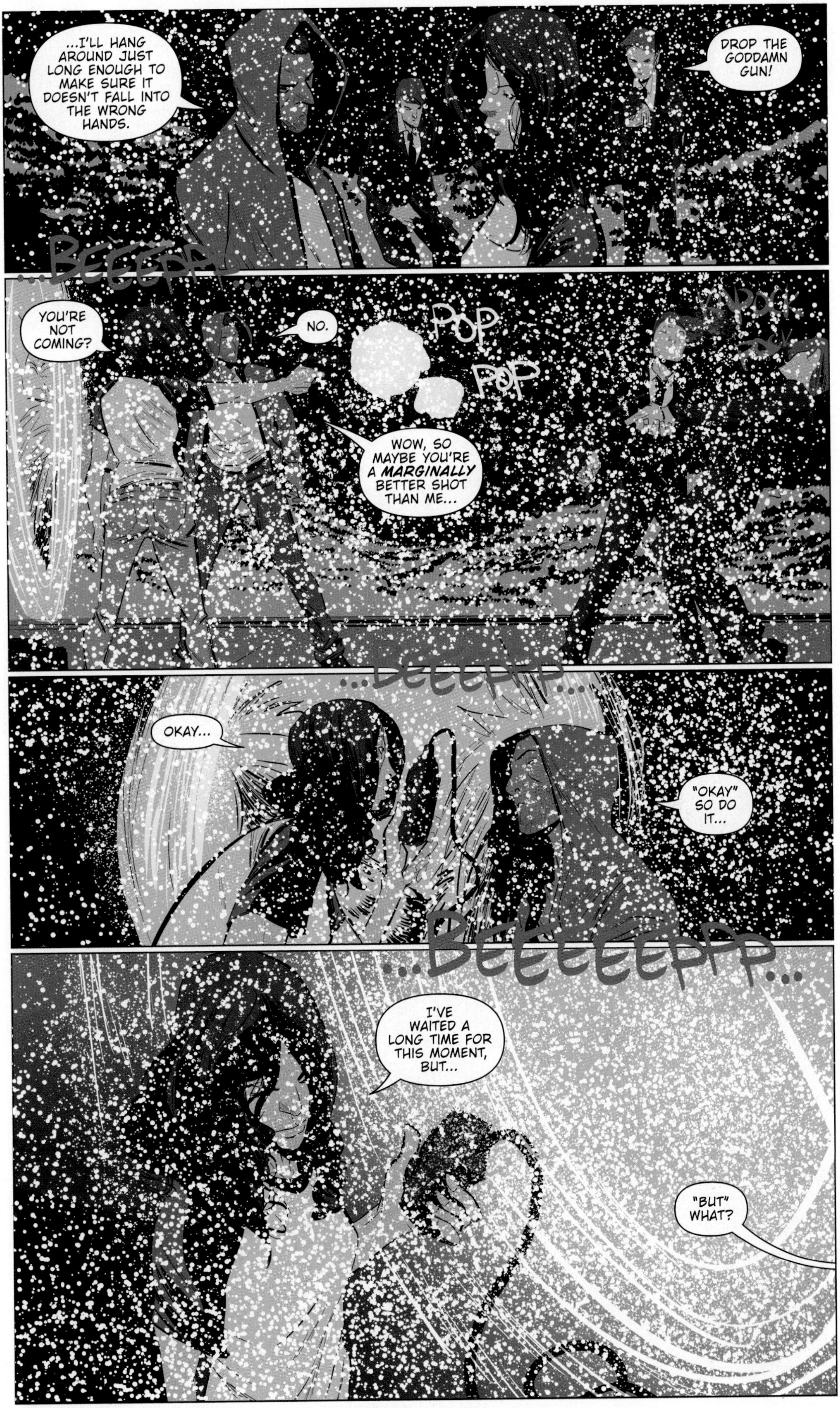
...I'LL HANG AROUND JUST LONG ENOUGH TO MAKE SURE IT DOESN'T FALL INTO THE WRONG HANDS.
DROP THE GODDAMN GUN!
YOU'RE NOT COMING?
NO.
POP
POP
WOW, SO MAYBE YOU'RE A **MARGINALLY** BETTER SHOT THAN ME...
OKAY...
"OKAY" SO DO IT...
I'VE WAITED A LONG TIME FOR THIS MOMENT, BUT...
"BUT" WHAT?

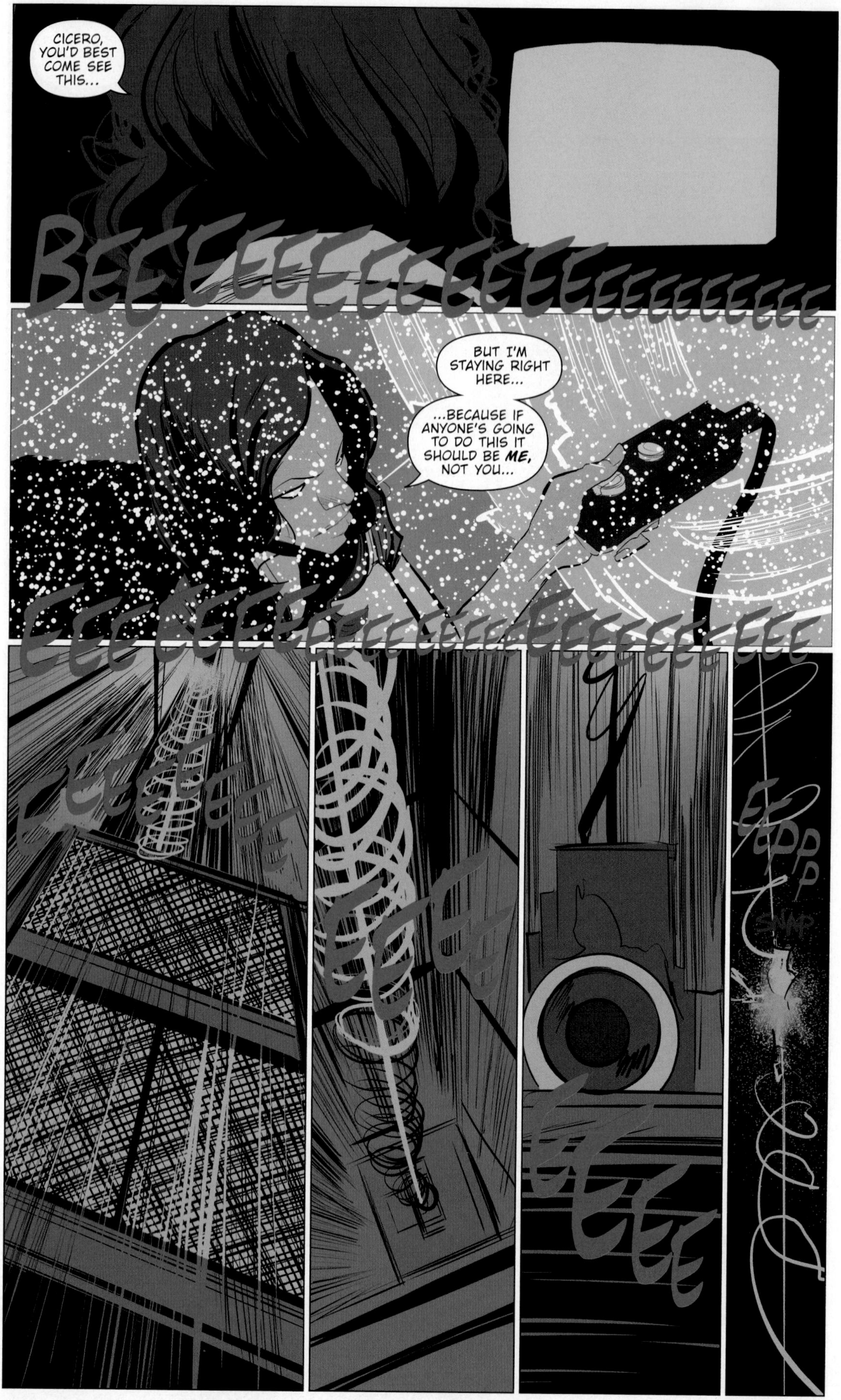
CICERO, YOU'D BEST COME SEE THIS...
BUT I'M STAYING RIGHT HERE...
...BECAUSE IF ANYONE'S GOING TO DO THIS IT SHOULD BE *ME,* NOT YOU...
EEPPP
SNAP

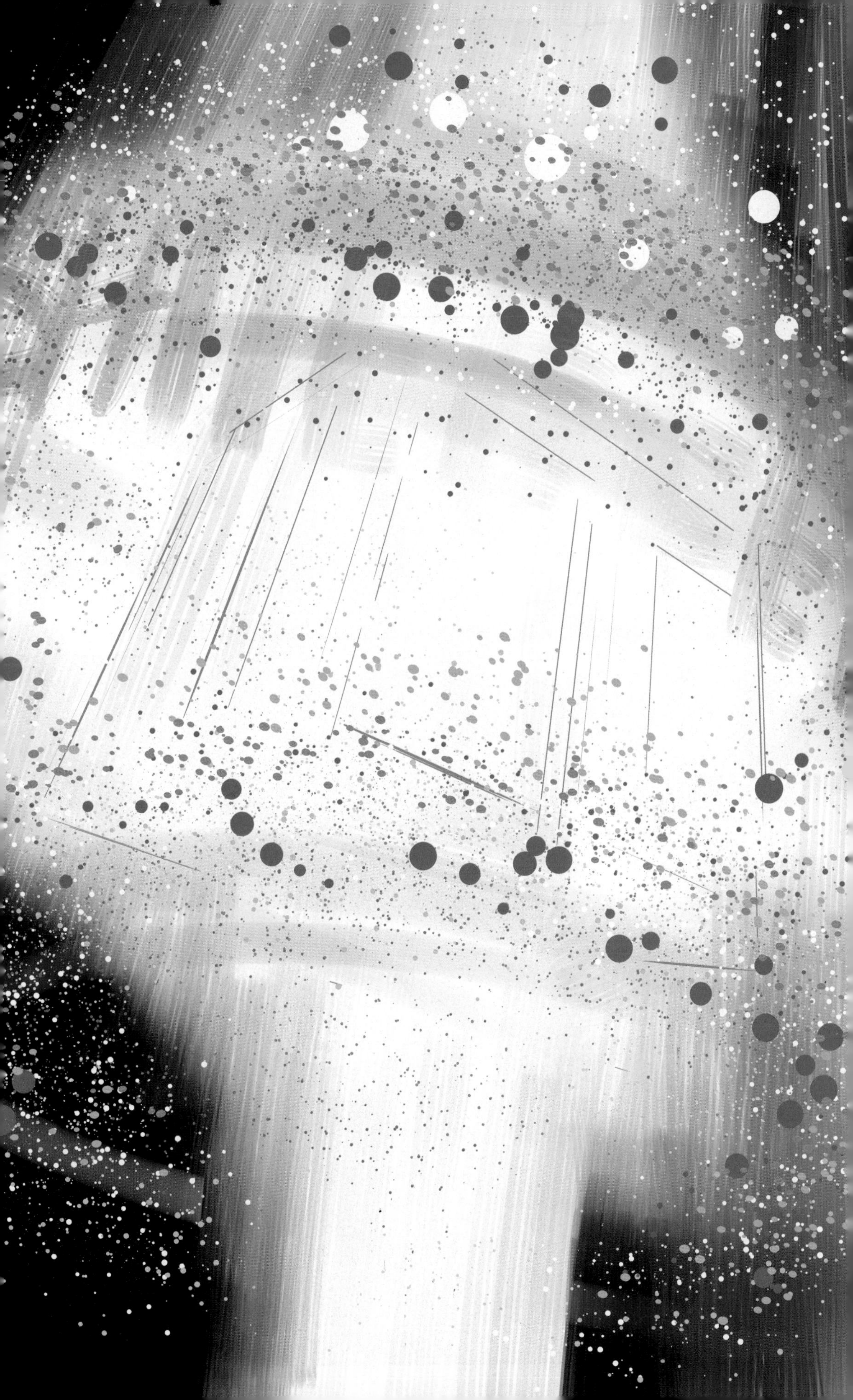

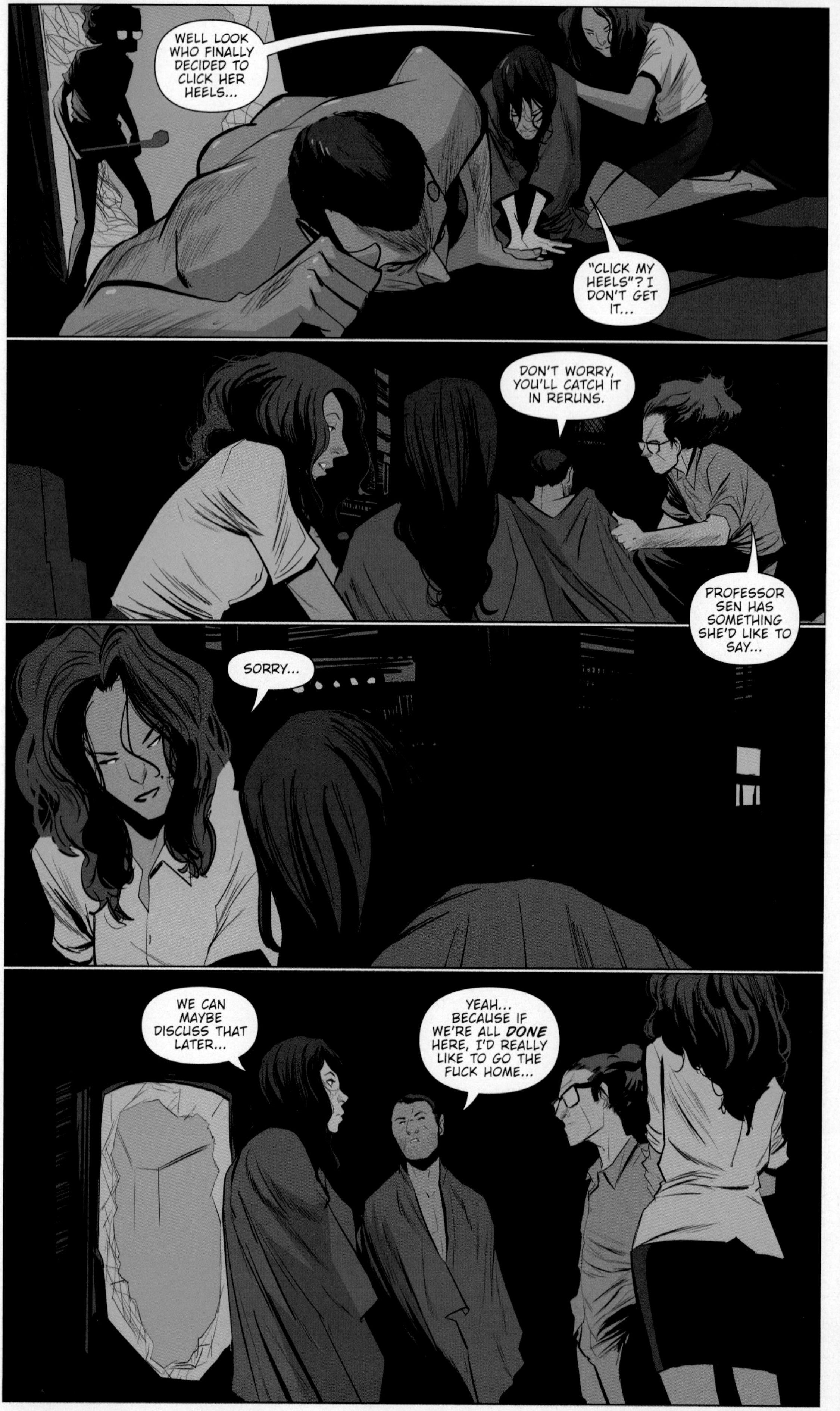
WELL LOOK WHO FINALLY DECIDED TO CLICK HER HEELS...
"CLICK MY HEELS"? I DON'T GET IT...
DON'T WORRY, YOU'LL CATCH IT IN RERUNS.
PROFESSOR SEN HAS SOMETHING SHE'D LIKE TO SAY...
SORRY...
WE CAN MAYBE DISCUSS THAT LATER...
YEAH... BECAUSE IF WE'RE ALL *DONE* HERE, I'D REALLY LIKE TO GO THE FUCK HOME...

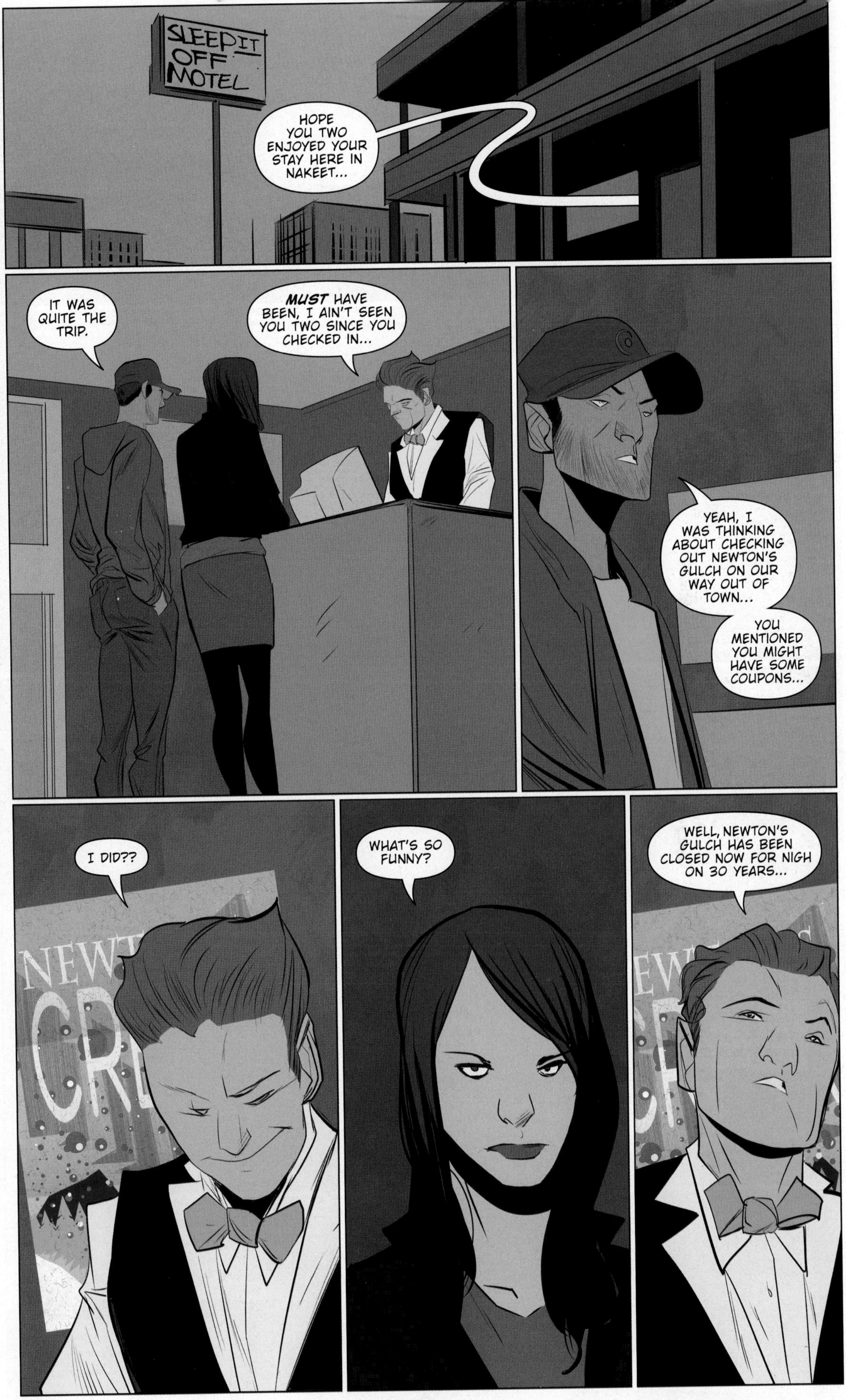
SLEEP IT OFF MOTEL
HOPE YOU TWO ENJOYED YOUR STAY HERE IN NAKEET...
IT WAS QUITE THE TRIP.
MUST HAVE BEEN, I AIN'T SEEN YOU TWO SINCE YOU CHECKED IN...
YEAH, I WAS THINKING ABOUT CHECKING OUT NEWTON'S GULCH ON OUR WAY OUT OF TOWN...
YOU MENTIONED YOU MIGHT HAVE SOME COUPONS...
I DID??
WHAT'S SO FUNNY?
WELL, NEWTON'S GULCH HAS BEEN CLOSED NOW FOR NIGH ON 30 YEARS...

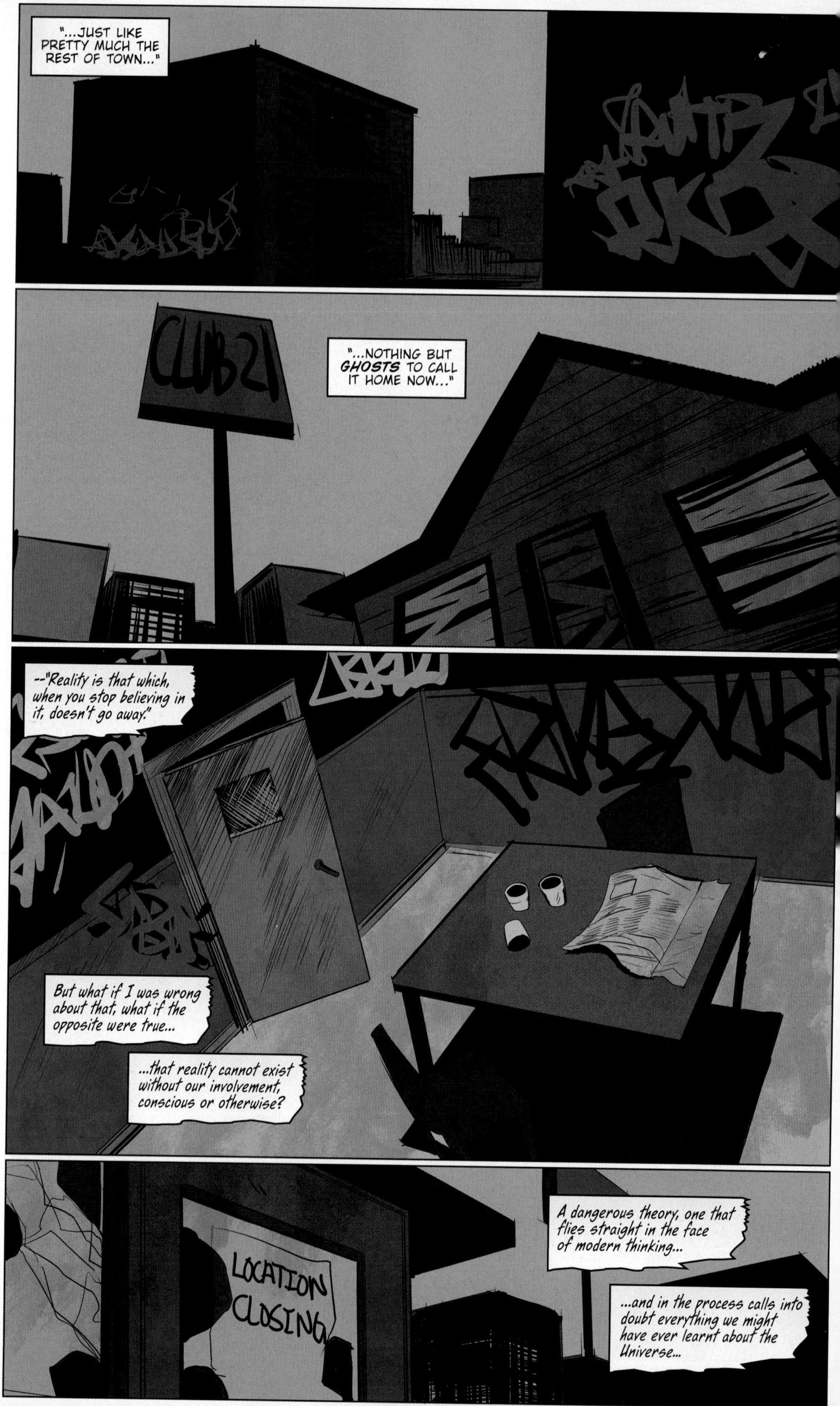
"...JUST LIKE PRETTY MUCH THE REST OF TOWN..."
CLUB 21
"...NOTHING BUT *GHOSTS* TO CALL IT HOME NOW..."
--"Reality is that which, when you stop believing in it, doesn't go away."
But what if I was wrong about that, what if the opposite were true...
...that reality cannot exist without our involvement, conscious or otherwise?
LOCATION CLOSING
A dangerous theory, one that flies straight in the face of modern thinking...
...and in the process calls into doubt everything we might have ever learnt about the Universe...

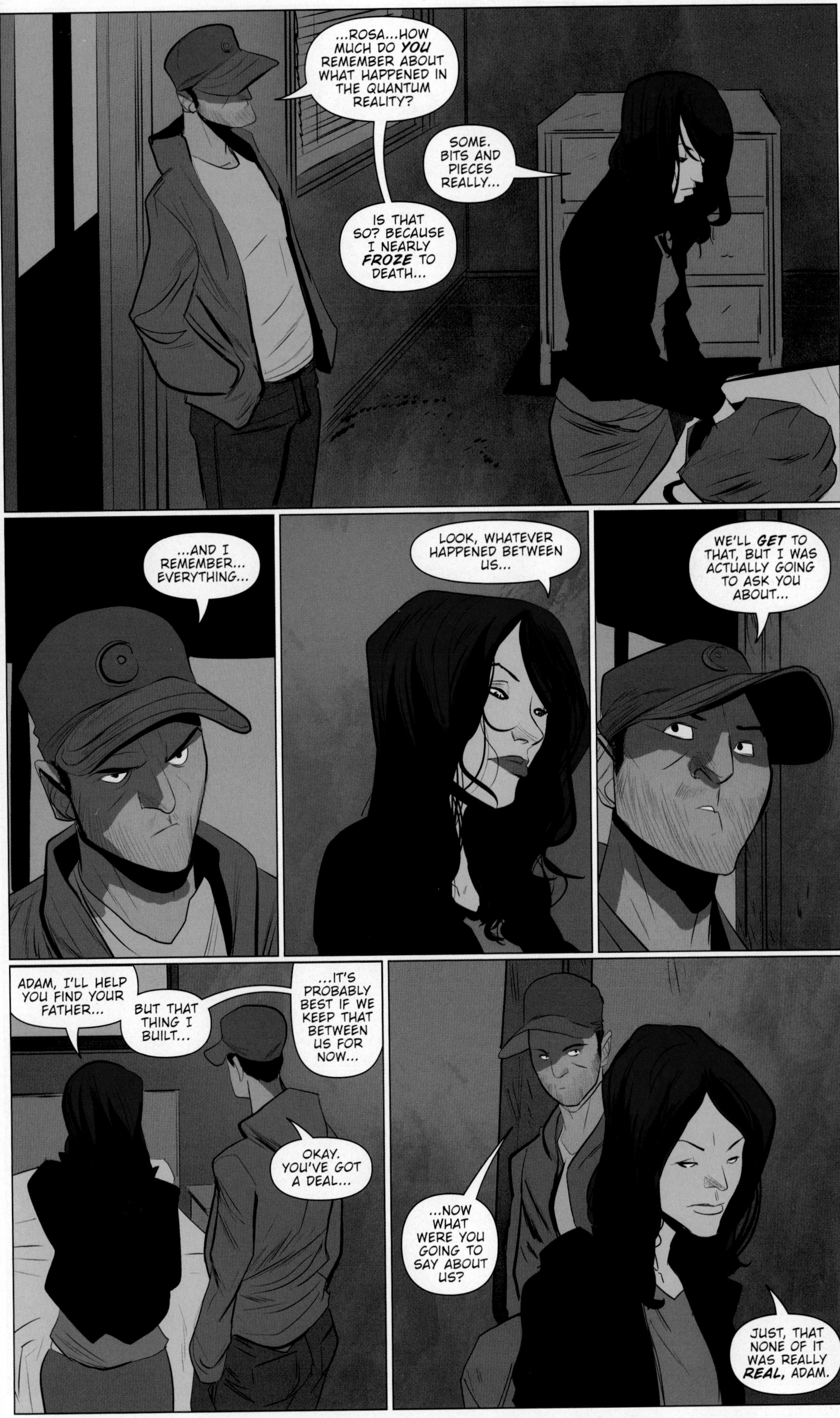
...ROSA...HOW MUCH DO *YOU* REMEMBER ABOUT WHAT HAPPENED IN THE QUANTUM REALITY?
SOME. BITS AND PIECES REALLY...
IS THAT SO? BECAUSE I NEARLY *FROZE* TO DEATH...
...AND I REMEMBER... EVERYTHING...
LOOK, WHATEVER HAPPENED BETWEEN US...
WE'LL *GET* TO THAT, BUT I WAS ACTUALLY GOING TO ASK YOU ABOUT...
ADAM, I'LL HELP YOU FIND YOUR FATHER...
BUT THAT THING I BUILT...
...IT'S PROBABLY BEST IF WE KEEP THAT BETWEEN US FOR NOW...
OKAY. YOU'VE GOT A DEAL...
...NOW WHAT WERE YOU GOING TO SAY ABOUT US?
JUST, THAT NONE OF IT WAS REALLY *REAL*, ADAM.

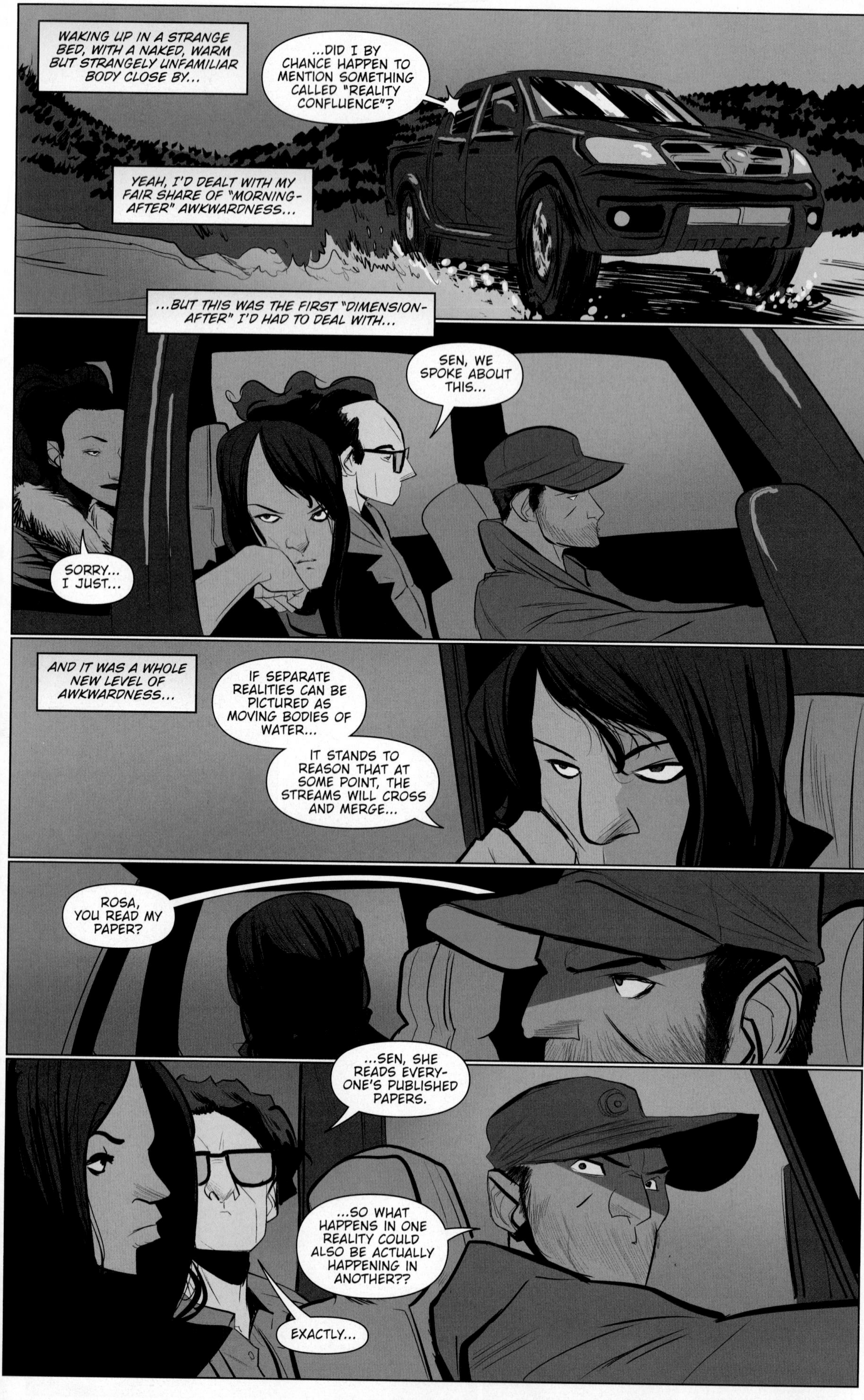
WAKING UP IN A STRANGE BED, WITH A NAKED, WARM BUT STRANGELY UNFAMILIAR BODY CLOSE BY...
...DID I BY CHANCE HAPPEN TO MENTION SOMETHING CALLED "REALITY CONFLUENCE"?
YEAH, I'D DEALT WITH MY FAIR SHARE OF "MORNING-AFTER" AWKWARDNESS...
...BUT THIS WAS THE FIRST "DIMENSION-AFTER" I'D HAD TO DEAL WITH...
SEN, WE SPOKE ABOUT THIS...
SORRY... I JUST...
AND IT WAS A WHOLE NEW LEVEL OF AWKWARDNESS...
IF SEPARATE REALITIES CAN BE PICTURED AS MOVING BODIES OF WATER...
IT STANDS TO REASON THAT AT SOME POINT, THE STREAMS WILL CROSS AND MERGE...
ROSA, YOU READ MY PAPER?
...SEN, SHE READS EVERY-ONE'S PUBLISHED PAPERS.
...SO WHAT HAPPENS IN ONE REALITY COULD ALSO BE ACTUALLY HAPPENING IN ANOTHER??
EXACTLY...

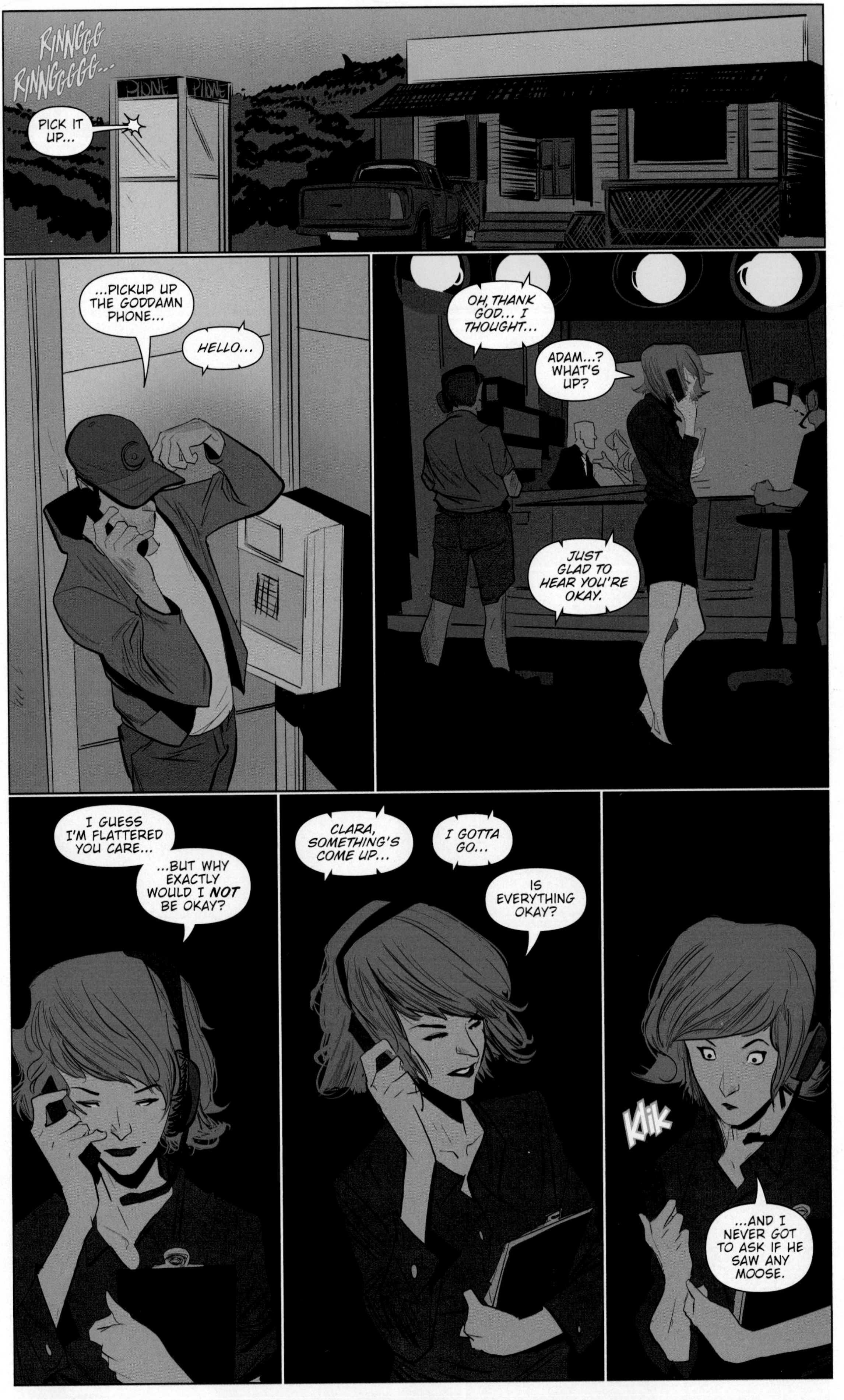
RINNGGG
RINNGGGG...
PHONE PHONE
PICK IT UP...
...PICKUP UP THE GODDAMN PHONE...
HELLO...
OH, THANK GOD... I THOUGHT...
ADAM...? WHAT'S UP?
JUST GLAD TO HEAR YOU'RE OKAY.
I GUESS I'M FLATTERED YOU CARE...
...BUT WHY EXACTLY WOULD I **NOT** BE OKAY?
CLARA, SOMETHING'S COME UP...
I GOTTA GO...
IS EVERYTHING OKAY?
KLIK
...AND I NEVER GOT TO ASK IF HE SAW ANY MOOSE.

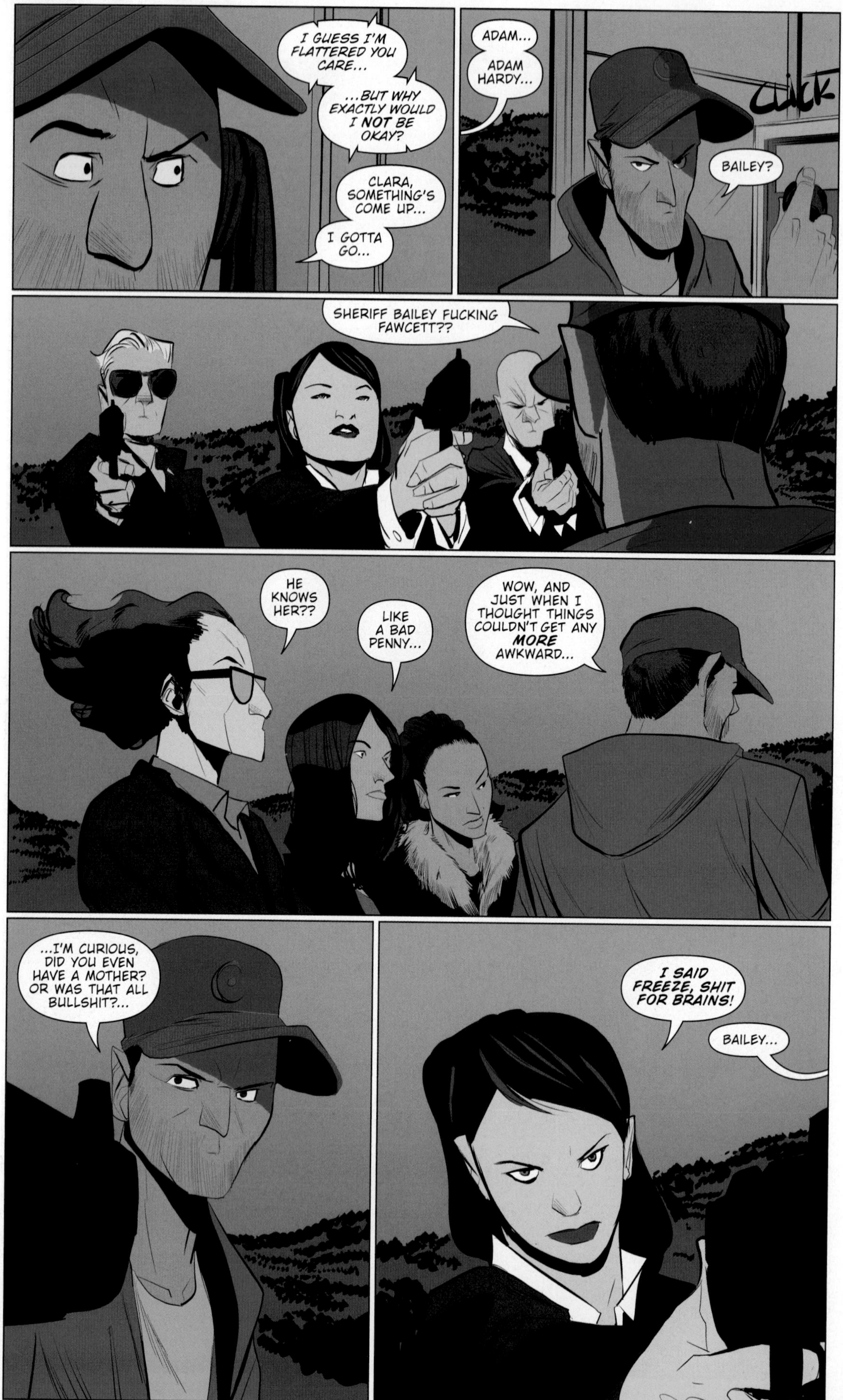
I GUESS I'M FLATTERED YOU CARE...
...BUT WHY EXACTLY WOULD I NOT BE OKAY?
CLARA, SOMETHING'S COME UP...
I GOTTA GO...
ADAM...
ADAM HARDY...
CLICK
BAILEY?
SHERIFF BAILEY FUCKING FAWCETT??
HE KNOWS HER??
LIKE A BAD PENNY...
WOW, AND JUST WHEN I THOUGHT THINGS COULDN'T GET ANY MORE AWKWARD...
...I'M CURIOUS, DID YOU EVEN HAVE A MOTHER? OR WAS THAT ALL BULLSHIT?...
I SAID FREEZE, SHIT FOR BRAINS!
BAILEY...

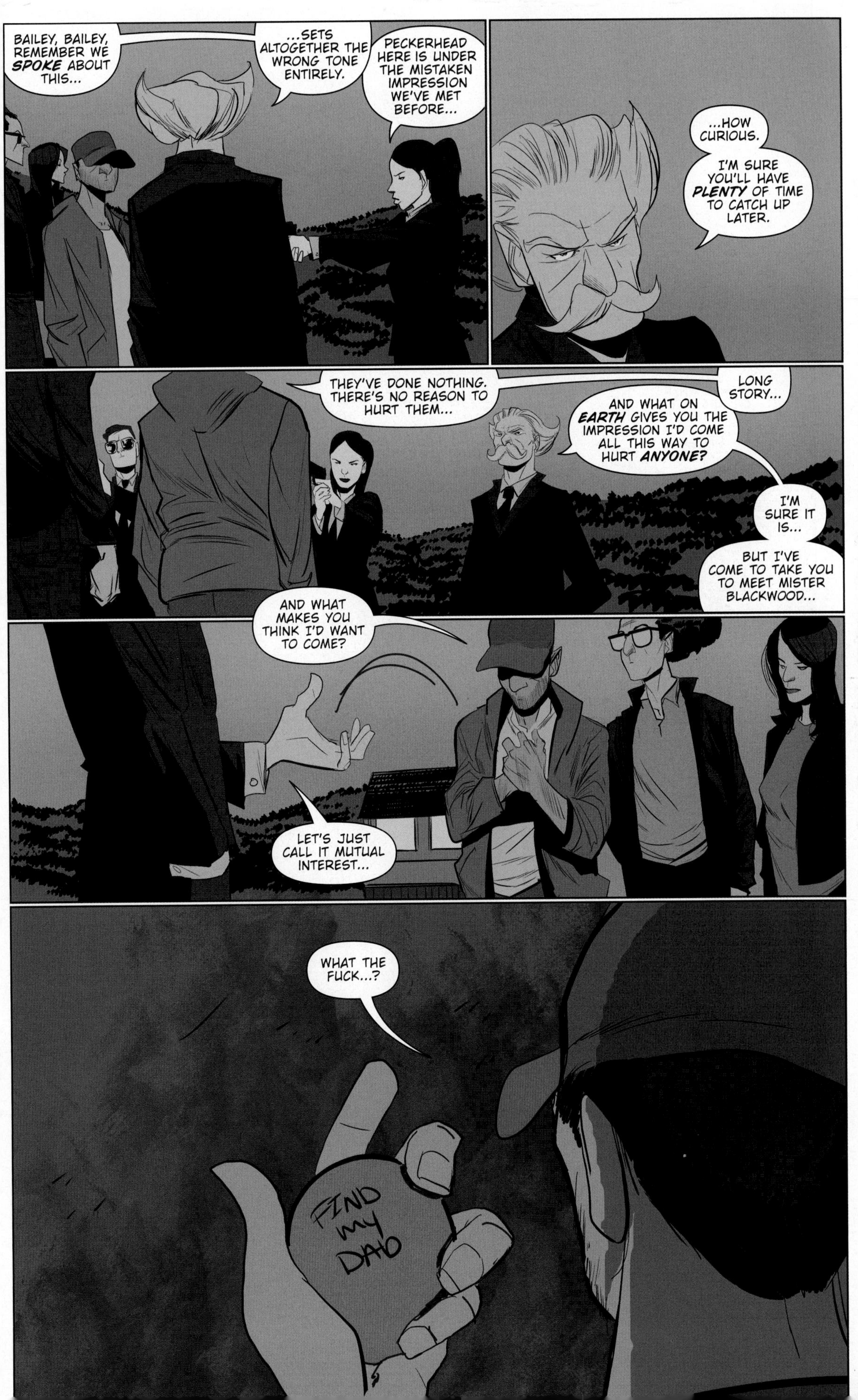
BAILEY, BAILEY, REMEMBER WE SPOKE ABOUT THIS...
...SETS ALTOGETHER THE WRONG TONE ENTIRELY.
PECKERHEAD HERE IS UNDER THE MISTAKEN IMPRESSION WE'VE MET BEFORE...
...HOW CURIOUS.
I'M SURE YOU'LL HAVE PLENTY OF TIME TO CATCH UP LATER.
THEY'VE DONE NOTHING. THERE'S NO REASON TO HURT THEM...
AND WHAT ON EARTH GIVES YOU THE IMPRESSION I'D COME ALL THIS WAY TO HURT ANYONE?
LONG STORY...
I'M SURE IT IS...
BUT I'VE COME TO TAKE YOU TO MEET MISTER BLACKWOOD...
AND WHAT MAKES YOU THINK I'D WANT TO COME?
LET'S JUST CALL IT MUTUAL INTEREST...
WHAT THE FUCK...?
FIND MY DAD

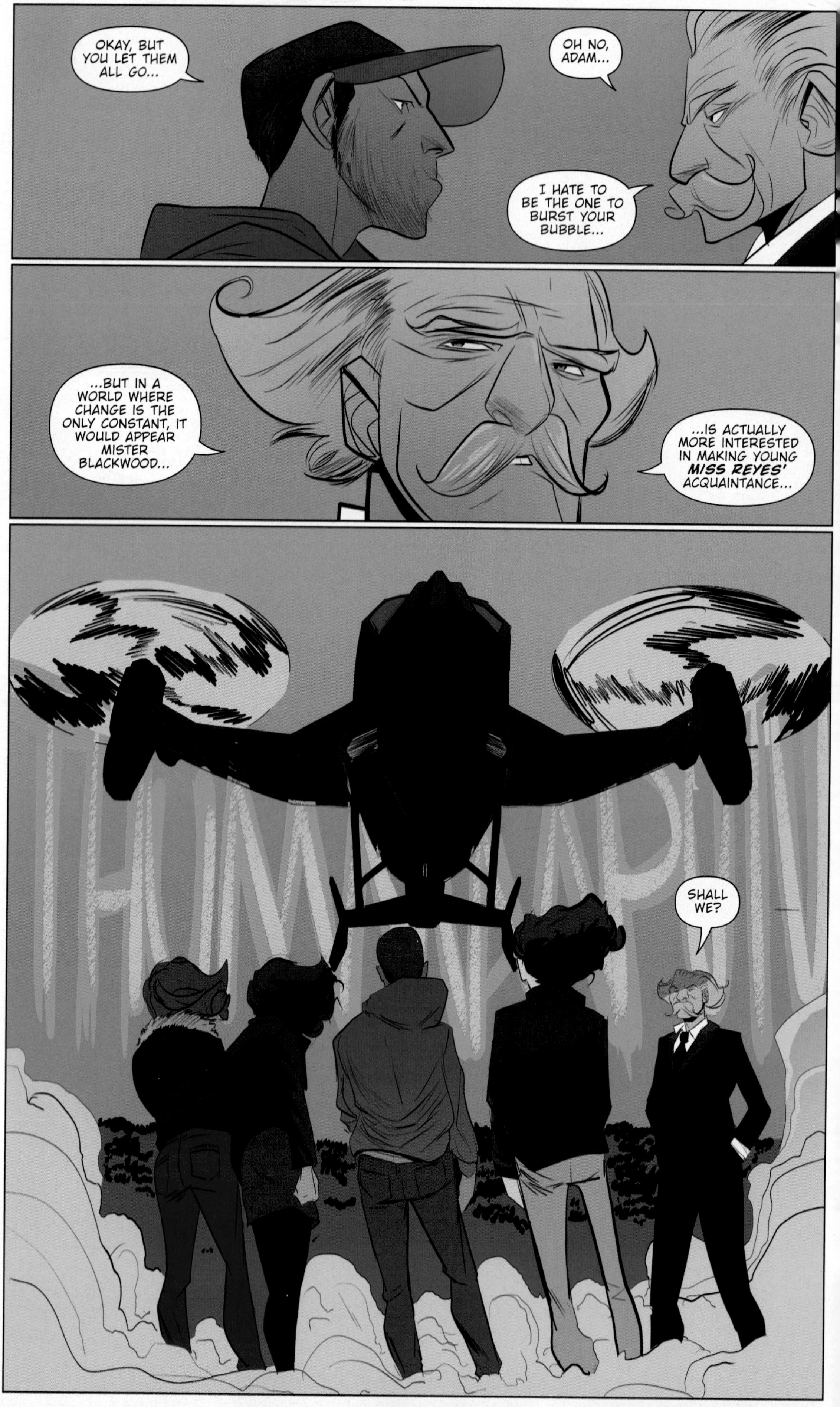
OKAY, BUT YOU LET THEM ALL GO...
OH NO, ADAM...
I HATE TO BE THE ONE TO BURST YOUR BUBBLE...
...BUT IN A WORLD WHERE CHANGE IS THE ONLY CONSTANT, IT WOULD APPEAR MISTER BLACKWOOD...
...IS ACTUALLY MORE INTERESTED IN MAKING YOUNG MISS REYES' ACQUAINTANCE...
SHALL WE?

Breakdowns and sketches by Robbi Rodriguez

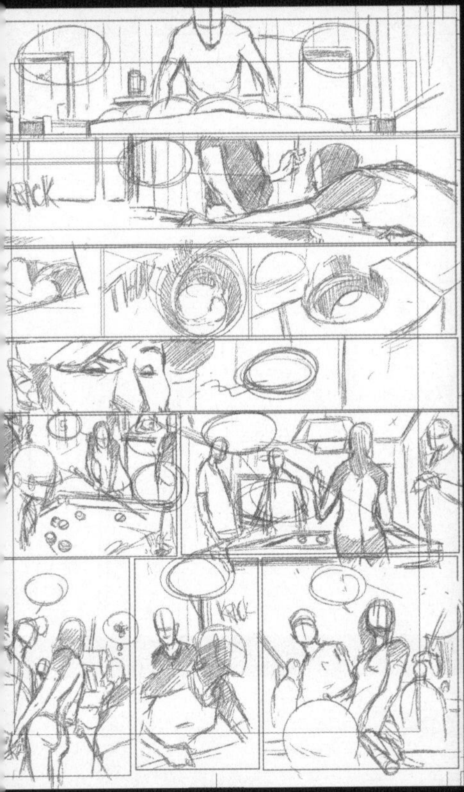

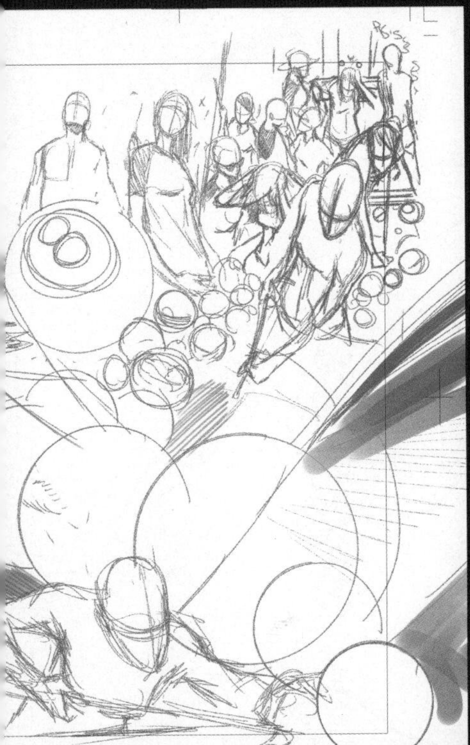

ISSUE #8

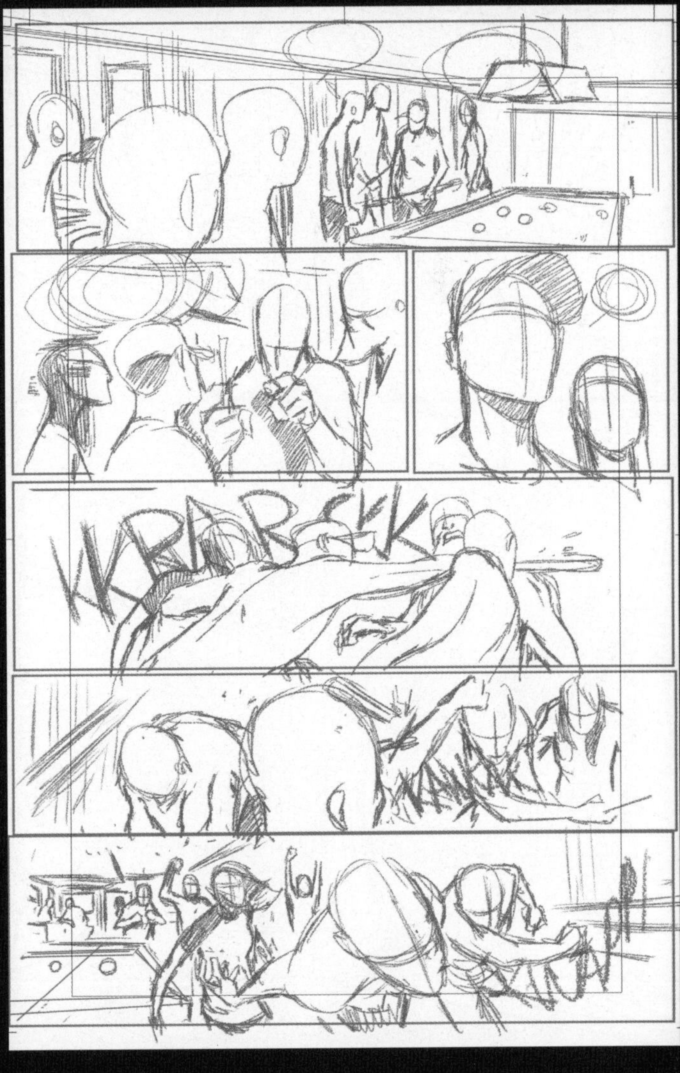

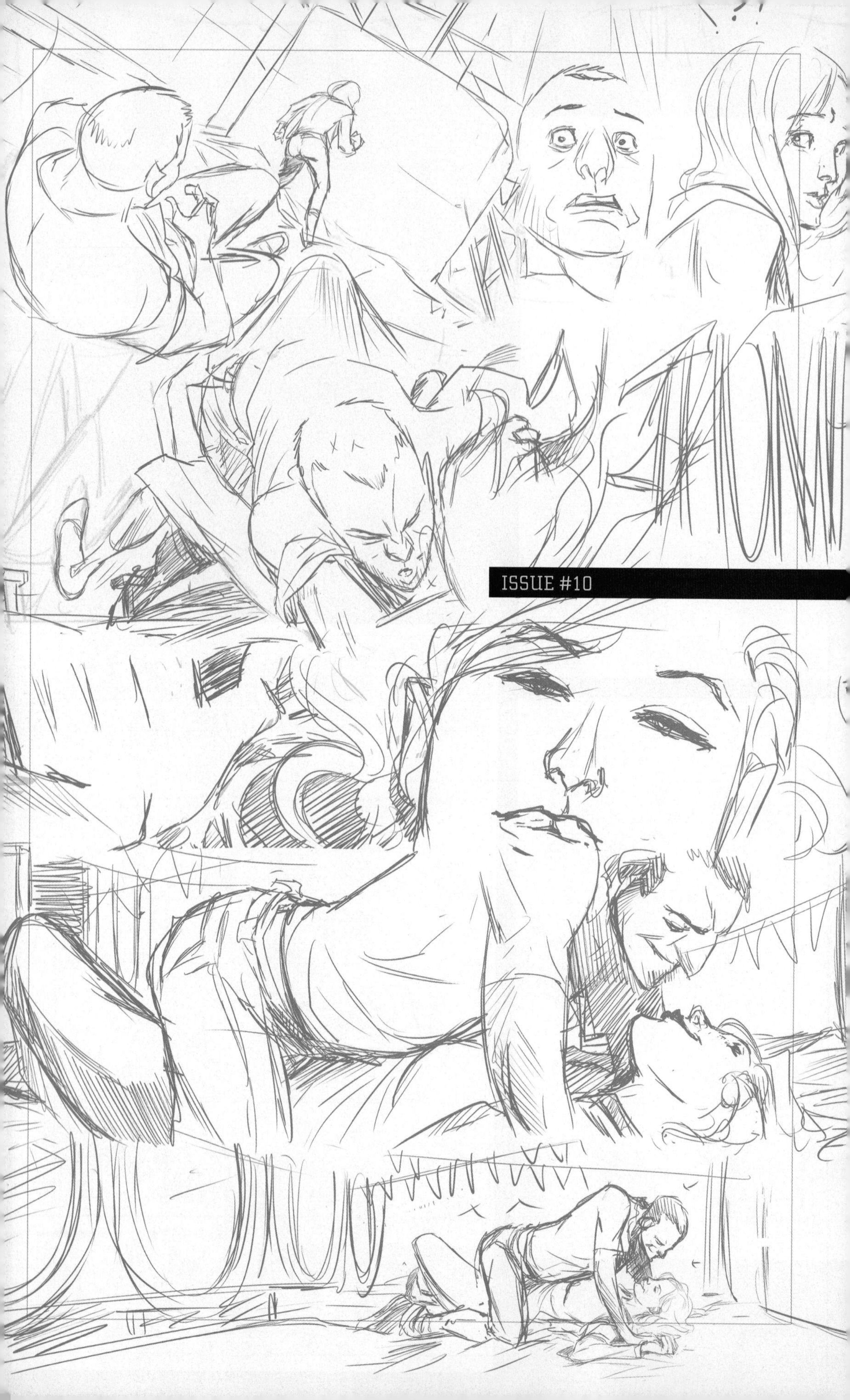

ISSUE #10

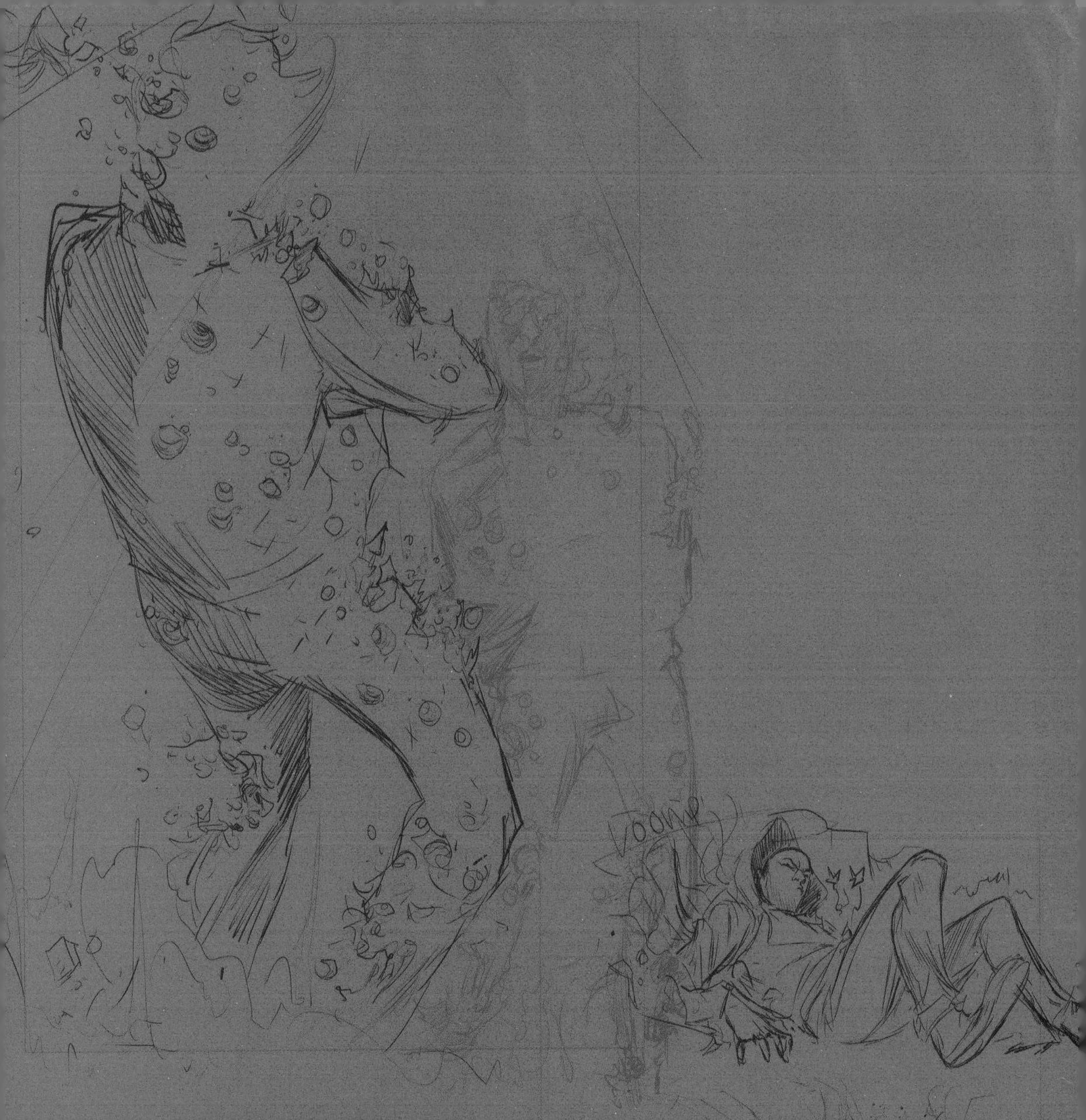

ISSUE #11

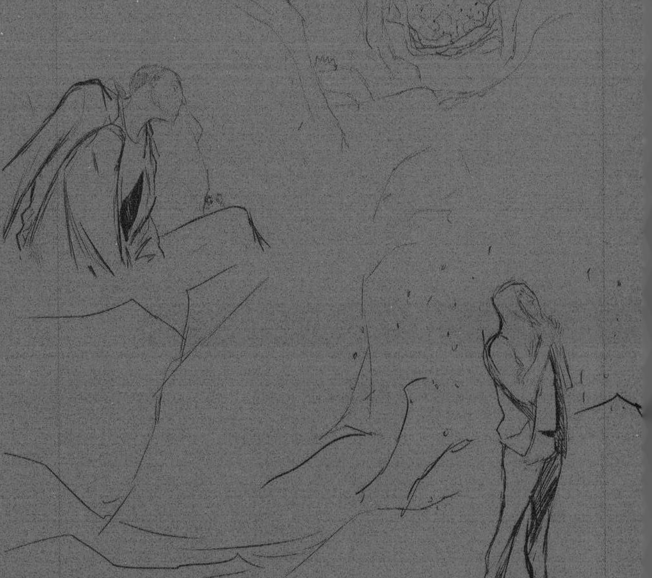

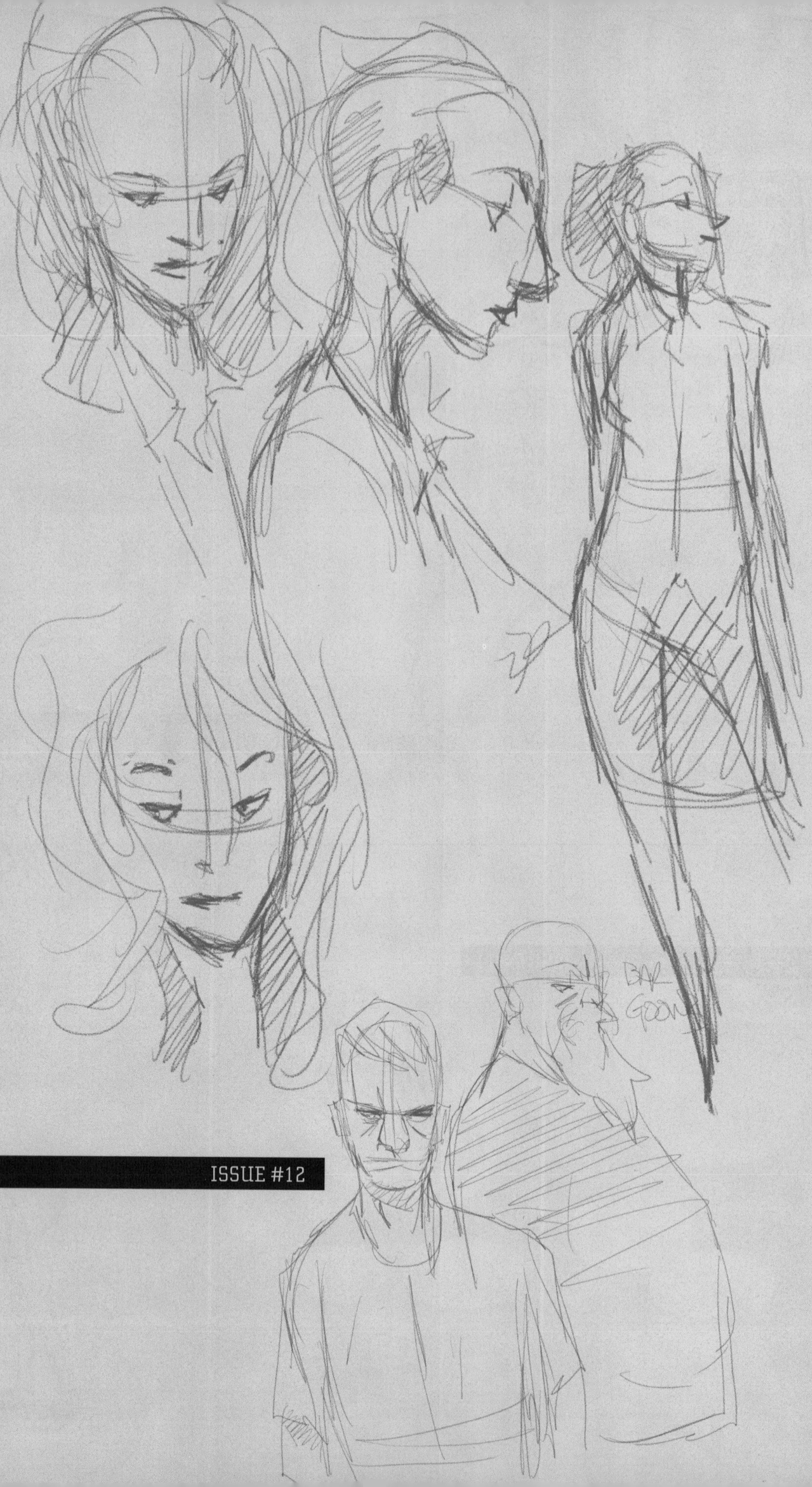
BAR
GOON

ISSUE #12

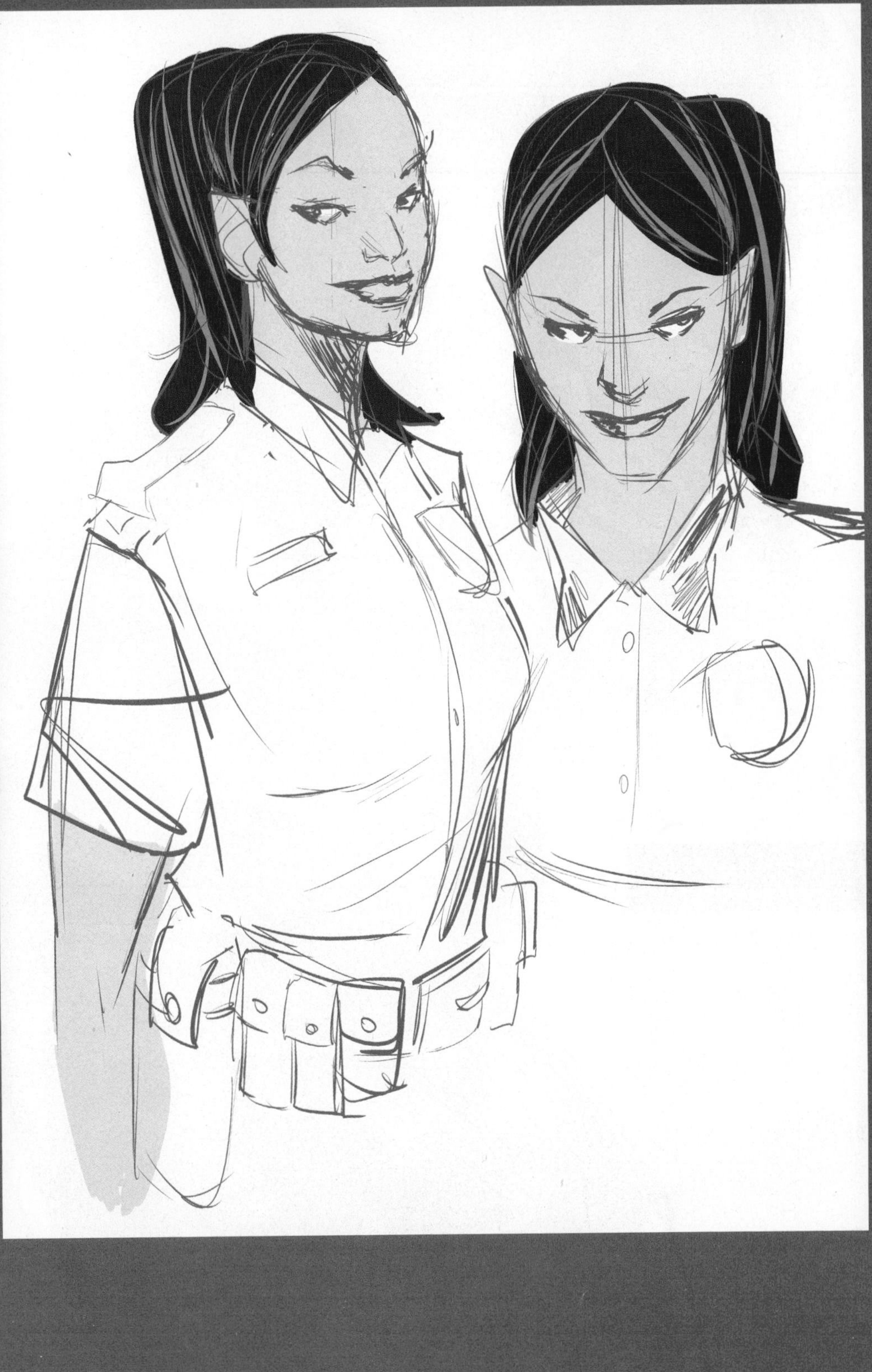

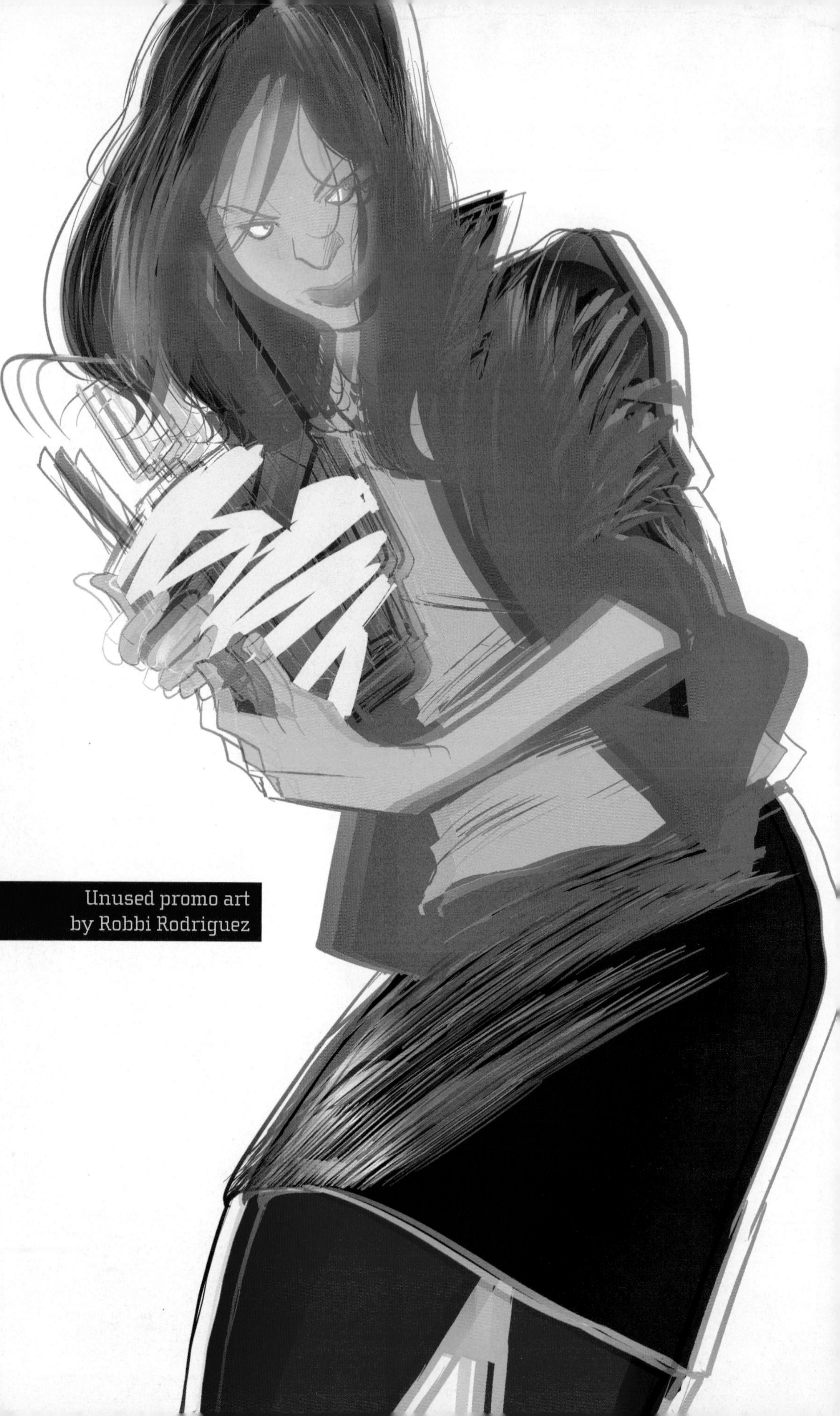

Unused promo art
by Robbi Rodriguez

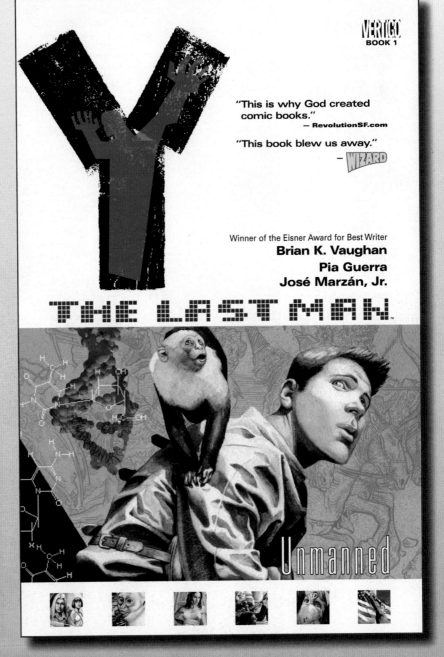

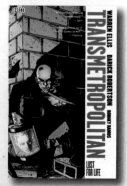